A GUY IN THE KITCHEN

Cavill's Classic Cooking

Ronald W. Cavill

PublishAmerica
Baltimore

First printing

ISBN: 1-60474-878-8
PUBLISHED BY PUBLISHAMERICA, LLLP
www.publishamerica.com
Baltimore

Printed in the United States of America

MAC -

THANKS FOR BEING SUCH
A GOOD FRIEND TO FREMIE.
NEXT BOOK WILL HAVE A
WALLEYE RECIPE!

RON

To the best "Sue-Chef" and partner
a man could ask for.

ACKNOWLEDGMENTS

I am not a professional chef.

I am a financial advisor, and a pretty good one at that, but we all have to eat and while eating out has its pleasures it is not something we want to do all the time. That brings us to why I wrote this cookbook.

My brother could not cook!

I was around 11 or 12 years old when I began to realize that my older brother would doggedly wait for me to come home from school so I could fix both of our growing bodies something to eat. How important and powerful I soon felt knowing that I controlled the destiny of someone much bigger and older than I! It was during those early years that I caught a real glimpse of what it truly was to become a Master of the Universe – *A Guy in The Kitchen*!

Power—raw power—was the real motivation behind my learning to cook!

I grew up in a time that many considered the dark ages. There were no malls and no fast food joints to hang out in after school. This was a time when we all suffered the terrible affects of The Dark Ages. No Malls! Oh sure, we had an A & W Drive-in but who had a car and enough money to afford a ***Big Frosty*** and a ***Deluxe Cheeseburger***?

The years have past since those days of "doctored" Chef Boyardee, and my culinary skills have modestly increased. My brother has also improved his grazing skills. He will proudly inform you that when Judy is out of town he now has a car and the money, and moreover, he knows quite well where the good restaurants can be found!

Gary still cannot cook!

Being motivated to power is one reason to learn to cook but having a good guide will inspire you to explore beyond merely cooking to eat, into the realm of creating for the pure enjoyment of it all. Nanny Lombardo was that inspiration in my life. I had worked in a supper club when I was in college and thought that I knew something of the mechanics of cooking but I really knew nothing about the art of cooking until Nanny came along.

I can remember those early years when Nanny and Poppy would come to visit us in Washington, D.C. from New Jersey. The old Chevy would pull up in front of our apartment and Pop would open the trunk to a veritable treasure of culinary delights. There would be a giant zucchini, wonderful cheeses, fresh vegetables, sausages, cans of Italian tomatoes with colorful labels, and even her own pots and pans. Initially, I would protest, "*Ma, we got stores here—we have the same pots and pans as you do—you gave them to us*". With her broad smile she would look at me and say, "*It's not the same.*"

So now we have motivation and guidance so the only ingredient missing in this recipe is appreciation.

Cooking is one of those marvelous activities that can give you both instant and lasting gratification. Think how many pleasant memories center around a meal you shared with someone special. How many childhood memories we have that are filled with the sweet smells of holiday meals. I will never forget my maternal grandmother's pantry and all those wonderful pies and baked goods.

Everyone in my office has always been appreciative of my creations—if for no other reason because most everyone appreciates a complimentary meal. For Patti, however, it was more than that. Patti would watch over my creations like a mother hen her brood of chicks. She would always mentally record the ingredients and then go home and duplicate the dish—the highest form of compliment! We have always had a full kitchen at the office so these happenings were frequent. She would always clean up after me and never meddle with the recipe by changing or suggesting changes to the formula (at least not in my presence), which could signal a lack of confidence in the cook. Remember that everyone in the kitchen is a *prima donna*—treat them with awe and respect!

Then there was Tausha. She came to work for me when she was still a student at the University of Colorado. It is unusual for young people to show as much interest in cooking as Tausha has, but I have had the pleasure of watching this person blossom into a very capable craftsman in the kitchen.

There is no doubt that one of the most inspirational things about cooking is watching someone else enjoy what you made; and then to see them take an interest in recreating your recipes or creating their own contributions, is the proverbial frosting on the cake! To that end everyone—at some time in their life—should have pals like Patti and Tausha who chow down all your creations as if they were manna from heaven.

Thanks everyone!

TABLE OF CONTENTS

MUNCHIES AND OTHER STARTER FOODS (APPETIZERS) 31

ALL THE SALAD YOU WILL EVER NEED 53

BOWLS AND SPOONS (SOUPS) 73

ON A BUN, IN A POCKET OR BETWEEN 2 SLICES 103

GEE WHIZZERS AND BIG DEALS (ENTREES) 137

PIZZAS AND BREADS 273

MANLY VEGGIES 285

DESSERTS 311

HOLIDAYS 323

BREAKFAST 339

WHAT TO DRINK 351
SHOPPING SKILLS 359

INTRODUCTION

As a professional investment advisor my mission in life is to help people make the most of their investments. If I have done a good job—and I usually do—then there should be a purpose, or and end result, behind good investing. I believe the ultimate objective in life is to live well, no matter how much money we have. My motto has long been, "*if you eat well you are living well.*"

This book is intended to help you eat well. Not fancy, but well. It is a collection of fairly simple recipes and general food wisdom. It is not a gourmet cookbook (nor is it canned stew) it is classic ordinary food that can be prepared easily and possibly served with a little flair to enhance the event.

This book is intended for three broad audiences that share a common seam—to eat well without complex preparation time and within budget.

The first group is the wheelers and dealers of the world who have found themselves to be successful at their respective professional callings' but have not achieved success in the kitchen to match, because they did not have the time or the motivation to cook. With careful reading of this book we could turn dealmaker's into meal makers. Picture it—from chairman of the board to a kitchen guy by simply reading this handy collection of great food thoughts. Wow!!

The second group is populated by the growing number of young Turks who are beginning to experience the thrill of running with the tall dogs, and have correctly determined that the road to success may very well pass by a stomach or two. These people already know that cooking is cool but they were, unfortunately, too focused on arriving that they did not learn to feed themselves because they were too busy clawing their way up the ladder.

The last group—and this may well be the largest group—comprises those who sooner or later find themselves faced with the need—or desire—to alter their cooking and eating habits. For some it will mean learning to cook for themselves without the aid of a helper (like Mom or a spouse), and for others it will be the need to adjust to a smaller number of people at the table. The most troublesome adjustment for this group is when you sit down to the table and the only one there is you!

For many people these later life changes can be trying but they need not be fatal. I always wince when I hear people say that it is not worth the effort to cook for just one or two people. Sure it is. It only takes a lot of effort to *think* about it. If it is worth eating it is certainly worth a little effort to prepare it properly.

So, to that end this collection of recipes is especially dedicated to those in each group who think cooking is too bothersome and difficult. I want to convince you that it is not impossible to maintain a professional competitiveness, balance family and social needs, and still be successful in the kitchen. Eating is one the higher forms of social behavior and I believe it should be a fun experience as well. Next time you have a hard day at the office come home and fix a nice meal and you will be surprised how it can change your entire attitude. Moreover, when you fix that nice meal to share with someone, there is a strong possibility that it may change more than your attitude!

I will show you that the recipes in this collection are—for the most part—quick and easy so you will not be able claim the excuse of," *it takes too long*".

I will also attempt to encourage those who need to cook healthier. Not every recipe wins the ***Happy Heart*** award, but many of them do and I will identify them for you. My main concern in recent years has been the same as most people in that I am concerned about fat content and ultimate cholesterol control. This is not a health book just a collection of basic food recipes which happen to include a few that are also healthy. There is also a lot to be said about eating fresh natural foods without preservatives and chemicals. You will find that I like to start from scratch whenever possible, (there is only one recipe that calls for cream of mushroom soup from the can) and you will too once you see how easy it really is.

The second most frequent comment I hear concerns portions. "*How do you make Chile for one?*" Simple—you don't. You make it for 8 or 10 and invite us all over to watch the game, or you make it for 8 or 10 and eat it for

8 or 10 days straight! Actually, maybe a combination of the two would work better.

The point is that most things not only keep well overnight (or over a couple of nights, unless it is fish), but in many cases the taste actually improves with a little aging. Forget the stigma of "leftovers" and be willing to make some portions that you can keep in the fridge for a day or two and revisit later. Now that does not mean that you make up four portions of an item and then wolf them down in one sitting-discipline is still in vogue. I often cook up a number of things on Sunday after the football game or a day on the boat and refrigerate them for easy meals during the week when my time demands are greater.

We have all heard of people who turn up their noses and whine about how they could not possibly eat the same thing twice in the same week as if it were some kind of a social disease. The same people, however, will order the Big Burger in a restaurant five days a week or eat commercially-prepared foods that were made days or even weeks in advance. If you knew how many restaurants were serving you frozen entrees and how chemically preserved those items were, you might reconsider your eating out habits. I am not only referring to the obvious "fast food" places, but a surprising number of tablecloth and credit card restaurants as well.

One parting observation is that cooking can also be a great mid-life crisis reliever.

This collection does not follow an ethnic theme even though there are a lot of Italian goodies, nor does it concentrate on a single issue like health or cost of preparation. It is an attempt to give you a mix of fairly easy recipes for solo eating as well as some *gee whizzers* for sure-fire entertaining.

I have spent my entire adult life trying to help people become comfortable with their money and their investments to the end that it creates a better life for them. This has rarely been an easy job but on more than one occasion, it has been a rewarding one. In that spirit, I hope that this book will help to make you comfortable in your own kitchen and thereby improve the quality of your life. Cooking, eating and sitting around the table in conversation with our friends and family is a passtime that is worth preserving.

BOUN APPETITO!!

KITCHEN NEEDS

You do not need Emeril's kitchen to prepare good meals, but some tools and doo-dads are needed. If you are starting out or even starting over, it makes sense to make an investment in your kitchen. Well, it makes sense if you plan to eat for some time. If, on the other hand, you think that eating may be a passing fad, then you are in luck—don't bother!

Let me pass on some tips I have learned over the years that might make your preparation easier. Remember, the right tools can make the job so much easier and enjoyable. Imagine what it would be like trying to run your office without a proper computer, a fax machine and a cell phone. The same concept applies to your kitchen. You can do a respectable job with very few kitchen tools, but in the final analysis, better equipment does mean a better finished product, even in the kitchen.

CUTTING BOARDS—This is one tool that is indispensable. You are always cutting, chopping and dicing things. I like wood and if you clean it after each use, you can keep it sanitary. I recommend that you use hot soapy water and a bristle brush immediately after each time you cut fish or fowl on it. If you clean it with bleach from time to time, it will be sanitary and should last for a long time. Be sure you buy hardwood like maple, which is much better than oak. Wood is also better for keeping an edge on your knives. You may wish to consider a number of cutting boards in different sizes and shapes if you plan to do some entertaining. This way everyone can have their own cutting board.

KNIVES—You could really get by with only three basic knives. The first would be a 10 or 12" chef's knife for the big stuff. Then a 6" utility and a 3" paring knife will round out your set. A boning knife is a good second-string addition, as is a good 10" carving knife for slicing the turkey. A serrated bread knife can also be helpful when you want to enlarge your holdings. Please do not wash them in the dishwasher—wash and dry them by hand. Also, try to keep them in a wooden block on their sides or on the heel and not the sharp edge. These two measures will help them retain their edge much longer. A sharp knife is both an efficient and safe knife. I look for a Wusthof Trident knife when I want high quality. If you buy a surgical sharpening stone, you will get the best edge that can be maintained with a few strokes on a steel each time you use the knife. A good knife does, in fact, last a lifetime and might be a factor in your will, so consider that when you look at the price tag.

SPOONS—This is an important part of cooking. You need a number of wooden spoons for stirring and poking. Wood is the best material for your pots and pans since it will not harm your non-stick surfaces. Metal can beat up on those nice cooking surfaces. Plastic is O.K., but excessive heat will melt or deform plastic and they don't age with the kind of character your wooden ones will. It is important to look cool while you cook. You need a couple of slotted spoons and a large ladle or two, and they can be plastic since they do not spend much time in or on the cooking surface.

POTS & PANS—Once again, a few items can go a long way if they are the right few items. In pots and pans, larger is better than smaller. If you only have one stockpot, you should make it a 10 or 12-quart size since you **can** always make soup for two in a 10-quart, but it is a little difficult to make chile for 12 in a 2-quart model. Your sauté pan should also be a large one in the neighborhood of 10" or 12" with a deep base to it. After you acquire a large 10" or 12" pan, you will want to get a 7" pan for omelets and other small orders. If you then have a 3-quart saucepan, you can make just about anything. As you can expand, it is wise to add smaller capacities and maybe duplicate a 2 ½ to 3-quart size since that is the most common in recipes. I have always preferred the heavy-gauge commercial stainless steel, and there is some benefit to some kind of a non-stick interior on your smaller (omelet-sized) sauté pans. There has been some concern that aluminum causes senility, but I can't seem to remember at this time! Calphalon has become a popular alternative in recent times, but I do not care for it. I find it very difficult to clean and that most foods stick to the bottom no matter how careful you are to use slow and low heat. All Clad, on the other hand, makes a real fine heavy stainless steel commercial grade product that I also use and like a great deal. The nice thing about these better pieces of equipment is that they are all open stock so you can buy a piece at a time. You will also want to acquire at least one large cast iron frying pan.

BAKING PIECES—Everyone needs at least three pieces of corning ware. One should be deep and one should be large enough to hold four chicken breasts and the other one big enough to hold two chicken breasts. A big blue enameled turkey roaster is perfect for the holiday bird and weekend lasagna. Pie dishes should be ceramic if you can find them, but glass will substitute and they should be deep. As you add to your baking pieces, you will want to look at some pottery items and maybe a bean crock.

BOWLS—You will want an assortment of bowls for prep work. I think that ceramic bowls always look nice and seem to do well when you are baking something. You can always display these bowls as they add a nice feel to your kitchen. You should also consider a nested set of stainless mixing bowls. The most important thing for a man to remember is think ***BIG*** when using mixing bowls. You are going to spin about a third of the stuff on the floor when you have a bowl that is too small, so remember to use a size bigger and you will have less cleaning to do later. If you have a dog, then smaller bowls will work from the dog's point of view.

ELECTRONICS—There are a lot of fine gadgets out there and I am certain that they have value, but in my experience I find that most things can be done manually. The only need I have had for a food processor is to blend things like salsa. A simple two-speed blender will not only handle most of your needs, it will also mix up those frozen drinks you need while you are cooking. A Kitchen Aid mixer can be a good investment if you do a lot of baking and if you make your own sausages, but in the meantime there is little that cannot be done better or more efficiently by hand. Pizza dough, for example, seems to come out better if you do it by hand. A microwave can be super for making popcorn, reheating certain leftovers, and an occasional frozen prepared item, but I find little value in it for "honest" cooking.

GADGETS—Yes, you need a few things.

A good easy to use corkscrew should be the first investment you make. Do not buy a plastic one or some other flimsy contraption. Make sure it is a good heavy metal one with the T-handle on the top and the collar shaft that keeps the thing straight on the bottle. A good corkscrew will definitely make the rest of your kitchen work more enjoyable.

You do not need a garlic press. Lay the garlic on your cutting board and smash is with the flat side of a knife blade.

You will need a metal grater. A nice large four-sided stainless steel model will serve all your needs and hold up in the dishwasher. You can buy this in the grocery store.

Skewers are indispensable if you grill shrimp and kabobs. Buy a set of metal ones so you can use them over again.

If you are going to cook pasta (and you will), you will need a colander to drain the stuff. There are some nice colorful, inexpensive plastic ones in the marketplace that do the job just fine. This is the big kind that looks like a bowl with holes in it and not the wire strainer that has a wooden handle attached to it. You also need a strainer for draining rice and vegetables, etc., so get one of those too but do not forget the colander. It sure beats having to pick it out of the sink when it all falls in there from the cooking pot you are trying to drain by using the cover or some other device.

Lastly, you should own a Mouli rotary grater so you can grate your hard Italian cheeses onto your pastas and dishes right at the table. If you are going to make pizza (even the frozen ones), you will need a heavy-duty pizza wheel to cut it with. Buy an industrial strength wheel and it will also double as a good herb mincer. Lay your fresh parsley or basil on your cutting board, run the wheel back and forth over the herb, and you have instant mincing! It works for nuts and garlic as well.

PANTRY ITEMS

It is no great mystery that good ingredients lead to a good finished product. What is true in all aspects of life is doubly true of cooking. If you begin with marginal quality, you will most likely end up with a marginal product.

As I have said earlier, it is always preferable to use fresh products whenever you can obtain them. Why buy frozen green beans when the market has fresh beans year around? It is not only going to give you a better product, it will also give you a new outlook on life. It can be fun going to the farmer's market, and it may even help reduce your stress level to put on some jeans and go interact with those people. It is refreshing to discover—or be reminded—that some people do live differently than you do. Who knows, you may even give up your law practice and become an organic farmer.

What follows is some basic commentary on some of the ingredients you will find in the recipes contained in this collection.

ASPARAGUS

The thing you have to get used to is that you are not cooking for Grant's army so you can afford the things you may have been passing by for many years. Asparagus is one of those things that you do not buy by the bushel. Choose the moderately-sized ones that tend to favor the thinner size, and remember that the woody base needs to be removed. I break them at the point of least resistance to assure the most tender part of the asparagus makes it into the saucepan.

BASIL

This is one of the most wonderful fresh herbs you can use. If you start some basil in the summer, you can grow it indoors all year long. Pick off only the leaves and they grow back on. If you must buy it at the store, be sure the leaves have not turned black. You can store it in a glass of water with a plastic bag over it to retain the moisture and it will last for a number of days. Break the basil leaves apart rather than cutting them (your fingers will smell really nice!). Steel from the knife or scissors can discolor the leaf. When you use fresh basil, do not overcook it. It can be added toward the end of the cooking process and it will flavor just fine. Your pesto will be terrific only if you use fresh basil.

CHEESE (HARD)

There are a number of good Italian grating cheeses. I tend to like the pecorino romano but a good reggiano, a locatelli or asiago can do just as well. Remember, cheese, like wine and olive oil, varies in taste according to the region it comes from, so while you will find subtle similarities and differences, it is ultimately a matter of taste. Experiment until you find your own favorite. Cut off a slice and eat some with fresh Italian bread so you can learn the taste of each type of cheese. What is critically important is that you grate freshly. That terrible substitute in the cardboard container that is sold as grated cheese is closer to sawdust than cheese. Grated cheese loses its flavor the longer it has been grated, so it is best to grate it directly on or into the food rather than buying it grated. Keep your hard cheese wrapped tightly to prevent it from drying out. Good fresh grating cheese should be a little on the yellow side when it is fresh.

CHEESE (SOFT)

Cottage cheese in no substitute for ricotta cheese. I know cottage cheese and believe me, cottage cheese is no ricotta. I am happy to report; however, that I have tried the low-fat version of ricotta and it does work. There is also a major difference between fresh mozzarella and the packaged stuff. If you buy the fresh stuff, you should plan to use it that same day. I recommend using fresh on a mozzarella and tomato salad since the taste is so dominate. It also makes a difference in the stuffed shells, but lasagna may not know the difference since there are so many other tastes present and the added moisture from fresh may make your lasagna a little runny.

CHEESE (OTHER)

This is the big fat offender. There are some low-fat products making their way into the marketplace, and you should use them in most cases. There are times, however, when nothing else will do but a 60% or 70% brie. What can replace a fine gorgonzola or Vermont cheddar? Truly, one of the gourmet food categories is cheese. If you are going to blow it, you can blow it in fine fashion at the cheese counter.

CHIVES

This is a versatile spice that everyone should have in his or her cupboard. I use it in scrambled eggs, on chicken, in soups, and over salads. If you can find it fresh, it is a delightful addition to some pasta sauces. This is another item you can grow in your kitchen or in your back yard.

GARLIC

You can never have too much garlic in the house. I had a friend in college, Jerry Marinelli, who would carry the stuff in his pockets and eat it like peanuts. What a complexion that guy had! Garlic will keep in your vegetable bin for a long time if it has not been peeled. Try one clove in your green beans or spinach while it is cooking. You can use the whole clove in cooking and when you do this, you can use a lot of it. When I make a chicken, for example, I will use an entire knuckle (that is the whole thing) for the marinade and sauté. If you sliver the garlic, you open it up, which releases more of its bouquet, so you can use less. If the garlic is crushed, you release all the juices and even less will go farther. Never burn the garlic — it is awful when you do. Garlic powder is an acceptable substitute (in a pinch), but please, do not use garlic salt.

HERBS & SPICES

Most dried herbs and spices do have a fixed shelf life. If you are not using them within a few months, you should buy smaller quantities. Dried varieties should usually be added to the recipe early on, while fresh ones can function well when added more toward the end of the recipe, requiring less cooking time. Be willing to experiment with different tastes. Vary the amounts and substitute spices in various recipes. When you use fresh herbs and spices, you will need to increase the amount significantly since the fresh selections simply take up more space to provide the same amount of flavoring.

LEMONS & LIMES

If you drink your scotch or bourbon on the rocks, a twist of lemon makes a nice touch and smoothes it out a little more. In addition to being critical in the bar, it has much usefulness in the kitchen. I like to use fresh lemon juice in my summer salads and I substitute lemon for vinegar in a lot of recipes. Both lemons and limes make for a great marinade ingredient. Don't forget the health benefits in a tall cold glass of water at mealtime. Dress is up with a slice of lemon hanging on your best wine goblet, and you have not only a healthy statement but an elegant one as well.

MUSHROOMS

This can be a very satisfying side dish all by itself, but in most cases it is part of the recipe. Domestic white mushrooms will do justice to most any recipe, but do not overlook the benefits of a porcini or a chanterelle when making that special dish. If you use a porcini or other dried mushroom, you should put them in a cup of water and bring them to a boil, turn off the heat, and let stand for 20 minutes before you use them. You will want to use the mushrooms and the juice you obtained from cooking them. Mushrooms all offer a distinctive taste, and your preference for them will grow in time.

OLIVE OIL

This may be the single most important item in your kitchen. If you regard your oil as simply a lubricant for your cooking, you might as well use Quaker State or Pennzoil. If, on the other hand, you realize that the oil is an important ingredient in your recipe, you will have a much different approach to the matter. I use olive oil for almost everything except for popping popcorn and baking. In all my cooking I use Extra Virgin Olive Oil, and if you are careful, it does work in most recipes. Extra Virgin is the most delicate of olive oils, so you must be careful not to burn it. Olive oil should never get so hot that it is smoking (which is not the same as steaming), which means that it is burning. If you burn the oil, you will replace a subtle delicate flavor with a pungent yucky one. Olive oil is like wine in that each region produces a different oil. You should sniff and taste it much the same as you would a good red wine.

I recommend using only Italian oil but would consider a Greek oil if I could not find Italian. Keep the oil sealed and out of sun light, or it will spoil. It does have a self life of six months to one year if it is sealed and kept in a dark cupboard, but if you use it for most of your cooking, it will be gone long before then.

ONIONS

When you need to buy onions by the pound, buy yellow onions. When you buy your onions according to your recipe, you will most likely buy white, Bermuda (red), or Spring onions (little green onions), and on those special occasions when you can, get a hold of some Vidalias. Onions will keep for a few weeks in the bottom of your refrigerator if they have not been cut. Once you cut your onion open, you should store it in a zip-lock bag. If you cut off about 1 ½ inches from the end and slap that end "back on" if you do not use the entire onion, it will help keep it fresh for six or seven days. It is also helpful if you do not peel the onion. When you reuse it later, you can take off the exposed face by removing a thin slice. The rest of the onion will be as fresh as when it was first cut. Onions are cheap, so do not use the ends in your cooking. The best part of the onion is the center cut. White onions make good cooking onions, as well as salad or sandwich onions. They are versatile. A red onion does very well in salads or on a burger, but it does not stand up as well as a white or yellow onion does when cooking for a long time. In other words they sauté fine, but if the cooking time is for one hour in a stew or a pasty, you would be better off using the yellow or white onions. The Spring onions, of course, can be eaten in hand and do well in salads or other recipes were there is no serious cooking time.

Vidalias are clearly for eating raw. Onions can be offensive, but I promise you that an honest Vidalia begs to be eaten raw. Try them sliced thin over some fresh crusty Jewish Rye with seeds and some chunky peanut butter for a great easy sandwich.

PARSLEY

This is another item you can grow in your kitchen or back yard. Fresh parsley can be added to almost any recipe other than Cherries Jubilee. It is a great decorative item and refreshes your palette quite nicely after any meal. Had too much garlic and you want to give your guest a goodnight kiss? No problem—chow down on your parsley and pucker up, baby!

PASTAS

You do not need to buy designer pasta to get good stuff. You also do not need to make your own or buy the fresh stuff, because none of your friends will know the difference anyhow. I have found that De Cecco has the best overall product on the market. Silver Palate makes some good specialty things like pepper pasta, as well. One unmistakable truth is that if the pasta sticks together when it cooks, you have the wrong brand. The cheap stuff sticks together, and makes it hard to cook with. In my recipes, I do not instruct you to salt the boiling water that you will cook the pasta in because I assume you either know that or will read the box or bag and figure it out. Most recipes call for an immediate "dressing" of the pasta so it is unnecessary to do anything else to the cooked pasta. If, on the other hand, the pasta may have to sit for some time before it is "dressed", you can add one teaspoon of olive oil to the boiling water just before you drain it, and that will help keep the pasta from sticking together *after* cooking.

Experiment with different types of pastas and make substitutions in your recipes. Do not feel obligated to always use penne in a particular recipe when a rotini or a raditori will give you the same culinary response with a different aesthetic presentation. The most important thing in substituting is to not cross pasta "classes". There are only two "classes" of pastas, so this is easy to control. You have the Heavy Duty stuff in one class and the Delicate stuff in the other. Heavy Dutys are the rigatonis down through the pennes and are basically the pastas that will take a little extra cooking and a heavier sauce without falling down on you. The Delicate angel hairs and spagettinis, and even some narrow gauge spaghettis, require lighter sauces. They should not be overcooked, and do not stand by after cooking very well. They need to be consumed quickly after cooking. You should never use anything but a very delicate sauce on these pastas. Avoid meat sauces, and never use a thick cheese-based sauce. I recently had a spagettini at an Old Town Alexandria restaurant that had a Béchamel sauce on it, and the pasta looked like wallpaper paste. This was a restaurant that has a good reputation and has been in business for a long time. Anyone can make a mistake. The most important thing about pasta is—do not overcook it!

POTATOES

The first reaction most people have to potatoes is, "*How common*". Sure, and also how fundamental, how nutritious, how easy, and how overlooked. A potato can be a wonderful source of vitamins and minerals with nearly zero fat and no cholesterol. In most parts of the country, you will find three varieties of potatoes and these will meet all of your cooking needs.

Idahos, Russets or Bakers are the most common and versatile of the three. They are great for baking, mashing, and using in most every recipe that calls for potatoes without specifying what kind. This is the best potato in the world for French fries, hash browns, and other fried potato recipes. Hand pick them, and make sure they are firm and have no black spots on them when you buy them.

White or New Potatoes are not as big as Bakers, so they do better boiled (with their skins on) and in potato salads. They are somewhat sweeter than a Russet (Idaho) and do not deep fry well.

Redskins are also sweeter to the taste and are a good alternate as a whole boiled potato. They make a nice potato salad and often turn up in a New England Lobster Boil.

SALT & PEPPER

I am not going to discuss the merits of high blood pressure or premature senility. I like salt and pepper. You decide and you use as much as you like. You will not find measurements for salt and pepper in this collection. I will tell you, however, that if you are going to use it—use fresh. Invest in both a salt and pepper mill. Freshly ground beats the stale old box stuff, hands down. It also looks cool when you are grinding it out. You can find coarse ground sea salt in most grocery stores today.

TOMATOES (FRESH)

Listen closely Grasshopper, for if there is wisdom, here it is: Grow your own tomatoes! If there is one single ingredient that can make you a hero, it is *fresh* tomatoes. There are simply some things that I will not make if I cannot get fresh tomatoes. Next to fresh from your own garden is an honest farmer's market. I absolutely will not buy anything other than cherry tomatoes in the super market. Find roadside stands and farmer's markets and make it worth your trip. Remember, when they pass salad stage, they are right for lots of pasta recipes, and when they are past some of the pasta recipes, they are still good for salsa. Si, those jalapenos will make them sparkle!

TOMATOES (CANNED)

Italian tomatoes in the can should be one type—San Marzano. This is the type of tomato not the brand. Asti, Rosa, Cento, and other labels offer the San Marzano tomato. If you cannot find a San Marzano but can find the Sclafani label, you are in luck. These tomatoes might come from Venezuela, but they originated in Italy so they work quite well and are found on many an Italian's table. I have often driven to Elizabeth, New Jersey for my canned tomatoes, because they are that important to my recipes. Whole Italian canned tomatoes can be selectively used in place of fresh tomatoes in some recipes. Crushed tomatoes are also key when making certain sauces. When you need a sauce, I prefer to use puree instead of sauce, simply because puree has nothing but tomatoes in it—no salt—no anything.

TOMATOES (DRIED)

If you live in Sicily, the climate is perfect for sun drying tomatoes. If you live most anywhere else, you should buy them in the store since it will be a lot easier. Sun dried tomatoes offer a rich and robust flavor that has very little in common with the other tomatoes mentioned above. If the recipe calls for fresh tomatoes, you will find that sun dried do not work very well as a substitute, and vice versa. A little of these tomatoes go a long way.

TORTILLAS

Fundamentally, there are two basic types of tortillas and one variation of one of those types. Flour tortillas—the white ones—are the most versatile and can be used with anything that you would use "ordinary" bread for. That is to say, they can make nice sandwiches for fine stand-alone eating. They are most commonly associated with Mexican or southwestern cooking but they are becoming more and more common in all sorts of uses. They are sturdy and can stand up to smothering—as in a burrito—and are yet much lighter than a hot dog bun. Flour tortillas are used to make fajitas and burritos and when they are deep-fried, they become chimi's.

Corn tortillas come in either the traditional yellow corn or a more eclectic blue corn variety. The most common use of this tortilla is fried into a corn chip for dipping in your salsa. You can buy them in the grocery store in a bag, or pick up the fresh tortillas and quarter them and cook them yourself in corn oil for a homemade freshness. You also find them used in taco shells, enchiladas, and tacitos. They are not real tasty just out of the package like a flour tortilla is, but they may be healthier since they are always lower in fat and cholesterol.

ZUCCHINI

Here is another much-maligned vegetable simply because it is so abundant. We all know of the versatility of this vegetable, but we sometimes overlook one other good feature, and that is its long shelf life. This is an important item when you are cooking for only a few people and need to be able to retain things in your pantries and refrigerators. Like potatoes, they can be baked, boiled and fried and can be fixed solo or as part of a combination of other vegetables.

A WORD ON MEASUREMENTS

If you plan to do any baking, you need to invest in a couple of measuring cups and a set of measuring spoons. It is impossible to bake properly without a proper measuring cup and set of measuring spoons.

Cooking, however, is a very different story. If you have hands and eyes, you can cook. Honest! In most recipes, it is not critical to have exact measurements. I have never used measuring instruments when preparing any recipe so you should regard my recipe instructions as *approximate* measurements only. When you are dealing with herbs and spices, it is all a matter of personal taste, and you should feel comfortable experimenting with your own measurements. I will oftentimes alter amounts depending on my own taste desires at the time I am preparing the dish. Some days I feel like an oregano man, but on other days I may feel more like a basil guy, so I will favor one or the other accordingly. If you are feeling real rakish, you might even substitute marjoram for oregano!

The point here is that you want to develop liberty in your seasonings and be comfortable in your preparation techniques. I guess one of the reasons why I was the Boy Scout Spaghetti Dinner cook for 10 years is that I have never been able to properly quantify the recipe to 500 servings of spaghetti. With 10 or 11 containers bubbling away, I just add a handful of this and a couple of shakes of that—well, you get the idea. Remember, this is supposed to be fun so don't let too much structure squelch that fun. It is also quite alright to taste test and sniff the product while it is in process. Remember that eating is a sensory experience. If you cannot distinguish certain tastes, do not be discouraged. Keep at it, and in time it will come to you. The truth of the matter is that, in most recipes, it will make little difference if you use ½ tablespoon or ¾ of a tablespoon. Of course if you smoke, you probably have no taste buds, so all of this is for nothing. Quit smoking and your sex life and dining pleasure will increase dramatically!

The same can be said about servings. Who am I to tell you how many servings there are to a recipe? Four chicken breasts might suggest four servings, but what if two people eat them? Figure it out for yourself! The easiest thing is to make way more than you think you need. There is no law against leftovers, but it is a crime to run short! Never come up short—make lots—it is what the Italians call abudanza!

Beyond that, all you need to remember is that **Tbsp** = Tablespoon And **tsp** = teaspoon.

(The Tablespoon is the big one—that is why it gets an upper case "T")

MUNCHIES AND OTHER STARTER FOODS (APPETIZERS)

BIG DEALE HOT CRAB DIP

If you are ever near Galesville, Maryland, there is a lovely little spot on the West River called ***Pirates Cove*** that begs at least one special-occasion meal. The food is decent, and the atmosphere can be charming with the water views and the fireplace in the winter. If you stop, you need to have a drink in the bar and ask about Joe Knox, the bartender. Joe served up drinks and chatter at Pirates Cove for over 40 years! Joe has sailed off to the Great Beyond, but his unusual trade mark bow tie made from a ***$100*** bill lives on. Joe introduced me to a fine hot crab dip at the bar, so I decided to try my hand at it. This is my version.

1 lb. crabmeat
1 8 oz pkg cream cheese
½ cup sour cream
1/3 cup sharp cheddar cheese –grated
1/3 cup pepper jack cheese –grated
2 Tbsp mayonnaise
1 Tbsp country mustard
1 Tbsp chives
1 Tbsp milk
1 ½ tsp Worcestershire sauce
1 tsp marjoram
½ tsp dry mustard
1/4 tsp garlic powder
paprika
Juice from 1/2 a lemon

You can use a lesser expensive crabmeat for this recipe provided it is fresh. I prefer to use Lump crabmeat, but Special will work for landlubbers—try to avoid Claws since it tends to have foreign matter in it.

In a large bowl mix all of the ingredients EXCEPT crabmeat, lemon juice, a little cheese, and paprika. Once these ingredients have been blended, you can now squeeze the lemon over the crabmeat and fold it into the mixture.

Prepare a 1 quart corning or similar deep dish by rubbing the inside with butter and then adding the ingredients from the mixing bowl. Spread the remaining cheese on top, dust with paprika, and bake in a preheated 350-degree oven for 30 minutes.

This is clearly **NOT** a Happy Heart item, but it definitely a Happy Palette number.

You can use the leftovers as the main ingredient in *Crab Town Muffins*

ANNIE'S CRAB BALLS

Ann is a good friend, and she had teamed up with me to do a holiday dinner party so I could meet one of her dear friends. As I was trying to decide what to do for an appetizer, I remembered some crab balls I had eaten in Annapolis just a week earlier. I had been back East for a few days and wanted to consume as much crab as I could while I was there. At one meal, I ordered crab balls and was delighted at how yummy they were and how easily they went down. I reasoned that I could reproduce them at home, and this is the result. I think the best part of these crab balls is the simplicity of them. Buy the best grade Blue crab meat you can find, and you won't be disappointed with the results.

2 lbs. Lump crab meat
1 lemon
2 eggs – beaten
2 Tbsp mayonnaise
1 Tbsp stone ground mustard
1 Tbsp sour cream
1/2 cup Italian breadcrumbs
1 Tbsp fresh chives

Mix all of it, reserving half of the breadcrumbs, together in a large bowl. Press the crabmeat into balls the size of a golf ball, and compact them firmly. Place the remaining breadcrumbs on a large flat plate and roll the crab balls in the crumbs, being careful to fully coat them. Put a dozen crab balls on a plate and cover with wax paper. Refrigerate for at least one hour but no more than four.

Preheat the corn oil in a deep fat fryer to 375 degrees. Cook the crab balls for four to five minutes and serve hot. If you make a dozen of these, you might be lucky and have enough left over to make two crab cakes that you can freeze; but you will want to eat them soon, maybe the next day for breakfast!

You can mix up a bunch of these and pop open a nice bottle of Fume Blanc along with a fresh *Tomato & Mozzarella Salad* for a complete no-fuss meal.

COLORADO RED SALSA

When I lived in Colorado, salsa became as basic as butter on bread. Every Southwestern, Mexican, or Tex-Mex eatery served a compliment of chips and salsa before every meal. The most basic salsa is a tomato-based, but many varieties can be found in the Southwest. Salsa is most commonly found next to a big bowl of corn chips but don't forget that it makes an excellent topping on broiled fish, juicy steaks, and even ladled over a couple of sunny-side-up eggs for breakfast.

The quality of the tomatoes is paramount to this recipe. Home grown is obviously the best tomato, but in the off months when all you can get is the cardboard excuse for tomatoes in the store, you need to let them mature in a brown paper bag on the counter for a few days after you buy them.

4-5 large ripe tomatoes
1 8 oz can tomato sauce
3 whole jalapeno peppers
2 slices large white onion
2 Tbsp dry cilantro – or 4 Tbsp fresh cilantro
2 tsp crushed red pepper
1/4 tsp garlic powder
juice from ½ lime
salt & pepper

Quarter the tomatoes and lightly pulse them in a food processor so they are chunky and of a rich consistency. Chop the sliced onion into a mixing bowl. Dice the jalapeno peppers, being careful of your hands and eyes since these peppers can be strong. Add the remaining ingredients to the mixing bowl and salt and pepper to taste. This salsa does best when it has 30 minutes or so to sit in a covered container on the kitchen counter.

Serve with a variety of corn chips.

You can heat the corn chips in a conventional oven for a few minutes to achieve an additional crispiness. You can also make your own chips by deep frying fresh quartered corn tortillas for a few minutes until they become crisp. Add salt to these chips and they are terrific with your salsa!

Salsa itself is a ***Happy Heart*** item since it possesses no fat itself. Watch the corn chips—look for the ones made without tropical oils or use baked products.

This recipe is also a key ingredient in *Houston Chicken Breasts*.

TRAIL DRIVE SALSA

Most of us enjoy anything done on the grill or over an open campfire. There is something very basic and relaxed about that kind of food. This salsa brings that grilling experience to any meal we might fix following this starter. I like to do this over a wood fire for a good wood flavor in the salsa.

1 ancho or pablano pepper
2 jalapeno peppers
2 tomatillos
10 cherry tomatoes
3 medium ripe tomatoes*
2 slices white onion – diced
1 Tbsp fresh cilantro – diced
1/8 tsp garlic powder
juice of a lime
salt & pepper

Put the peppers and tomatillos over the hot coals of your fire and turn frequently so they blacken evenly. The cherry tomatoes should be done on a skewer so you don't lose them between the grates. Remove the items from the grill and allow cooling on a cutting board. Carefully, cut the ends from the peppers and butterfly them so you can clean the seeds from them. Be careful not to touch the peppers with your hands—use a fork.

Place the peppers, cherry tomatoes, and tomatillos in a blender and grind finely. Blend the ripe tomatoes so they are moderately chunky. Add the remaining ingredients to a mixing bowl and blend until it is well mixed.

Serve at room temperature with warm tortilla chips.

* Fresh ingredients are really important to this recipe—if you cannot get honest vine ripened tomatoes, forget the recipe and go eat out in a restaurant instead.

SUSIE'S SALSA

When we entered the Colorado BBQ challenge in Frisco, Colorado, we submitted our salsa for judging. Unfortunately, we did not have an adequate supply and only finished in the top 10. However, one member of our team had more to do with our winning the People's Choice Award for our BBQ than any other person and so very much liked my salsa, that I decided to name it after her. Incidentally, it was a unanimous decision among the rest of our motorcycle group that this is a first place winner.

2 pablano peppers
6 large ripe tomatoes
3 Tbsp corn oil
1 8 oz can tomato sauce
2 cloves garlic
1/3 cup corn –frozen
3 slices white onion –diced
1 tsp oregano
2 Tbsp cilantro –fresh
juice of ½ lime
salt & pepper

Marinate the peppers and tomatoes with corn oil in a large metal bowl. Roll the tomatoes and peppers around in the bowl to fully cover all items with corn oil. Roast the peppers and tomatoes on a wood fire until the outsides turn black.

Remove the items from the grill and place them on a cutting board. Carefully, cut the ends from the peppers and butterfly them so you can clean the seeds from them. Be careful not to touch the peppers with your hands – use a fork.

Place the peppers and tomatoes in a blender and grind to a chunky consistency. Add the remaining ingredients to a mixing bowl and blend until it is well mixed. Serve at room temperature with warm tortilla chips.

HONEST GUACAMOLE DIP

Cooking is not rocket science—you can do it with simple ingredients. The trick to this recipe is getting good avocados, and that is not something that you can find at all times of the year. When you do buy them, you will probably have to allow them some time to soften up before using them. You can use this recipe as a straight dip before a meal in concert with other munchies, or as a companion to a number of entrees found in this collection. However you serve this, you can rest assured that it will be a hit.

4 or 5 ripe avocados
1 large ripe tomato
2 Tbsp white onion – diced
1 Tbsp sour cream
1 Tbsp fresh cilantro
½ tsp crushed red pepper
½ tsp garlic powder
juice of a lime
salt

Cut the avocados from end to end rotating the blade around the large seed in the middle. If the avocado is properly ripened, the two halves will pull clean away from the seed. Remove the seed with a spoon and spoon the avocado meat from the skin into a mixing bowl.

Add all of the remaining ingredients and blend with a fork into a fairly smooth consistency. Cover and place in refrigerator and then allow to stand on the counter for at least fifteen minutes before serving. If it comes out with a flat taste, you simply need to add more salt.

This dip is an ingredient used in *Bandito Nacho Grande Platter, Taos Enchilada Stack*, and a twist on *Houston's Chicken Breasts.*

BANDITO NACHO GRANDE PLATTER

There are times when you have the whole gang over to watch the big game or to celebrate a house warming and you need to put out an extra special nacho platter. This is that platter. This can be an easy item **IF** you have the chile made ahead of time, and if you have a need for salsa and guacamole in addition to the amount needed for the nachos. In any case, it is a good idea to set out some salsa and guacamole with plain chips, so go ahead and turn the affair into fiesta.

1 large bag sturdy tortilla chips
1 cup *Big Ron's Original Colorado Chile*
1 cup Monterey Jack cheese – shredded
1 cup sharp cheddar cheese – shredded
2 Tbsp spring onions – diced
1 Tbsp jalapeno pepper – sliced
3 Tbsp *Colorado Red Salsa*
3 Tbsp *Honest Guacamole*
3 Tbsp sour cream

The best way to do this is to build it like you would a house from the ground up. Place a layer of chips on a large heat-resistant platter. Then add chile over that layer and continue with more chips and the cheeses mixed together with the spring onions, and then top with one more layer of chips and cheeses on the top. Scatter the jalapenos on the very top and slip into the oven on the broiler setting for a few minutes until the cheese begins to melt and spread evenly.

Remove from oven and dollop the salsa, guacamole and sour cream around the sides and top of the nachos and serve immediately.

This is a real honest sitting-around-the-campfire-after-robbing-the-Overland-Stagecoach kind of nachos. Break out the good Corona and Dos Eqquis and listen for the strolling mariachis to arrive.

DENVER CHICKEN WINGS

If my heart is in Denver, my stomach cannot be too far away. I have always enjoyed the interesting blend that Denver offers by way of culinary roots. The Southwestern influence is obvious. It should be said that this influence is a very simpatico one, and I like that. Denver does not have the stratified image of Santa Fe' which appeals to a different side of me. Denver also has a strong Italian culture and some fine neighborhood spaghetti places. My wings are a blend of the these two cultures, so they acquire the Denver label and should easily make you forget Buffalo or Hoboken or any of those places in no time at all.

16 chicken wings
½ cup olive oil
juice from 2 limes
3 Tbsp grated Romano cheese
2 Tbsp chives
1 Tbsp cilantro
1 tsp cumin
½ tsp cayenne pepper
½ tsp garlic powder
salt & pepper

Lay the wings on a wooden cutting board and separate them by cutting them at their joints with a large sharp knife. Discard the bony end. Spread the chicken wings in a large shallow baking dish, being careful that none of the pieces jump on top of each other. They will marinate better this way.

Salt & pepper the wings. Mix the remaining ingredients in the measuring cup with a fork so they are well blended.

Pour the mixture over the wings, cover and refrigerate for 8 to 12 hours.

Preheat oven to 450 degrees.

Bake wings with cover on for 15 minutes. Remove cover and reduce heat to 350 degrees. Bake for an additional 1 hour and 15 minutes.

This is a great appetizer or even a main course with a tray of fresh vegetables and fruit. The skin on the chicken is the only fat offender so this could be a ***Happy Heart*** item if you only eat a few as an appetizer.

TRADE WINDS CHICKEN WINGS

Legend has it that Columbus arrived in the Islands just as Happy Hour was getting underway. The friendly locals were serving up *Planters Punch* and some of these wings to the sounds of a steel band. That is honestly how they got the name Trade Winds Chicken Wings. I was in the Bahamas last year, and I learned this secret from a man named "Island". Ya, Mon, it is true!

16 wings
1/3 cup soy sauce
1/3 cup rum
1/3 cup brown sugar
3 Tbsp olive oil
½ tsp ginger
1 Tbsp sesame seeds
1 Tbsp chives

Separate the wings at their joints with a large sharp knife and discard the bony ends. Lay the wing pieces in a shallow corning baker so that all pieces marinate evenly.

Blend all the ingredients together with a fork, pour over wings and refrigerate for 4 to 8 hours.

Bake—uncovered—in preheated 400-degree oven for 1 1/4 to 1 ½ hours or barbecue on a grill until crispy.

NOTE: This is a great marinade for chicken breasts or other parts of the chicken done on the grill in the Good Old Summer Time.

CROSTINI OLIVIO

Crostini may have its origins in Tuscany, but is a sure hit on any table. Most recipes with few ingredients place a heavy emphasis on the quality of each item, and fresh is often the deciding factor. This recipe is no exception to this rule and is best made with fresh buffalo mozzarella and either garden fresh tomatoes or sun-dried tomatoes. If you buy the mozzarella fresh, it only comes in one basic size somewhat smaller than a baseball. A plate of crostini, a bowl of soup, and a nice bottle of wine can make an easy Sunday evening meal.

1 loaf of French bread
1 ball of fresh mozzarella cheese
1 6 oz jar of Kalamata Kopanisti *
4 ripe fresh Roma tomatoes
garlic powder
2 Tbsp fresh basil – finely chopped
Extra Virgin olive oil

Cut the French bread on a 45 degree diagonal into 1 inch thick pieces. Brush each slice of bread with a fine film of olive oil and garlic powder and toast on your grill. Turn the bread once so it toasts on both sides.

Spread a layer of Kalamata on the bread followed by a slice of mozzarella and then a slice of tomato. Sprinkle some basil on the tomato and place on the middle rack of a 400-degree oven and bake until cheese begins to melt.

Serve hot from the oven.

If you are unable to find the Kopanisti, you can make your own by finely chopping some black Kalamata olives with olive oil, oregano, and garlic powder to form a paste-like mixture.

If you use Italian bread, you need to cut it down the middle first and then slice it. The pieces should be no larger than the slice of tomato.

PAISANO OLIVE SPREAD

This is a simple appetizer that goes well with some good Italian or French bread or even some nice crackers. You can make this ahead of time and refrigerate for days before you use it. It goes well with a cold beer, iced tea, a red wine, or strong liquor over the rocks. It has a bold and assertive flavor, so the drink needs to be able to stand on its own. A nice counter point to this spread would be creamy Brie that has been popped in the microwave for about 30 seconds.

2 garlic cloves
9 oz salad olives w/pimentos
6 large black olives w/pits
6 large Sicilian cracked olives
6 sun-dried tomatoes
1 tsp capers
3 Tbsp Extra Virgin olive oil
½ tsp cilantro
½ tsp crushed red pepper
black pepper

Drain the salad olives and trim the black and Sicilian olives from their pits. Blend the garlic well in the blender so it becomes fine. Add the olives and sun-dried tomatoes together and quickly pulse them with the garlic bits. Do not blend them into a paste but keep the consistency coarse Place the mixture in a mixing bowl and add the olive oil, cilantro, crushed red pepper and capers. Add a couple of twists of the pepper mill over the mix, and stir with a wooden spoon. Allow olive mix to stand at room temperature for 30 minutes before serving. If you do not have fresh bread or bread sticks, then use crackers because the bread is really critical. Consider putting out a couple of small bowls of this during cocktails before a nice dinner of *Ron's Rigatonis and Meatballs*.

This is an absolute ***Happy Heart*** recipe. The olive oil is a great HDL booster and garlic is good for your heart and your nagging arthritis!

WAREHOUSE MUSSEL'S MARINARA

Sometimes the best eating comes out of the strangest places. Denver had a Mexican restaurant in one of the worst neighborhoods that was a citywide favorite. Rockville, Maryland has a reputation for a string of Italian restaurants in an industrial section nestled amongst some auto body shops. For a brief period of time, there was a nice place in a row of warehouses that did not last long but made a lasting impact on me for their treatment of mussels. This is very inexpensive seafood that begs to be in a tomato marinara with a loaf of Italian bread next to it.

1 lb. mussels
1 35 oz can Italian tomatoes – crushed
1/3 cup olive oil
4 cloves garlic
4 spring onions
1 Tbsp parsley
½ cup white wine
1 ½ tsp marjoram
½ tsp crushed red pepper
salt & pepper

Scrub and clean the mussels, being careful to remove all their beards and discarding any broken or gaping shells. Keep the mussels in cold water until you are ready to cook them. Sliver and dice the garlic and dice the spring onions up to the first junction on the onion stem.

In a large saucepan or a small stockpot, heat the olive oil and then sauté the garlic—do not allow the garlic to turn brown. Add the remaining ingredients and simmer for 30 minutes. Add the mussels, cover and cook an additional 10 minutes.

Serve in soup bowls with plenty of French bread to soak up the sauce.

This is a 100% ***Happy Heart*** item that is also a CASH FLOW CHAMP. Mussels are so inexpensive in comparison to clams and oysters.

You may very well have a lot of the sauce left over when the mussels are eaten. If you do, you can use it to make *Mason-Dixon Line Jambalaya* found elsewhere in this collection.

OYSTERS ITALIANO

Oysters are the "Blue Chips" of the food world. You can use them in any "portfolio" in any number of ways. They can be fried, baked, broiled, or eaten raw. They can be a main course, appetizer or a main ingredient in everything from main courses to salads. On a trip to Italy many years ago, we ate in a little seaside trattoria that initiated my interest in Italian preparation of seafood. On that particular evening the place was actually closed, but the owner happened to be there and opened the doors for my friend and me and fixed dinner for the two of us. Can you imagine the NYSE opening on a Saturday just so you can sell your Disney stock?

12 fresh oysters
1 15 oz can tomato sauce
½ cup grated mozzarella cheese
3 Tbsp green pepper – finely chopped
3 Tbsp pepperoni – finely chopped

1 Tbsp marjoram
1 Tbsp olive oil
1 tsp allspice
1/4 tsp crushed red pepper
black pepper
rock salt

In a sauce pan heat the olive oil and add the tomato sauce, marjoram, allspice, red pepper, and black pepper to taste and cook over medium heat for 10 minutes. Add the green peppers and pepperoni and turn off heat.

Open oysters and discard the half without the flesh.

Place oysters on a bed of rock salt in a metal baking pan. Spoon the tomato sauce mixture over each oyster and top with a portion of grated mozzarella.

Bake in a preheated 450-degree oven for 10 minutes and serve hot.

If you make up two dozen of these things and a serving of *Crostini Olivio* along with a nice cold bottle of Fume Blanc, you can do a nice Sunday evening light meal for two with little or no fuss.

JOHN B'S WORLD-FAMOUS ONION RINGS

When you cruise on the Chesapeake Bay, you will invariably visit Annapolis. It is a lovely old community, but it is also too crowded and boat traffic is congested all summer long. A short sail from Annapolis will bring you to Herring Bay and the peace of the Rockhold Creek. At the mouth of the Rockhold, you should stop in at Skipper's Pier to sample the local color of this fishing community. John B. used to own this place and often held court at the dock bar while his lovely wife, Sherry, kept the wheels running on their prize on the bay. The steamed crabs were always a favorite here, but the onion rings were homemade and always served as a compliment to a dozen steamed crabs and a couple of cold beers. They are easy to make at home if you have a deep fat fryer.

4 medium white onions
2 cups Bisquick
½ cup grated Romano cheese
1 ½ cups Beer

Peel onions and slice them into 3/4" to 1" slices and separate the rings.

Mix Bisquick, grated cheese, and beer into a smooth batter.

Dip onion rings and deep fry in 400-degree corn oil until golden brown. It makes one grand mess, but this is not something that you make everyday so do not let it get you down.

Serve hot with lots of cold beer.

IRON GATE HUMUS & PITA CHIPS

Washington provides those rare moments in the summer when the humidity is bearable and the light breezes actually make living there a pleasure. When those rare combinations do occur, you must forsake the indoor dining places and eat outside. Unfortunately, there are not enough outdoor eating-places when the conditions are right. One exception is the Iron Gate Inn which has lovely grape arbors overhanging the courtyard patio. The Iron Gate serves Middle East cuisine so humus is a given on their menu. I have eaten it in the Middle East as well, and that is probably why I always associate it with sun-drenched lazy afternoons with little or no cares. It is also very easy to make and is a ***Happy Heart*** item even with the pita chips added to it.

1 16 oz can ceci beans (chick peas)
3-4 Tbsp olive oil (Extra Virgin)
½ tsp garlic powder
juice of 1 lemon
paprika
6-8 pita pockets

In a processor blend the ceci, olive oil, garlic powder and lemon juice until a smooth consistency develops.

Cut pitas into strips and bake in 450-degree oven until the edges begin to brown—approximately 5-6 minutes.

Drizzle a little olive oil over humus, garnish with paprika and serve with warm pita for dipping.

Pretty easy stuff and you don't need an oil well to afford it.

ALL THE SALAD YOU WILL EVER NEED

ANTIPASTO CLASSICO

I think that the key to a good antipasto salad is abundance. It needs to be big and contain everything but the kitchen sink. When I make mine, I make it on the largest platter I own and it weighs about 75 pounds when it is finished! I try to imagine that if John Madden were making it, it might look this way and that pushes me to really pile it on.

This is a dish that begins a feast. It can sit out on the table or highboard while people are milling around with a drink and talking. Provide small plates so each person can carry around their own creation. It also does well for a seated group. With all the variety it is sure to please everybody at the table.

1 head iceberg lettuce
1 can sardines
1 6 oz jar Cara Mia artichoke hearts
2 large ripe tomatoes
1 large green pepper
1 medium red pepper
8 spring onions
4 large slices Bermuda onion
2 Tbsp ceci beans
12 black Sicilian olives
12 stuffed green olives
12 pepperoncinis
12 slices Genoa salami
8 slices mortadella
8 slices provolone cheese
2 hard boiled eggs
1/3 cup Extra Virgin olive oil
1 Tbsp oregano
2 Tbsp grated Romano cheese
black pepper

Rinse the lettuce in cold water and break off the larger outer leaves to line the bottom of the platter. The lining should be 3 or 5 leaves deep.

Slice the green and red peppers into rings and place them around the platter. Section the tomatoes and alternate them with the peppers. Sprinkle the olives, pepperoncinis, pieces of the artichoke hearts and ceci beans randomly over the platter.

Role the salami, mortadella, and provolone into funnel shapes and rotate them around the outer edges, along with the sardines and spring onions. By this point, you should be developing a mound effect in the center of the platter. Lay the Bermuda onion down the center of the mound with slices of hard-boiled egg, making a border around the onion

Mix the olive oil, romano cheese and oregano in a mixing bowl by whisking it together thoroughly. Sprinkle oil mixture over antipasto; grind some fresh black pepper, and serve.

The only trick here is to make it look good. All you are really doing is being creative with the display. There is no cooking involved, just jar and can opening and placement.

If you have colored sheets, be sure you wash them in cold water or they will fade and look tacky.

INSALATA RONALDO

This was a ***TRAVELING LINGUINI BROTHERS*** original. I needed a salad that would compliment my *Veal Toscano,* so this was born to fill that need. This is a better summer salad because of the need for fresh tomatoes, but if you can find some good grape tomatoes or imported cherry tomatoes in the winter, you may discover a nice salad even in the middle of winter.

4 medium fresh tomatoes
1 6 oz jar of Cara Mia artichoke hearts
1 small green pepper
5 slices of Bermuda onion – thin
5 strips of fresh bacon
10 giant black olives
1/4 cup Extra Virgin olive oil
2 Tbsp Worcestershire sauce
2 Tbsp fresh basil – finely chopped
2 Tbsp Gorgonzola cheese – crumbled
juice from 2 lemons
Boston Bib lettuce
salt & pepper

Cut the bacon into 1-inch strips and cook until crisp. Remove from fat and place on a paper towel to drain.

Section and quarter the tomato and place in a mixing bowl. Chop the green pepper into nickel-sized pieces, cut the onion slices in half, slice the olives, drain the artichoke hearts, and add remainder of ingredients to mixing bowl. Mix and place in refrigerator for 15 minutes before serving.

Place large leaves of lettuce on each plate, top with salad mix, and then sprinkle bacon on the top just prior to serving.

NANNY'S SIMPLE LETTUCE SALAD

Sometimes the key to a simple dish is found in some little variation in the preparation that many cooks might overlook. This salad may have one of those little secrets in it. I think the key is crisp lettuce, and Nanny always used to soak her lettuce in cold water in the refrigerator for 20 to 30 minutes prior to making this salad. Try this technique anytime you use lettuce.

1 head of iceberg lettuce
1 medium white onion
8 – 10 Italian olives with the pits
6 – 8 medium pepperoncinis
2 Tbsp Extra Virgin olive oil
juice from 2 lemons
½ tsp oregano
salt & pepper

Shake excess water from lettuce, break apart by hand, and place in mixing bowl. Add remaining ingredients and toss well before serving.

This is a great salad to serve after a nice plate of spaghetti and meatballs. Italians tend to eat their salads after the main course on the firm belief that it aids in the digestive process. You will also find that your wine tastes better with the main course if you have not had a vinegar or lemon-based salad prior to the main course.

UNCLE JIMMY'S ITALIAN TOMATO SALAD

I remember one time hearing a relative say that all you needed to do to make Uncle Jimmy happy was to give him an Italian Tomato Salad. I thought how could that be? If you have ever come home on a warm summer day to a loaf of fresh Italian bread and one of these salads, you will understand the meaning of "simple pleasures". It is true—this is a fine repast all by itself with a loaf of bread or a compliment to almost any meal. I must warn you, however, that this salad only works with honest garden tomatoes—no substitutes please!

6 – 8 large fresh tomatoes
1 medium white or red onion
1/3 cup Extra Virgin olive oil
2 Tbsp Worcestershire sauce
1/4 cup chopped basil – loosely packed
½ tsp oregano
salt & pepper

Section the tomatoes and slice the onion using only the center portion of the onion. Mix all of the ingredients into a ceramic mixing bowl—not aluminum—and stir well.

Cover the bowl and refrigerate for not less than 20 minutes but not more than 60 minutes.

You must have some fresh Italian or French bread to soak up the juices. You may even want to drink the juice it will taste that good.

The salad is a true ***Happy Heart*** recipe, but be careful of the bread—no butter—you do not need it. If you want it to have real zero fat grams, have a whole grain bagel instead of the bread.

TOMATO & MOZZARELLA SALAD

There are limited ingredients in this recipe, and it is imperative that **ALL** items are fresh or else it will not work. You need fresh tomatoes, fresh buffalo mozzarella, and fresh basil. You may have to search for the buffalo milk mozzarella, but you will be in for a real treat when you find it. It is not easy to find and when you do, it will be quite expensive. Like many things that are simple, the beauty of that simplicity often strikes us. Go into any fine Italian restaurant and you will find this salad on their summer menu. Now you can create it yourself and be a hit the next time you entertain.

2 large ripe tomatoes
1 ball of fresh *buffalo* mozzarella
2 Tbsp of fresh basil – chopped
2 Tbsp Extra Virgin olive oil
salt & pepper

Take the best three or four slices of the center of the tomato for each serving. Do not pinch on this recipe. Cut an equal number of 1/4 to ½ inch mozzarella slices from the center of the mozzarella ball.

Lay the tomato slices on a flat surface, salt & pepper to taste, and then sprinkle the basil over the tomato and mozzarella. Alternate the tomato and mozzarella slices on a plate, and drizzle the olive oil down the center of the presentation.

Garnish with one or two whole basil leaves and serve at room temperature.

This is an excellent accompaniment for any veal or beef dish. It will not violate your red wine since it is not an overpowering or citric offering. If you wish to splash some balsamic vinegar on top of the tomatoes, that will add some additional zest! If you are serving fresh bread, it is nice to have it on the table when this is served so you can sponge up the juices on the plate when the salad is consumed. If the Godfather can do this, so can you!

MOM'S POTATO SALAD

As far back as I have memories, there is potato salad in those memories. When I was growing up (the first time), we spent our summers at our cabin on Lake Superior. The memories of blueberry pies baked in the wood stove or morning toast from the top of that wood stove are lasting ones. So are the times we would get in the boat and motor up to the picnic area for those afternoon lunches under those majestic Michigan White Pines. My Mom often made Potato Salad in those days and years later when I attempted my first picnic, I called her to get this recipe. Many things change in life, but I am certain this is the way it was done back in the "old days".

4 large white potatoes
6 radishes
2 ribs of celery
2 slices white onion – diced
2 hard boiled eggs
2 medium tomatoes
2 heaping Tbsp mayo
1 Tbsp parsley
paprika
black pepper

Cube the potatoes into 1 ½ inch square cubes and boil in salted water until cooked firm. (Approximately 15 minutes) Drain the potatoes, add the onions immediately, and let stand till they cool. Dice the tomatoes, celery, and hard-boiled eggs and slice the radishes.

Mix all ingredients together with a few turns of black pepper grindings and top with a dusting of paprika. You can refrigerate and serve later or serve it as soon as it is prepared.

If you have some bacon crumbs left over, they make a nice addition and so does adding a handful of frozen peas to the boiling potato water.

MILWAUKEE POTATO SALAD

If you happen to be in the great Midwest city of Milwaukee during the summer, you need to take in the ***Summer Fest*** activities down by the waterfront. The city hosts a series of fests that spotlight the ethic richness of this crossroads city. One of the highlights is the ***German Fest*** with the sounds of the ompah bands and the smell of bratwurst in the air. This German-style potato salad eats well when it is warm or cold, depending on the accompanying entrees. You can eat it at home, or take it along on a picnic in the mountains.

6-7 new white potatoes
3-4 slices of bacon – diced
3 slices of Bermuda onion – diced
1/3 cup wine vinegar
1 Tbsp sugar
1 tsp dry mustard
1 tsp salt
1 Tbsp flour
2/3 Cup Water
parsley
fresh pepper

Cut the potatoes in half and then slice into 1/4 inch slices. Bring a pot of water to a boil, add salt, and boil about 5 – 7 minutes until tender. Drain and set aside in a large mixing bowl while remaining ingredients come together.

While the potatoes are boiling, cook the diced bacon over moderate heat until crisp, then remove with a slotted spoon and set aside.

Add the onions to the bacon fat and sauté lightly. When the onions become limp, add the vinegar, sugar, dry mustard and salt, stirring until it comes to a gentle boil. Vigorously mix the flour and water together in a bowl, making sure all the lumps are gone. Add the water flour mixture, along with the bacon bits, and bring to a gentle boil for 2 minutes.

Blend the sauce into the potatoes, adding a sprinkle of parsley and fresh ground black pepper.

This salad goes well with *Championship Brats, Patti's Perfect Pork Chops*, and *Grandpa Fred's T-Bones.*

MICHIGAN COLE SLAW

I am certain that this recipe is common all over the country, but I remember it from my growing years and since those were in Michigan, I get to call it Michigan Cole Slaw. It somehow evokes memories of giant White Pine trees swaying gently in the breezes that come off the Great Lakes. I can recall those wonderful summer picnics down the beach from the cabin, and it brings to mind those pristine beaches and clear water with magnificent August sunsets. Pretty good stuff from a bunch of cabbage!

½ head cabbage
1/4 head red cabbage
2 large carrots
3 Tbsp crushed pineapple
3 Tbsp pineapple juice
2 Tbsp green pepper – chopped
1 tsp caraway seed
3 heaping Tbsp mayo
black pepper

Dice the cabbage and carrot together into a fine chop. Mix together the remaining ingredients and chill in refrigerator for at least 30 minutes before serving.

Cole slaw makes a nice topping for all of your barbecue sandwiches.

The Great Lakes are the world's largest body of fresh water.

CAESAR STEAK SALAD

There is a sort of mystique about having a Caesar salad prepared at your table that conjures up images of **Humphrey Bogart** and **Peter Lori** in white dinner jackets entertaining ladies with strapless evening gowns and wide brimmed hats. You should have a large wooden salad bowl to do this properly, and a tube of anchovy paste will solve the little fish dilemma. This salad requires a little bit of advance prep work if you want to serve it with a measure of flair.

1 lb. thin round steak *
1 head iceberg & romaine lettuce
2 slices Bermuda onion – diced
½ cup ceci beans
1 large egg
½ tsp garlic powder
3 Tbsp olive oil
½ tsp anchovy paste
½ cup croutons
juice from 1 lemon
2 Tbsp blue cheese – crumbled
3/4 cup Parmesan cheese – grated
black pepper

Cut the round steak into 2-inch squares and sauté in a pan with salt, pepper and garlic powder to taste. Be generous with the pepper.

In a separate holding bowl, wash the lettuce in ice-cold water and pat dry in paper toweling. Break up about one third to one half of each head of lettuce into pieces, add the onion and ceci beans, and set aside for the moment.

In your large wooden salad bowl, break the egg into the bottom and add the garlic powder, anchovy paste, and olive oil and whisk together with a fork until well blended.

Add the bowl of lettuce, steak, croutons, lemon juice, blue cheese and grated cheese and toss until well mixed. Grate fresh black pepper over salad and serve.

* You can use leftover flank steak, filet, t-bone or any other quality piece of meat to make this salad. You can also use cold grilled chicken breast as a substitute for the beef. If you like the anchovy taste, you can increase the measurement to 1 full tsp.

LAS CRUCES CHICKEN CLUB SALAD

This summer salad evokes days of the New Mexican desert, big wide-open skies, and the dry hot winds that sweep across the open land. This salad for two really does the job on a lazy summer day when you feel like doing a little grilling out of doors. If you can find some mesquite charcoal or smoker chips, it will enhance the flavor greatly.

juice of a lime
1 large chicken breast – boneless
paprika
salt & pepper
1 head iceberg lettuce
4 strips thick bacon
1 avocado – cubed
2 eggs – hard boiled
1 medium Bermuda onion – sliced
6 pepperoncinis
12 cherry tomatoes – sliced in half
12 baby corn cobs
red wine vinegar
Extra Virgin olive oil
white corn chips

Place the chicken breast in a sealable container, squeeze the lime over the chicken, and dust with paprika, salt, and pepper. Marinate for 4 to 6 hours.

On a hot grill, cook the chicken until done, turning once or twice. Set aside. Fry the bacon in a skillet until crisp. Remove and set aside. Drain all but 1 Tbsp of bacon grease. Sauté the onion until it just begins to turn limp.

In a bowl, break the lettuce and add the pepperoncinis, tomatoes, avocado, grilled onions and corn cobs. Crumble the bacon into the bowl and dress with vinegar and oil to taste (Remember—more vinegar than oil) and toss. Break up a handful of corn chips on the bottom of each individual salad bowl and then spoon the lettuce mix over the chips. Slice the chicken breasts on the diagonal, and lay an equal number of strips across the lettuce mound and crown with the egg quarters.

Try some fresh lemonade and an assortment of fresh-baked bread sticks and jump in the hammock after lunch. ***Happy Heart*** and happy dreams in the hammock!

SHRIMP & PASTA MEDLEY

This is truly a summer creation that becomes a medley because of the variety of ingredients found in the salad. I like to use as many as three or four different kinds of pasta and everything I have growing in my garden at the time. The variety of pastas provide eye appeal from the different shapes and colors that are missing when you use only one kind of pasta. If you keep your pastas in glass storage units like I do, you can grab a handful of whatever you like to mix and match. I like to use the spinach and tomato along with the basic pasta, so you get an Italian red, white and green effect. Try to use pastas that have a similar consistency so the cooking time is uniform. Cooking a big rigatoni and a small penne together, for example, will have the rigatoni under cooked while the penne is over cooked. Wheels, small shells, radatori, fusilli, rotini, cut ziti, and penne are all compatible in cooking time.

1 lb. mixed pasta
3/4 lb. medium shrimp
1 Tbsp olive oil
1 tsp garlic powder
3 oz frozen peas
½ cup green peppers
1/4 cup red bell peppers
2 medium tomatoes
10 black olives
2 slices Bermuda onion – diced
1 Tbsp fresh parsley
1 tsp cayenne pepper
1 Tbsp dill weed
3 Tbsp mayo
black pepper

Sauté the shrimp in the olive oil and garlic powder until they are completely cooked. Boil the pasta in salted water until al dente, add the peas, and drain immediately.

Dice the peppers and tomatoes and slice the olives. Add all ingredients to mixing bowl and mix thoroughly, adding more mayo if necessary.

Refrigerate at least 30 minutes prior to serving. If you use a no-fat or Lite mayo, this is a ***Happy Heart*** recipe.

CARLO'S HOUSEWARMING PASTA SALAD

When George and Patti bought a big old house on the water, one year I docked my boat in one of their slips. It was an unseasonably warm spring day, and I had spent most of the day recommissioning the ***"Little Duck"*** and did not feel much like fussing over dinner. Yet it was a perfect evening for eating on the boat as the sun set. This recipe fed four of us and helped to say, "Welcome to your new home."

3/4 lb. radatori (spinach, tomato & wheat)
1/4 lb. fussili
1/3 cup peas – frozen
1 Tbsp olive oil
3 links sweet Italian sausage – sliced
4 boneless chicken breasts – diced
juice of 1 lime
1 tsp garlic powder
1 tsp rosemary
1 tsp sage
½ tsp cayenne pepper
black pepper
6 oz artichoke hearts
6-8 green olives
½ green bell pepper – diced
4 Italian plum tomatoes – diced
1 hard boiled egg – diced
Good Seasons Italian Dressing made w/white wine vinegar & olive oil

In a sauté pan, heat the olive oil and sauté the sausage and chicken breasts with the garlic powder, rosemary, sage and lime juice. Set aside when cooked.

Meanwhile, cook the pasta in salted boiling water until al dente. Add the peas at the end of the cooking and drain water. Combine meats with pasta and allow a few minutes to cool.

Add remaining ingredients and about 1/4 to 1/3 of a cup of Good Seasonings dressing and toss. Serve at room temperature.

SICILIAN WHITE BEAN SALAD

This is one of those recipes that I started out with a basic concept for and just threw it together without any forethought. It is a definite ***Happy Heart*** contribution that is also loaded with good protein and fiber. This *IS* an offer you cannot refuse!

12 oz great northern beans – dry
1 2½ oz can white tuna in oil
1 cup frozen corn
1 large ripe tomato – diced
2 Tbsp Extra Virgin olive oil
1/4 cup Extra Virgin olive oil
3 spring onions – diced
2 tsp rosemary
1 tsp basil
1 tsp cilantro
1 bay leaf
juice of 1 lemon
dusting of garlic powder
dusting of cayenne pepper
black pepper
salt

Soak the beans in fresh water overnight. Discard the soaking water.

Rinse the beans and bring to a boil in salted water. Skim off the residue with a large spoon and discard. Reduce heat to a simmer and add the two tablespoons of olive oil, bay leaf, rosemary, basil and cilantro and continue to cook until beans become soft—45 to 60 minutes. When beans are finished cooking, add the frozen corn and salt and drain immediately into a large colander.

In a large mixing bowl, add the beans, tuna, garlic powder, cayenne, black pepper, lemon juice, and 1/4 cup of olive oil. Toss and chill for 30 to 45 minutes before serving.

This salad should be served on a bed of crisp lettuce.

BOWLS AND SPOONS
(SOUPS)

CALLING THE SIGNALS IN THE KITCHEN

My mother was fond of saying that the test of a good marriage is whether or not two people can hang wallpaper together. Along those same lines, the test of good cooking is being able to get the meal on the table and be more relaxed at serving time than you were when you started. I am aware that this is not the case with many people that I know, because many of them have asked me what the secret is to cooking cool.

The first thing is to *look* cool. Invest in some fun aprons or even a chef's jacket. The big boys wear them so why not you? So, while we are at it, why not *act* like the pros do.

Get a sous-chef. The pleasure of cooking can be greatly enhanced when you do it with someone who can be a good helper. Needless to say, a good helper can make all the difference in the world in creating the ambience and even the quality of the finished product. Let us not forget that much of the reason for cooking and eating is the social interplay that takes place before, during and after the meal. Some people are natural helper types and if you know one of those, you are extremely lucky and need not read any further. If, however, you are like most of us and either do not have a helper all the time or are not quite able to get it just right, here are some tips that will make your cooking come together a little better.

Location, location, location is a well-worn expression in real estate, but it can also apply to cooking, as well. Naturally, we would all do well to have designer kitchens, but the truth of the matter is that most people do not, and even those that do have one, do not know how to properly use it. In this case, I am talking about layout. You need a workspace to put these meals into production. In an ideal arrangement, you will have counter tops that are close to both your sink and stovetop. That counter top should afford as much premium working space as possible that is free of clutter and distraction. You do not need 30 feet of counter top to cook well. If you stand next to your sink and place one hand on the edge of the sink and extend the other hand down the counter, that is the premium workspace you need. This is logical since that is all you can reach. That premium workspace—"ground zero"—should have no machines, gadgets, or other obstructions because that is where most of your food prep will take place. If you can allocate another foot of counter top on the opposite side of the sink, that will come in handy later on. I mentioned earlier that it would be nice to be able to turn around or take one side step to the range top, but that is not as critical as being close to the sink for Stage One.

Do not worry if your cupboards and cabinets that house your gadgets and service pieces are not within easy reach of ground zero because the first step in good cooking logistics is to lay everything out ahead of time. I like to line up everything that I will need to create the recipe before I start. This practice gives me the opportunity to visualize the process and the end result. If you ever have a chance to be in the kitchen of a well-run restaurant, you will notice that all of the workstations have everything they need within arms reach and eyesight. The last thing you want to be doing when your hands have just come out of mixing meat is to be fumbling through drawers looking for a wooden spoon. I have, on more than one occasion, set out to make something only to discover midway through the recipe that I was missing a main ingredient, a critical tool, or a piece of cookware.

You want to line up your tools and wares on the outer ring of your prime work space so you can drag them into service at the appropriate time. Your cutting board and the ingredient you are working on should be at center court, and the other ingredients should be playing in the secondary line within easy reach. At this point in time, I like to set the cooking utensils on the stove. This tells you how many burners you will need and it gives you one more step in the visualization process. Remember, you can always prepare things in a mixing bowl at the counter and then take the mixing bowl to the waiting cookware on the stove.

To accomplish the set up, you clearly need to read the recipe or think out what you are making so you can round up the proper inventory of ingredients. At this point, you should have your bowls, spices, and other ingredients lined up in front of you.

Cooking is a fundamental management application of delegation of duty, coupled with good communication skills. It works something like this: If I were making *BOSS HOG*, for example, I would get out the big deep Corning and say, "O.K., Corning will house the pork shoulder when it is time." Then I would get out a large metal mixing bowl and say, "Yes, the mixing bowl will be responsible for the sauce!" It is a matter of choice as to what you call your ingredients, but if you use audibles while you work through the mental checklist, you will be certain to have all the players assembled prior to calling the play. It is at this point that the thought of talking to your Corning ware may be more acceptable than some of the nasty things that could come spilling out of your frustrated jaws in front of your best pal. A lot of the barking and snarling at one and other during the preparation process simply comes from bad planning.

Begin with the item that takes the longest to cook. For example, if you are having rice or potatoes and they take 30 to 45 minutes to cook and the main entree only takes 15 minutes, you should get your longer-cooking items started right away. If you think it through, it is possible to time things so they all come together at the same time, and you complete and set the table in one graceful movement. Incidentally, if you do not have time to set the table during the cooking time, it is always a good idea to set it before you begin the prep process. This is something your helper can do during a lull in preparations. Once again, setting the table in advance allows you to visualize the end product and that adds to the overall success of the project.

Keep your prime workspace as clutter-free as possible. Make good use of your sink. Throw meat wrappers, trimmings, dirty bowls, whatever, into the sink to get them out of your way and allow you maximum use of the prep space. You can always clean the sink later, or once again; your helper can do this as you go along. I should give a personal pointer at this juncture, and that is this helper business is dirty work, so you need to be mindful and give appropriate pats, pecks, plaudits and promises of things to come to your helper, or run the risk of facing a job discrimination suit!

Also, it does not hurt to have a cocktail or glass of wine handy during the prep time to keep everyone really cool and happy.

The objective is to keep your assembly space as functional as possible and that means retiring things that no longer have use in the recipe. Earlier,

I mentioned having a space on the other side of the sink. It is obvious that not everything can end up in the sink, and that is especially true of seasonings and other ingredients that get used again. I find it helpful to move the used items to the other side of the sink once they have been used. This can be particularly useful when the recipe has a lot of ingredients in it. I start with everything on my right (I am right-handed) lined up in the order of the recipe. Once I have added it to the mixing or cooking vessel, I then set it on the left side of the sink. This eliminates any confusion in larger recipes as to whether or not I added a particular item to the recipe if I am reading the recipe as I prepare it.

If you have timed things so that everything is coming together at the same time, you will find the excitement level increases geometrically at this point. This is a good time to remember that the objective is to *enjoy* the meal and not to spoil the ambience that the meal should be creating. In other words, this is not the time to worry about cleaning the kitchen. If you have been cleaning as you go along and your sink has been cleaned of all the garbage, you can dump a lot of pots and pans into the sink. In any case, do not worry about it. If you returned refrigerated items to the refrigerator when you were finished with them, you can simply dish up the meal, turn the lights out in the kitchen, and clean up later that night or, if romance dictates, remember that you can even clean up the next morning!

BIG RON'S ORIGINAL COLORADO CHILE

I think this is the one true universal. It seems to me that everyone likes chile and almost everyone makes it. Chile may have become as American as apple pie or hot dogs. It is the staple of every football game gathering, whether in the parking lot at the stadium or in the comfort of your living room. There are as many ways of making chile as there are people who make it, and there are also many ways of serving it, as well. I have two basic rules about chile and they are: make it simple and make it big. Three or four days later, this chile is superb over a dish of rigatoni with grated pecorino romano cheese on it.

Like Colorado's mountains, this is a big serving recipe and therefore requires a large stockpot. I use a 10 or 12-quart heavy gauge aluminum stockpot because I like to prepare everything in the stockpot and eliminate the use of a frying pan. An 8-quart will work, but it gives you less working room in the pot.

4 – 5 lbs. ground meat (You can use any grade of beef, pork, or turkey. I like a mix of all three.)
1 tsp garlic powder
1 32 oz can whole Italian tomatoes
2 28 oz cans tomato puree
4 – 5 Tbsp red chile powder
4 – 5 Tbsp cumin
4 – 5 bay leaves
4 – 5 Tbsp cilantro
1 Tbsp crushed red pepper
1 52 oz can of kidney beans *
2 14 oz cans of black beans
2 14 oz cans of pinto beans
¼ cup yellow corn meal
¼ cup milk
salt & pepper

Brown the meat in the stockpot with the garlic powder, salt and pepper. When the meat is gray in color (some red and pink can remain), drain the excess fat into a colander and discard. This solves some of the problem of the fat content in the meat.

Add the can of whole tomatoes, half the chile powder and cumin, cover and cook on medium heat for about 30 minutes. The tomatoes should break down by now, but if large chunks persist, you can help them along with a large wooden spoon. If you do not like chucks of tomato in your chile, run them through the food processor for a moment before adding to the stockpot. Now add the tomato puree, the rest of the cumin, chile powder, bay leaves, cilantro, and red pepper. Allow chile to simmer another 45 to 60 minutes on low heat.

Blend corn meal and milk to a smooth consistency in measuring cup and add, with kidney beans, in the last 15 minutes of cooking.

Serve with shredded sharp cheddar, sour cream, diced white onions, corn chips, and flour tortillas on the side.

*Dry pinto beans can be used as the only bean in this chile, and they do add a different flavor. Soak and cook according to package and once fully cooked, you can add them to the recipe in the last 15 minutes just as you did the canned kidney beans.

COPPER MOUNTAIN CHILE & RICE

In the winter of 1991, I was skiing in Colorado with my good friend, Brad Pelsue. Since Brad is much younger than I am, he had succeeded in skiing my legs off by about 3:00 P.M. and had left me at the bottom of the mountain while he made one more run before calling it quits. As I reclined on an outdoor picnic table near the American Eagle lift, I overheard a lady telling her friend about chile and rice and how her children enjoy it. I am sorry that I did not get the name of the mystery lady, but since I was at Copper Mountain, I decided to name it after that great ski resort. I had often made chile and pasta, but had never tried the chile and rice combination. When I returned home, I made some and discovered that it was a hit with adults and children alike. Here is a very easy item once you have the chile on hand.

6 cups *Big Ron's Original Colorado Chile*
1 cup long grain white rice
½ cup sharp cheddar cheese – shredded

Heat the chile over moderate heat while cooking the rice according to package instructions. I prefer "regular" rice but in a pinch, if you are really tired from skiing all day and still want to serve a hot meal, then Minute Rice will work as well.

Fill soup bowls half full with rice, layer with shredded cheese, and top with approximately 1 to 1 ½ cups of chile.

That is it. You will have four to six good servings from this recipe.

Serve with *Nanny's Simple Lettuce Salad*, a loaf of fresh French bread, and a bottle of very cold beer for the adults, and soda for the kids.

MID-VAIL BLACK BEAN & CHICKEN CHILE

A couple of years ago while skiing my favorite mountain we stopped for lunch at Mid-Vail. It was one of those unforgettable days when all the conditions were just right. The sun was intense, the snow perfect, and my companion most agreeable. It only seemed right that a new item on the menu would make a real lasting hit. What follows is merely my own interpretation of that offering and may be different from what is being served at Mid-Vail today, but it serves my purpose nonetheless.

3 large boneless chicken thighs – diced
1 Tbsp olive oil
1 6 oz can tomato paste
1 tsp ground cumin
½ tsp chile powder
½ tsp cilantro
½ tsp marjoram
½ tsp allspice
1 12oz bag dry black beans
2 Tbsp cumin
1 Tbsp chile powder
1 Tbsp cilantro
2 large tomatoes – diced
1 cup chicken broth (2 cubes)
salt & pepper

Prepare the black beans by soaking overnight, draining, rinsing and then boiling in salted water for 1 hour. Remove 2 cups of beans after they have cooked, puree in blender, and set aside.

Sauté the chicken thighs in the olive oil with salt and pepper until golden brown. Add the tomato paste and turn until it is fluid. Add the cumin, chile powder, cilantro, marjoram, and allspice. Continue to cook on low heat for an additional 15 minutes.

Combine the chicken mix with the black beans, the bean puree, the chicken broth, the additional cumin, chile powder, and cilantro and simmer an additional 30 minutes.

Add the diced tomatoes. Salt and pepper to taste and simmer an additional 30 minutes.

This is a ***Happy Heart*** item until you drop a dollop of sour cream on top of each bowl as you serve it. In any case, a nice big slice of corn bread and a cold beer will put you right on top of the mountain.

PEPI'S GOULASH SOUP

Gasthof Grammshammer in Vail is one of the best places in the world to sit out on the porch, watch the people go by, and eat Goulash Soup! It does not matter if it is the peak of the ski season or the middle of the summer; this is a year-round favorite. You have a perfect blend of nature—the beautiful mountains and blue skies, humanity, and graceful architecture inhabited by gentle, happy people. Given this environment, how could the food be anything but good? If the food happens to be outstanding, as is the case here, you need nothing more for the moment.

I actually had my first Goulash Soup in another outdoor bierstube on the side of a vineyard near Ludwigsburg, Germany. It, too, had that lasting memorable quality to it. I hope you will find an occasion to turn this recipe into that kind of an experience.

1 lb. lean stew meat
1/3 cup flour
1/3 cup corn oil
1 35 oz can Italian tomatoes – blended
1 Tbsp paprika
1 tsp parsley
1 tsp Kitchen Bouquet
½ tsp caraway seeds
½ tsp thyme
1 bay leaf
1 large potato – diced
salt & pepper

Cut the stew meat into smaller pieces and mix in the flour seasoned with salt and pepper so that the meat is lightly coated. Sauté in the corn oil in a 4-½ quart saucepot. Add oil if necessary.

As soon as the meat is browned, you can add the tomatoes, paprika, parsley,

Kitchen Bouquet, caraway seeds, thyme, and bay leaf and reduce to a simmer. Simmer for at least 1 hour and 30 minutes to fully tenderize the meat.

Add the potato and continue to cook for an additional 20 to 30 minutes. Prior to serving, or at the table, you can add a dollop of sour cream and stir into the soup.

On a cool autumn day, this goes well with a bottle of beer and a loaf of French bread.

THE POLISH NAVY SOUP

Some people refer to this as Senate Bean Soup but since I make mine with kielbasa and navy beans, it seems more logical to call it Polish Navy Soup. You remember I said that I name things after friends and memorable experiences, and I often wonder if we have any friends in the Senate. I could not give my soup their name. This is a great stick-to-your-ribs kind of soup that goes well after an autumn day on the water or upon returning from your college homecoming football game.

16 oz dry great northern beans
2 Tbsp olive oil
2 garlic cloves
1 celery rib – diced
½ lb. kielbasa *
2 tsp tomato paste
2 cups chicken broth (2 bouillon cubes)
1 Tbsp chives

1 Tbsp parsley
3 bay leaves
6 cups water
¼ cup carrots – diced
salt & pepper

Soak the beans in cold water for 8 to 12 hours. Be certain there is sufficient water to cover the beans with 2 inches of water. Drain and rinse the beans with fresh water.

In a heavy stock pot, heat the olive oil, garlic and celery over medium heat, add the sliced and halved pieces of kielbasa and sauté until golden. Add the tomato paste and stir frequently to keep from burning. Cook until paste is diluted and acquires a golden glow. Add all the remaining ingredients, except the carrots, and increase the heat to medium high. Bring to a boil for 5 minutes. Lower heat and simmer for 2 hours or until beans become tender. Remove a cup of beans, puree and return to the stockpot with the carrots and lots of black pepper and salt, as needed. Simmer for an additional 20 minutes.

This is a high fiber ***Happy Heart*** entree that goes well with a nice turkey sandwich on whole wheat bread.

* This is another soup that lends itself well to the leftover ham bone, which is how the Senate does it because when it comes to pork, they are the experts. If you have a ham bone left from another meal, you can toss it in the stockpot instead of the kielbasa. Instead of sautéing, just put the ham bone and all the other items into the pot and cook away.

GRANNIE'S FRENCH PEA SOUP

My maternal grandmother—a French Canadian—was one of the best cooks I can remember. Her house was always filled with warm and wonderful aromas from the oven and the stove. True to those promises, there were always goodies stashed in her pantry. At the turn of the century, as a young woman, she worked as a pastry cook in a hotel in the heart of the mining country of northern Michigan and learned her trade well. I regret that I did not have the opportunity to work with her in her kitchen and preserve some of her recipes firsthand. This is how my mom and I remember this soup.

1 ham bone (smoked picnic shoulder with meat left on it)*
3 quarts water
2 cups split green peas
2/3 cup yellow onion – diced
2 chicken boullion cubes
2 bay leaves
1 Tbsp parsley
½ tsp thyme
1 tsp black pepper
1/2 cup carrots – sliced
1 large potato – diced
salt

* Any leftover ham bone will do, just as long as it has sufficient meat left on the bone. I like a picnic shoulder, but it does not matter.

Inspect your ham bone and remove any accessible fat and hide. Rinse and clean your dry peas to check for any foreign objects.

In a large stockpot, place the water, ham bone, peas, onions, boullion, bay leaves, parsley, thyme, and black pepper. Bring water to a rapid boil, and then reduce to a simmer. Cover partially and cook for approximately 1 hour. Add the carrots and potatoes and cook an additional 1-hour. Remove the ham bone, trim the meat from the bone, and return the meat to the soup. The bone you can give to your favorite pooch.

This is an easy recipe that requires very little tending once it is started. It is a great weekender since you need not be fussing over the stockpot, and you can do other things while it cooks. It is a good use of that leftover piece of ham from a prior meal.

Check the flavor and add salt, as needed. Depending on the amount and saltiness of the ham, you may only need a little salt. Serve this soup with a heavy rye bread, some sharp cheese, and a good European beer.

MANHATTAN DELI LENTIL SOUP

New York may be the pits in many respects, but you have to admit that some of the food in that city is unparalleled in many ways. The delis are legendary and serve some kind of soup, but most of them serve lentil soup. No matter where you live, you should get in a cab, on an airplane or a train, and go to Manhattan for the day and have some lentil soup and a pastrami sandwich. Or just make this soup and stay at home and gaze at the mountains.

5 cups water
3 beef boullion cubes
8 oz lentils
1 stalk celery – chopped
1 large carrot – chopped

4 plum tomatoes – diced
1 bay leaf
1 Tbsp chives
1 link kielbasa – diced
½ box frozen spinach
salt & pepper

Heat the water in a 3-4 quart pot until it comes to a boil. Add the boullion cubes, reduce the heat to medium and continue cooking until the boullion dissolves.

Add the lentils, celery, carrot, and bay leaves and cover and cook for 30 minutes. Add the tomatoes, chives, kielbasa, salt and pepper, and cook an additional 30 minutes. Add the spinach and cook until well mixed. Turn off heat and let stand on stovetop for an additional 30 minutes.

The best soup will be that which you serve the following day, but if you really must have some, you can return the heat until the soup is hot to eat.

Some people like to grate parmesan cheese over the bowl before serving or add a tablespoon of rice to the bowl. If you like crackers, a handful of oyster crackers lends a nice touch.

MID-WINTER VEGETABLE BEEF (CHICKEN) SOUP

This soup is welcome any time of the year, but the preparation lends itself to a nice, snowy winter day. It is the kind of thing that gives your kitchen a nice warm feeling, with an aroma that makes you feel snug and homey. It takes some time to prepare, so you can enjoy the fireplace and even find time for romance while it is cooking. In other words, it is not so demanding a recipe that you cannot do other things while it is coming together. I use a 10 quart stockpot to fix this recipe. It will keep in the refrigerator for five days and a couple of weeks in the freezer.

1 ½ lb. beef shank w/bone (or 1 ½ lb boneless chicken thighs)
1 Tbsp olive oil
1 Tbsp onion – diced
1 35 oz can Italian tomatoes
5 bay leaves
3 beef bouillon cubes
½ green pepper – diced
4 celery ribs
2 carrots
2 potatoes
1 medium zucchini
½ cup green beans
1 Tbsp parsley
2 tsp salt
1 tsp basil
1 tsp black pepper
½ tsp thyme

Cut the beef into bite-size cubes and sauté in olive oil and onions in stockpot over medium heat. Include the bones. Add the Italian tomatoes, cover and simmer for 60 minutes until tomatoes begin to breakdown. Add one can of water, bay leaves, bouillon cubes and green peppers, cover and cook an additional 30 minutes.

Cut the celery, carrots, potatoes, and zucchini into good-size pieces and add to the stockpot. Cut the beans into two inch lengths, and add them along with the parsley, basil, thyme, salt and pepper and cook over low heat an additional 30 minutes.

If you like additional vegetables, you can add some frozen corn and peas to the soup 5 minutes before you serve it. If I have cauliflower in my refrigerator, I usually put some of that in the soup the same time I put in the rest of the raw vegetables to cook.

This soup is so hearty it makes a meal in itself with a salad, nice fresh bread, and a block of stout cheese. The chicken version is a ***Happy Heart*** winner.

Never cook with a wine that you would not drink.

WATERMAN'S CRAB SOUP

One of the things I like most about the Chesapeake Bay is the careful preservation of the past that you find in the waterman's way of life. I love to cruise over to ***Tilghman's Island*** and poke around all the old crab boats and the skipjacks. You will find a hearty breed of men and women that have carried on a tradition of working the waters for generations, and their food reflects that tradition. The locals use any grade of crabmeat, including claws and other leftovers.

corn oil
½ cup onion – diced
1 stalk of celery – diced
½ cup carrots – diced
1 35 oz whole Italian tomatoes – chopped
5 cups water
2 chicken bouillon cubes
2 bay leaves
1/4 tsp black pepper
1 Tbsp jalapeno peppers – diced
2 tsp Worcestershire sauce
1 Tbsp Old Bay seasoning
2 potatoes – diced
1 ½ cups corn
1 cup peas
1 cup lima beans
1/4 cup fresh parsley – chopped
1 lb. fresh crab meat
juice of 1 lemon
salt
***1 link cooked Italian sausage – sliced ***

In a large stockpot, pour a couple tablespoons of corn oil and sauté the onions and celery over medium heat for about 3-4 minutes. Add the tomatoes, water, and chicken bouillon and bring to a boil. Add the carrots, black pepper, bay leaves, jalapenos, Worcestershire, and Old Bay Seasoning. Reduce heat to a simmer for 30 to 40 minutes with the cover on.

Add potatoes and parsley and simmer for an additional 30 minutes.

Separate the crabmeat in a bowl—checking for cartilage—and sprinkle lemon juice over the crab. Add the crabmeat, corn, peas, and lima beans. Return it to a gentle boil, then turn off the stove and allow soup to stand for 10 minutes before serving. This soup will keep two or three days—maximum. It is seafood, but probably tastes best the next day, so if you make this a day in advance of your meal, it will work fine as a soup course that does not require any prep time the day of the meal. You can also make the soup right up to the point where you add the crabmeat, one day ahead of time. The tomato and vegetables benefit from a day of flavor blending, and if you add the crab on the day you serve the soup, it will have a nice fresh flavor.

Note—Using the sausage is not a Chesapeake Bay version of this soup, but you will remember that I named this "Waterman's" soup, so if you do use the sausage, then the water we speak of could very easily be the canals of Venice. Add the cooked sausage to the pot at the same time you put the crab in.

Serve crusty bread or oyster crackers with cold beer and a salad for a nice easy meal.

CRAB & CORN CHOWDER

It seems that everyone has a chowder recipe or at least a good place to buy chowder when they get the woolies for a bowl of it. Most chowder is made with clams, and when it is made with oysters, it is called stew. In this case, we look to the bounty of the Bay and make ours with good Chesapeake Blue Crabs and fresh corn from the August harvest. This is a hearty meal dish in itself, but you can also use it as a prelude to your holiday meals. I fixed this for Christmas dinner, and it was the smash hit of the entire meal. This one will get you noticed at the next dinner party.

1 Tbsp sweet butter
1 small red pepper – diced
1 small white onion – diced
1 rib celery – diced
1 baker potato – cubed
1 cup chicken stock
1 jalapeno pepper – diced
1 10 oz pkg. frozen corn
2 cups heavy cream
1 cup milk
1 tsp salt
1 lb. lump crab meat
4 spring onions – diced
black pepper

Sauté the peppers, onions and celery in butter over medium heat until onion becomes limp but not browned. Add chicken stock and 1 tablespoon of corn and cover and cook over medium heat for 15 minutes.

In a separate pot, cook the potatoes in salted water at a rapid boil for 15 minutes. Drain potatoes, reserving 1 cup of potato water.

Place the chicken stock mixture in a blender and run until mixture is smooth and consistent.

Combine chicken stock, potatoes, potato water, corn, and salt and bring to a boil. Reduce heat and add cream, milk, and crab meat. Simmer for 10 minutes and remove from heat. Sprinkle diced onions over each bowl and serve immediately.

Serve with a *Caesar Salad, Twice Baked Potatoes*, and *Christmas Pork Loin.*

YOOPER CORN CHOWDER

A ***Yooper*** is someone who comes from the Upper Peninsula of Michigan in contrast from someone who is from "Down Below"—meaning below the Straits of Mackinaw. Now, those Yoopers come from hardy stock—loggers, miners and other such people who extracted their living from an unforgiving land. I have seen winters so cold that—if your car started—it would run down the road like the tires were made of wood because they were frozen flat on the bottoms. I have seen snow so deep you had to tie red flags on your auto antennas so you could see each other approaching at intersections. And yes, Grasshopper, we walked to school in this weather without the benefit of buses or parental chauffeuring. Here is chowder that is worthy of that climate.

6 slices of bacon
1 small green pepper – diced fine
1 Tbsp jalapeno – diced fine
1 rib celery – diced fine
2 new potatoes – cubed
3 medium tomatoes – diced
1 10 oz pkg. frozen corn
1/8 tsp allspice

pinch sugar
1 tsp salt
2 bay leaves
1 cup white wine
2 cups light cream
1 cup milk
6 spring onions – diced
black pepper

Fry the bacon in a large pan until crisp. Remove and drain on a plate with a paper towel to absorb excess fat. Crumble and set aside.

Discard all but about 1 Tbsp of bacon fat. Sauté green pepper, jalapeno, and celery in bacon fat on medium heat for about 5 minutes, and then add tomatoes, potatoes, corn, allspice, sugar, salt, bay leaves, and wine. Cover and cook over low heat for about 20 minutes. Stir in cream, milk, and fresh ground black pepper to taste. Bring to a boil and then reduce to a simmer for an additional 10 to 15 minutes.

Serve the chowder in large bowls with portions of the bacon and spring onions on the top of each serving. This can become a meal in itself or the prelude to the *Caesar Steak Salad***.**

S.S. HESPER LOBSTER BISQUE

In all my travels, I have only been to the state of Maine once, but I have spent more than a few hours with my friends Steve and Mary on Steve's catboat the ***HESPER***. A catboat is a type of sailboat that is indigenous to the East Coast from Cape Cod to Cape May. In all of the Chesapeake, I have only seen two or three of these boats under sail. A catboat is a commodious craft that conveys a warm, friendly feel to it. This soup fits that role.

1 1 1/3 lbs. fresh whole lobster
3 3/4 quarts water
1 cup dry white wine
½ cup white onion – diced
1 large carrot – diced
1 celery rib – diced
1 tsp thyme
6 peppercorns
1 medium potato – cubed
16 oz frozen corn
1/4 cup light cream
8 asparagus tips
1 Tbsp chives
1 Tbsp bacon pieces
salt

Bring the salted water to a rapid boil and plunge the live lobster in the water headfirst. Boil for 18 to 20 minutes and remove.

Add wine, onion, carrot, celery, thyme, peppercorns, and potato to the water and continue to cook on medium heat. Remove the lobster meat from the tail and claws, dice into one-inch pieces, and set aside. Remove the tomalley from the body of the lobster and discard. Return the shell and legs to the stockpot and continue to cook for 15 to 20 minutes. Remove two slotted spoons' worth of potatoes from stock and set aside with lobster meat. Cook stock an additional 1 1/4 hours.

Remove lobster shells and discard. Add 3/4 of corn to hot stock, spoon vegetables in, and blend into a smooth puree. Return blended stock to stockpot and add 1/4 cup cream, lobster, potatoes, and remaining corn and heat until consistency develops.

In a small sauté pan, you can heat the asparagus tips until tender.

Top each bowl of bisque with two asparagus tips, a sprinkle of chives, and bacon bits.

RED BELLS AND BLUE CRABS SOUP

We first did this soup for a Thanksgiving dinner for 10 people where we served the traditional turkey and all the trimmings, plus a standard Italian compliment of pasta. This soup was the hit of the entire meal. Even though it is a cream-based soup, you can make most of it the day before and, thereby, cut down on preparation time the day of the meal. Of course, you can always eat any kind of soup out of a cup, but this one begs for the fine china.

4 medium red bell peppers
1 medium Vidalia onion
1 stick of sweet butter
1 bay leaf
1 ½ Tbsp paprika
½ cup flour
1 ½ quarts chicken stock
1 cup whipping cream
1 lb. lump crab meat
1/8 tsp cayenne pepper
2 Tbsp fresh chives
salt

Dice the peppers and onions into small pieces and sauté in the butter over medium heat until the peppers and onions begin to become limp. Do not brown!

Combine the flour, paprika and cayenne pepper in a small mixing bowl, and then slowly add the flour mix into the peppers and onions, stirring to a full consistency. Add the chicken stock, bay leaf and salt. Simmer for 10 minutes over medium heat.

Remove the bay leaf and set aside. Pour soup into blender and puree the mix on high speed. The soup may be refrigerated at this point and completed the next day.

Return the pureed soup to the pot, bring to a full boil, and add the cream and crab, stirring consistently to separate the crabmeat. Serve in large soup bowls and sprinkle ½ tsp of fresh chives on top of each bowl just as you serve it.

Fresh French bread or crusty bread sticks are a must for this soup.

ASPARAGUS & BACON SOUP

A good cream of asparagus soup is a welcome item on any menu, but unfortunately, the cream makes it a high cholesterol offender so many people tend to shy away it. This recipe solves that problem because the soup does not call for any cream yet still provides all the richness that asparagus affords.

1 10 oz pkg. frozen asparagus
3 slices of bacon – sliced
2 slices of Bermuda onion – diced
2 cups chicken broth
2 Tbsp tomato – diced

In a 3-quart saucepan, boil the asparagus in the chicken broth until the asparagus is soft and limp.

Sauté the diced bacon in a small frying pan until it is crisp, remove from the pan with a slotted spoon, and place it on paper towels to absorb the grease.

Retain about 1 Tbsp of bacon grease in frying pan, and sauté the onion until it is soft and translucent.

Add the onion to the asparagus, and puree in a food processor. Return to sauce pan, and salt and pepper to taste while reheating.

Serve in individual bowls with a tablespoon of bacon bits and tomatoes ladled over the top of each bowl.

Enjoy your ***Happy Heart*** soup with a simple salad and mineral water.

THE CAMPBELLS' WEDDING SOUP

Don't bother looking for this in the soup section of your supermarket, because this is not made by the Mm...Mm... Good people. When my pal Arch married Gina, I wanted to do a soup that reflected their personalities. Here is a classic ***Happy Heart*** item that is low on fat and high on satisfaction. A delicate marriage of the common but fiber-rich ceci bean with graceful and elegant shrimp, surrounded by the warmth of good chicken broth, and held together with a little of Popeye's favorite. What's not to like about it?

Simple, stylish and satisfying—just like his movie reviews!

6 cups water
6 pkg. Herb Ox chicken broth
½ lb. medium shrimp
½ cup ceci beans – drained
6-8 large spinach leaves
2 Tbsp fresh chives – chopped

Bring the 6 cups of water to a fast boil in a 3-quart saucepan.

Peel and set aside the shrimp while the water is coming to a boil.

When the water begins to boil, add the chicken broth and shrimp and continue to cook for 3 to 5 minutes until the shrimp turns pink.

Cut the spinach into 1/4 inch strips and add to the boiling water, along with the ceci beans. Cover the pot, turn off the heat, and chop the chives.

Ladle the soup into individual bowls, sprinkle a few chives on the top of each bowl, and serve hot.

This soup is quick and easy and will be a sure starter for any elegant meal.

Holding your securities in "street name" with a broker guards against having the stock or bond "called" and not getting the notice. due to mailing errors.

DOCTOR NANNY'S CHICKEN SOUP

The healing virtues of chicken soup have long held sway in a number of cultures. This is one that has been in our family for a long time. Not only does it have the magic of getting you back on your feet, it is also a great holiday soup before the big meal because it is light and does not compete with the tastes of the main course. It may take awhile to make, but if you are feeling a little under the weather, just the smell in your kitchen will go a long way toward getting you well again.

4-5 # whole frying or stewing chicken
3 bay leaves
3 chicken bouillon cubes – Knorr®Extra Large
3 stalks of celery w/tops sliced in 2" strips
3 thick carrots – sliced in 2" strips
1 medium onion – diced thick *
salt & pepper
2 cups white rice or small pasta

Remove the insides of the chicken and soak in ice water for one hour. Place chicken in a 10-quart. stockpot and cover with 2-3 inches of water. Add bouillon cubes, salt and pepper, and bay leaves. Bring to a rapid boil and reduce heat, cover, and simmer for 1 to 1 ½ hours. When chicken meat is easily separated from the bones, remove it from the pot. Add the vegetables (eliminate the onion if this is a get-well soup and not a starter soup) and allow the stockpot to simmer for an additional 45 minutes. Meanwhile, separate the skin and bones from the chicken, discarding these items and setting the meat aside until the vegetables have cooked for 45 minutes. Return the meat to the pot, and turn off the heat.

In a separate pot, cook the rice or pasta according to the package directions. Put a ladle of rice or pasta in a soup bowl, and then fill with the chicken soup mix. Serve hot with nice crusty bread or crackers.

Happy Heart, Happy Tummy, Happy Camper !!

ON A BUN, IN A POCKET OR… BETWEEN 2 SLICES

HEROS, HOAGIES, & SUBS

No matter what they are called, they are a popular treat for all age groups and ethnic origins. It is a great summertime treat when you have been out of doors all day. A hoagie with a cold soda and some potato chips with pickles and olives is a satisfying treat in anybody's book. There is no real secret to making a good sub other than FRESH! I find that if you buy the cold cuts and bread a few hours prior to making the subs, you will never go wrong. A good, crisp sub roll is half the taste, so if you are unable to get them baked for you, look in the frozen food case for Pepperidge Farm short French breads that you bake yourself. There is no question that subs have as many different possibilities as there are people willing to eat them. The two classics, however, are the Italian Hoagie and the Tuna Fish Sub.

Italian Hoagie

Danish ham
mortadella
Genoa salami
cappacola
provolone cheese
shredded lettuce
sliced tomato
sliced white onion – paper-thin
Italian oil – olive oil w/ oregano & basil

Slice the roll end to end and put two layers of each meat on the roll. Top with lettuce, tomatoes, and onions, and then squirt oil over the top and some on the inside of the top slice of the roll. To make the oil, fill a squirt bottle (the kind that you use for ketchup on picnics) half full of Extra Virgin olive oil and add 1 Tbsp of oregano and 1 Tbsp basil. Allow to stand for at least one day before using.

Tuna Sub

1 12 1/2oz can white tuna in water
1 hard boiled egg – chopped
2 strips of bacon – crumbled
1/8 tsp garlic powder
2 Tbsp mayo
lemon juice
shredded lettuce
sliced tomatoes
sliced white onions – paper thin

Mix the tuna, egg, bacon, garlic powder, mayo and a squirt of lemon juice to make the tuna salad. Spread on roll and top with lettuce, tomato and onion.

PONCHO'S CHEESE STEAK

Most people know that south Philadelphia provided the roots for the famous Philly Cheese Steak sandwich, and that no other place in the world does it quite the same way. To find the roots of this next item, however, you will have to go considerably south of Philadelphia for this old favorite. A few old Texas Rangers that I once knew told me this might have been the real reason so many people wanted to catch Poncho and his boys. If you do not have a large cast iron frying pan, forget about trying this recipe. Go out and rob a Wells Fargo stagecoach and buy a good camp-size iron frying pan.

1 very large cast iron frying pan
1 lb. top round steak – thin cut
2 Tbsp corn oil

1 large Bermuda onion – sliced
2 green peppers – sliced thin
1 Tbsp jalapeno peppers – diced
garlic powder
salt & pepper
4 slices Monterey Jack
4 large tortillas
½ cup Colorado Red Salsa
juice of 1 lime

Most round steak that you buy that says "thin sliced" is not thin enough, so you should first slice the steak to about half the thickness of what came from the market. Lay it on your cutting board and shave the sharpest knife you have across the top of the meat. No piece should be larger than a dollar bill.

Sauté the peppers and onions in a large, iron frying pan with the corn oil, salt and pepper. Cook until the peppers and onions begin to turn limp. Move the peppers and onions to one side of the frying pan and add the jalapenos to that mixture. Place the steak on the free side of the pan and salt, pepper, and use garlic powder with a liberal hand. Fry until the meat is brown all over. Cut the lime in half and squirt the lime juice on the meat and cover with monterey jack.

Make four separate portions of the meat and cheese and continue to cook for a few more minutes, until the cheese begins to soften.

Place the meat and cheese in the center of the tortilla and top with the onions and peppers. Spoon some salsa on and roll into a burrito shape. Serve an order of *Honest Guacamole* and *Real French Fries* with ice-cold Corona and the rest of the lime cut up for the beer. Ole!

SLOPPY WHO

Everybody makes this, but nobody admits that they serve it to anyone other than the kids. That's fine, so next time you have ***Tony the Tiger*** and a bunch of kids over, here is a fun item to fix for them. It is quick and easy, and you do not have to buy that stuff in the can to make it come out right. This recipe is a good year-round fixer because it warms you in the winter and is quick to fix in the summer so you do not overheat your kitchen. You can throw this together in very little time. I resisted the idea of calling it Sloppy Joe, simply because they make everyone who eats them "Sloppy".

1 ½ lbs. lean ground beef *
½ tsp garlic powder
3 Tbsp green pepper – diced
3 Tbsp Hunt's ketchup
1 Tbsp Dijon mustard
1 Tbsp parsley
2 slices white onion – diced
salt & pepper
*** Ground turkey is a fine substitute.**

Brown the ground meat, green peppers, garlic powder and salt & pepper in a sauté pan and drain the oil when it is browned. Add the ketchup, mustard and parsley and simmer for 15 minutes. Add the diced onion, stirring into the meat, and allow to cook an additional 2-3 minutes.

Serve in a pita pocket for a ***Happy Heart*** if you used the ground turkey. A whole wheat bun is also a good choice. If you used a lean beef and drained the fat from it after it cooked it, you still have a solidly healthy meal.

You can do some carrots sticks, celery and other raw veggies to accompany the Sloppy Who. Call it "Sloppy Whoever You Are Fixing It For".

WEENIE ROLLERS

We have all had a hot dog that remains firmly etched in our memories. Maybe it was that special day at the ballpark or a picnic in the country. For me, it was Sideroff's or the Windmill at the Jersey Shore. Those big, plump dogs with the crunchy skin topped with mustard and onions were worth the drive every time. The "dog", while it is clearly one of America's favorite foods, does not often find itself on our home table unless it is to feed the kids. Too bad. Part of this problem, I think, is what passes for hot dogs in the average super market. If you live near New York City or in parts of Jersey, you can get good hot dogs, but for the rest of us, we are not so lucky. I have found that National Hebrew Dinner Franks are as close to "Jersey Shore Dogs" as you can find.

4 National Hebrew Dinner Franks
4 large flour tortillas
4 slices – cheddar cheese
4 spring onions
lettuce
Country mustard

Grill the dogs on the grill or on the broiler.

If the tortillas are not fresh and supple, you can renew them by placing them in a large baggie with 2 toothpick-sized holes and heat in microwave for 20 seconds on high heat. This will make the tortillas easier to work with.

Chop lettuce and onion into a fine mixture.

Lay tortilla flat and place 1 slice of cheese in the center. Place hot dog on one end with a ribbon of mustard on top of it. Spread a dusting of lettuce and onion on the remaining side of tortilla.

Beginning with the end containing the hot dog, roll the tortilla, forming a nice, fat weenie roll.

These dogs compliment any relish tray and a bowl of *Michigan Cole Slaw* for a nice lunch. If it is a summer day, serve beer.

If you live in California, throw out the dog and substitute with sprouts, avocados, and smoked turkey breast and call it a "High Roller". Serve mineral water, of course.

L.A. DELI CHICKEN SALAD

No cookbook would be complete without the ever-present chicken salad sandwich. This is a Left Coast version of the old standard. You can use any leftover chicken that you might find in the refrigerator. It can be fried, grilled, boiled, or rescued from the chicken stockpot. I like to use cold leftover *Santa Fe Chicken Breasts* that have been grilled over cherry wood, but you do what you like because it's your lunch.

2 cups diced chicken meat
8-10 pecans – chopped
6-8 bread & butter pickle chips – diced
2 slices Vidalia onions – diced
1 tsp parsley
4 Tbsp real mayonnaise
salt & pepper

Mix all ingredients into a mixing bowl until thoroughly blended. Chill for 30 minutes and serve on whole wheat bread with bib or romaine lettuce. A tall glass of iced tea with a fresh strawberry garnish, carrot sticks, and radishes are a nice complement.

PLEASE do not put your good cutlery in the dishwasher—it will cause them to become dull.

ESCANABA BOLOGNA SALAD

Escanaba, Michigan sits on the northern tip of Lake Michigan and with a population of 14,000 people, is one of the largest towns in the Upper Peninsula. You will not find this town recommended as a destination by *Travel & Leisure*, nor will you find a write-up in *Gourmet* magazine, and come to think of it, that may be the best reason to visit this quiet little community—it is off the beaten path. In the early part of this century, the cruise boats that filled the Great Lakes from Chicago to Escanaba carried the likes of Louis Armstrong, Earl Hines, and other jazz legends that entertained their well-heeled passengers. If you stay at the hundred-year-old House of Ludington overlooking the Lake, you will feel as if you have stepped back in time. The Log Cabin restaurant, as well as The House, will tend to your fundamental dining needs, and you can be on your own for the rest of your meals. You can pack a sack of these sandwiches and go to the city dock and fish for perch some afternoon. A simple recipe for a simple place and time. Incidentally, if you are going to do this the right way, you need one of those heavy metal hand grinders that you secure to the edge of your counter top. More authentic!

1 lb. bologna – not sliced
2 ½ Tbsp bread and butter pickles
3 Tbsp mayo

NOTE: You can buy your favorite bologna at the deli by asking them to simply give you a whole piece of it.

Cut the bologna into chucks that will fit into the hopper of the hand grinder, and grind into a mixing bowl. Periodically, add some pickles into the hopper along with the meat, so they become ground into the same consistency. Add the mayo to create a nice smooth salad which can be served on a Kaiser roll with fresh lettuce and sliced tomatoes.

Make some fresh lemonade; grab a big bag of chips, your favorite pal, and head out to the park for a picnic!

CRAWDADDIES & CRABS IN THE HIP POCKET

Baltimore and New Orleans share a common thread based upon the water in the form of *beautiful swimmers*. The crawfish and the crab are major staples in the seafood market of each city. Both swimmers are delightful when steamed and seasoned and eaten with fresh corn on the cob and pitchers of ice-cold beer. Pick'n crabs and daddies on a hot summer day on a picnic table near the water is an ideal way to spend an afternoon. This recipe does away with the mess, and turns the swimmers into an elegant sandwich offering.

½ lb. crawfish (cooked)
½ lb. lump crab meat
1/3 cup pistachios
4-6 spring onions – diced
juice of 1 lemon
3-4 Tbsp mayo
½ tsp paprika
3/4 cup bean sprouts
4 pita pockets – whole-wheat
diced tomatoes & avocados

Pick the meat out of the crawfish and mix with the crabmeat, pistachios, onions and lemon. Stir to mix lemon over the meat. Add mayo and paprika and blend well.

Chill for 1 hour.

Scoop crab and crawfish mixture into open pita pockets and top with generous portions of bean sprouts, diced tomatoes & avocados.

Serve with kosher dill pickles, potato chips and homemade lemonade.

A.J.'S HOMETOWN PASTIES

I am fortunate in that I have a sister-in-law who is a real gem. Judy (my brother calls her A.J.) is one of those people who always makes you feel more at home in her house than you do in your own. There is always a comfort level in her home that is sort of like a warm pasty. I grew up in a part of the country where pasty shoppes outnumbered the hamburger outlets. Because of the abundance of pasty shoppes, I never really knew of anyone who actually made their own pasties until I ate Judy's, and I must confess that this may not actually be her recipe. She has told it to me so many times, but as with most things, I only retain some of the input. In this recipe we use prepared piecrusts, but you can always make the crust from scratch if you so prefer.

1 pkg. Pillsbury pie crusts (2 crusts)
1 lb. lean ground beef (ground round)
2 medium baking potatoes
1 medium rutabaga
1 medium yellow onion
1 Tbsp parsley
butter
salt & pepper

Peeling the rutabaga is a yeoman's task. Those critters have a tough skin—be careful. If you simply cut off the ends like you would an onion and then slice it into ½ inch thick slices, you can trim the outside, dice them into ½ inch cubes, and place them a mixing bowl. You really only want the inside portion of the rutabaga anyhow. Wash and dice the potatoes (you can leave the skins on) and dice the onion. Add potatoes and onions to mixing bowl.

Crumble the meat into thumb-size chunks and add them to the mixing bowl, along with the parsley, salt and pepper.

Combine the mixture in the bowl.

Lay out a pie crust on a floured surface. Pie crusts should be at room temperature so they are pliable. Roll the crusts into a thinner crust about 1/3 larger than the original crust. Cut into three equal sizes. Fill the half of the pie crust facing you with the mixture. Top with a pat of butter. Fold the back half of the pie crust forward and crimp the edges shut, forming a sealed half moon.

Place the pasties on a cookie sheet and bake in the middle of the oven at 400 degrees for 50 – 55 minutes.

If you do not use ground round, you will obtain a little too much fat in the pasty and it can run out into your oven, making a mess.

Some people like ketchup on their pasties. Some people eat them with their hands, while others eat them with a knife and fork. In the old days, a pasty was eaten with your hands and there was no discussion on the matter. You can simply trim the crusts and make them whichever size suits you.

If you have some crisp Milwaukee pickles, they go well with your pasties. A small salad and a cold drink will make a fine meal anytime of the year.

Pasties actually came to America in the dinner pails of the Cornish miners. It was said that a good pasty could survive a fall down the mineshaft and still be intact and eaten at mealtime. Ours are not quite that sturdy. You will find pasties in almost every community of the Upper Peninsula of Michigan and in a few of the northern-most communities of Lower Michigan. Mackinaw City, for example, is a good pasty town, but Detroit is not.

Hope this item makes you want to "***Say Yes to Michigan***" and maybe take a trip to the U.P. and see the Soo Locks and visit an iron mine.

Sault Ste. Marie, Michigan is the third oldest city in the United States.

KIMMIE'S KALZONES

It really is true that anything that you can buy in a restaurant, you can make at home. It was not too many years ago that we thought pizza only came from a deliveryman and not from the oven. Calzones are easy to make—they just take time because the dough has to rise. They can fit into a busy work schedule around the house because the prep time in between the dough and the baking is quite short. My neighbor made these for us one night when we were relaxing on the back of my boat watching the sunset.

DOUGH

1 pkg. dry yeast
1 cup warm water
1 tsp salt
1/4 cup Extra Virgin olive oil
3 cups flour
1 egg white – beaten

FILLING

½ lb. Italian sausage
8 slices stick pepperoni – halved
1/4 cup green peppers – diced
2 cups mozzarella cheese – shredded
1/4 cup Romano cheese – grated
1 6 oz can tomato paste
1 tsp basil
1 tsp oregano
1/8 tsp garlic powder

Dissolve yeast in warm water and let stand for 5 minutes. Combine salt, oil, and flour—one cup at a time—in a large mixing bowl. When you get a large ball, knead it on a floured surface for about 5 minutes. Place in a well-oiled large bowl, cover, and set in a warm place to rise for 1 hour.

Fry the sausage in a large pan, breaking it down into small pieces. Drain off the cooking fat, and refrigerate the meat in a large bowl until the dough is finished rising.

Combine the remaining ingredients with the sausage and mix well.

Roll out the dough so it forms a large rectangle. Spread the filling in the center of the dough and fold the dough closed sealing the seam. Turn the calzone over so the seam is down and pinch closed the ends. Score the top of the loaf and brush with egg whites.

Bake in a 400-degree oven for about 25 minutes or until golden brown. Serve hot.

There is no substitute for good diversification in your portfolio. The market will always cycle up and down, but rarely do all sectors move in the same direction.

BARBECUE BEEF, PORK AND CHICKEN

Some will justifiably argue that there is nothing this side of heaven that can compare to a good barbecue sandwich—the slow-cooked Carolina "pulled" style where the meat literally falls off the bone and melts in your mouth. Surprisingly enough, there are only two secrets to success and they are: 1) lots of time and 2) a good sauce.

What follows on the next few pages is a basic barbecue sauce that has been modified for the three types of meats. I often interchange recipes and use any of the three on beef and pork ribs with equal success.

You can use lower quality cuts of meat for these recipes, since they all have to cook so long it is not important to get the best cut or the best grade of chicken.

The main component, however, is slow cooking, whether it is in a conventional oven or some kind of wood, gas or charcoal-fired device.

BOSS HOG

God created the pig to be barbecued! I can think of no finer way to fix a pig than to turn it into pulled pork sandwiches. This is one of those things that you can fix while you are doing all sorts of other things because it takes so long to cook. It is absolutely no maintenance once you get it set on slow cook time. You can go sailing for the day, go to a movie, shopping, flea marketing, whatever.

3 lbs. pork shoulder butt
1 cup white wine vinegar
1 15 oz tomato sauce
3 Tbsp Worcestershire sauce
1 Tbsp jalapeno peppers – minced

2 tsp Tabasco sauce
½ tsp garlic powder
½ tsp dry mustard
salt & pepper

Trim the fat and hide off the pork butt, being careful to clean away any bone splinters. Leave the bone in the meat as it adds flavor.

In a mixing bowl, mix well all the other ingredients and pour it over the pork in a deep-sided Corning with a lid.

Place the covered dish in a cold oven, set for 450 degrees, and bake for 30 minutes.

Reduce the heat to 250 degrees and continue cooking for an additional 6 hours.

Remove from the oven, discard the bone and any remaining fat, and separate or "pull" the pork with a fork so no big lumps are left.

You need to have some good buns or pitas, a side serving of *Mom's Potato Salad*, some *Michigan Cole Slaw* to serve on top of the pork in the bun, and some ice-cold beer.

You can serve four to six people if you really feel like sharing—or you can "pig out" for two and have leftovers for a few days!

BITCH'N BULL

For you Californians who like it a little hotter, we have turned up the heat a little on this one. Same basic recipe as the *Boss Hog* except for the introduction of the molasses, the use of red wine instead of white wine, and twice as many jalapenos to stoke up the fire.

3 lbs. beef chuck pot roast
1 cup red wine vinegar
1 15 oz tomato sauce
2 Tbsp Worcestershire sauce
2 Tbsp molasses
2 Tbsp jalapeno peppers – minced
1 tsp Tabasco sauce
½ tsp garlic powder
½ tsp dry mustard
salt & pepper

Trim away excess fat from beef roast and place in a shallow Corning with a lid. The choice of Corning is determined by the cut of meat. With the pork, you need a deeper dish since it is a tall roast; however, the beef roast is longer and wider and not as tall, so a shallow dish works better. You want the meat to be fairly immersed in the sauce.

Mix the sauce ingredients in a mixing bowl until they are well blended, pour over the meat, and place the lid on the Corning. Put the Corning in a cold oven and heat to 450 degrees for a period of 30 minutes. Reduce the heat to 250 degrees and continue cooking for an additional 6 hours.

Remove from oven and take out any bones and fat as you separate the meat with your fork into an even consistency. A whole wheat bun topped with a slice of fresh white onion makes an unbeatable combination. Throw in a side order of *Uncle Jimmy's Italian Tomato Salad* and some corn on the cob and you have an easy and enjoyable meal just right for eating on the patio.

CRAZY COYOTE CHICKEN

Coyotes love chicken, but if one ever got ahold of this recipe, it would drive them crazy. In fact, you might find this one so good that you may want to howl at the moon after you have eaten it! Go ahead and do that if you like—it is a common thing in the Southwest.

This recipe calls for a whole chicken, but you can use parts if you would rather have only one kind of meat in the barbecue.

4 lbs. whole roasting chicken
1 cup white wine vinegar
1 15 oz tomato sauce
4 spring onions
2 Tbsp Worcestershire sauce
2 Tbsp jalapeno peppers – minced
2 Tbsp German mustard
2 Tbsp honey
1 tsp Tabasco
½ tsp garlic powder
salt & pepper

Clean out the chicken and place it in a deep corning dish. Salt & pepper the chicken. Mix the sauce ingredients in a mixing bowl until they are well blended, pour over the chicken, and place the lid on the Corning.

Put the Corning in a cold oven and heat to 450 degrees for a period of 30 minutes. Reduce the heat to 250 degrees and continue cooking for an additional 4 ½ hours.

Remove from oven and use two forks to remove the bones, skin, and grizzle. As you remove the bones, etc, you successfully mix the meat into the sauce, creating a nice consistent pulled mixture.

ROYAL CHAMPIONSHIP CHICKEN

When Colorado hosted their first-ever Kansas City BBQ Society Cook-off, I talked some of my friends from the Chief Hosa HMC to come up to Frisco and help me try to raise some money for a charity. Roger & Susie, Ray Bob & Toni, Bob & Kitty, Jim & Kathee and Brad & Georgi all turned out to eat, smoke, stoke coals, turn meat, and promote the end results. For us, the end results were one trophy and two ribbons, all done on two standard Weber grills! The original recipe was for 100 pounds of chicken breasts, but in this case I have trimmed it down to 5 pounds.

5 lbs. boneless chicken breasts
1 cup red wine vinegar
1 15 oz tomato ketchup
2 Tbsp Worcestershire sauce
1/3 cup Triple Sec
2 Tbsp honey
2 Tbsp brown sugar
2 tsp whole cloves
2 Tbsp jalapeno peppers – minced
2 tsp crushed red pepper
1 tsp Tabasco sauce
2 cloves garlic – crushed
1 Tbsp chopped parsley
salt & pepper

Combine all the items, except the chicken, in a large saucepan and bring to a boil. Reduce heat and simmer for 30 minutes. Allow to cool and refrigerate overnight. Wash the chicken in cold water and shake dry. Place the chicken breasts in large zip lock bags, fill with BBQ sauce, and allow to marinate for 3 or 4 hours. Grill on a hot hickory wood grill fire until cooked through. Baste with the sauce three or four times while they are grilling. Serve on a bun as a sandwich or on a plate with *Milwaukee Potato Salad* and cold beer.

CLARKE'S CHOICE

When we made our first trip to Sturgis, I was tapped to be the chuck wagon boss and fix a couple of meals for our motorcycle gang. Feeding 10 big men can either be real easy or an impossible chore, depending on how hungry they are. One of the guys in our group, Don Clarke, an ex-Viet Nam chopper pilot, made such a fuss over this recipe that I had no other choice than to name it after him. This is a nice combination of two meats that blend well with the long roasting time and excellent sauce.

3 lbs. beef chuck pot roast
3 lbs. pork loin roast
1 ½ cups red wine vinegar
1 cup tomato ketchup
3 Tbsp Worcestershire sauce
3 Tbsp molasses
4 Tbsp jalapeno peppers – minced
1 Tbsp brown sugar
2 tsp Tabasco sauce
1 medium onion – diced
1 tsp garlic powder
1 tsp dry mustard
salt & pepper

Trim the fat and hide off the pork loin and the beef roast, being careful to clean away any bone splinters. Leave the bone in the meat as it adds flavor. Cut the meat into large pieces to fit a large turkey roaster.

In a mixing bowl, mix well all the other ingredients and pour it over the meat in the turkey roaster with the lid on.

Place the roaster in a cold oven, set for 450 degrees and roast for 30 minutes. Reduce the heat to 250 degrees and continue cooking for an additional 7 hours.

Remove from the oven, discard the bone and any remaining fat, and separate or "pull" the meat with a fork so no big lumps are left.

You can serve the entire motorcycle gang (or the bridge club) in a nice, buffet style with lots of cold beer and videos of the last summer outing!

CHAMPIONSHIP BRATS ON THE GRILL

People from Wisconsin have a justifiable pride in their sausages. The Germanic immigrants brought their old country recipes with them, and they live on today in their summer sausages, liverwursts, and kielbasa. But the single rallying cry to a "Cheese Head" is "**BRATS**"! Bratwursts are not the same if you buy them outside of Wisconsin. The shipping and preservatives can steal the flavor, but even with those limitations, brats on the grill are still a summertime favorite all over the country. Here is a method that works with one-pound increments. It also works with 300-pound servings. Our Chief Hosa Motorcycle Club won the People's Choice Award with these brats at the Colorado BBQ Challenge in Frisco, Colorado in 1996, 1997, 1998, 1999 and 2000!

1 lb. fresh Johnsonville bratwursts (not frozen)
2 12 oz cans Miller beer
1 large yellow onion
black pepper

Slice the onion into 1/4-inch slices. Put the beer and onions, with a few twists of freshly ground black pepper, in a pot and heat to a gentle boil. Once you have a boil, drop the brats into the boiling brew. Reduce heat and simmer for 20 to 30 minutes.

Remove brats from beer and onions—save the onions. Grill—rotating—until brown and cooked through, which takes approximately 10 to 15 more minutes on medium heat.

Serve on hoagie rolls, kaiser rolls, or in a pita with the beer-flavored onions.

Chips, potato salad, pickles, olives, and plenty of cold beer will make an unbeatable lunch, summer picnic, or tailgate menu.

Go Packers!!

AN UNABRIDGED HISTORY OF THE BURGER

The Hamburger is so much more than just something we eat. The Burger is something we do, it is a way of life—it is life itself! The Burger is an institution that is uniquely American—in fact it is **America!**

I remember . . .

In the beginning, my dad would fry hamburgers in the cast iron frying pan with sliced onions. Most of the time, we would eat them naked on a plate with something not fun like cooked *carrots*. On occasion, we would stick it between two slices of Bunny Bread and make a sandwich out of it. Not much to write home about.

In 1961, it happened. I can remember it like it was yesterday. I pulled into the A & W Root Beer stand in my jet black 1947 Ford Coupe. I was wearing a white T-Shirt with a pack of *Lucky Strikes* rolled in the sleeve. James Dean had nothing on me. I pulled into a parking space under the canopy and a bright young car hop bounced over to my car and took my order. I did not even have to get out of my car! A large frosted mug of root beer and a hamburger deluxe! We are talking a burger on a real bun (not two slices of bread) with lettuce and tomato! A burger in your hand, ***Dion and the Belmont's*** on the radio, $2.00 worth of gas in the tank, and it is Friday night! The beginning of an era!

Life moved quickly, for in 1962 I was visiting my brother in Milwaukee when he took me to a different kind of a drive-in. No car hops—just a big open front on the red and white tiled building with a long counter that pushed burgers out like they were on a conveyor belt. The air was charged with electricity it was so exciting. On my brother's instructions, we each ordered 6 cheeseburgers and 6 orders of fries. The burgers were 12 cents and the fries 10 cents each, so it was no big financial deal. Welcome to ***McDonald's*** and the Golden Arches!

Unpeeled garlic will keep in the lower drawer of your refrigerator for a month or longer.

I remember taking a young lady to a McDonald's in Washington, D.C. as late as 1969 and having her ask me if we really ate these things in our car. On this occasion, I was driving my 1962 Nash Rambler American. A black convertible with a white top and red vinyl upholstery. How sweet it was! This was the first time she had eaten at a McDonald's, and we had just finished eating our way across Europe the prior year. Amazing!

I remember meeting R. David Thomas at one of his earlier restaurants in Denver in 1976 and thinking how revolutionary he was to be serving "fresh" burgers instead of the customary fare that was being served at the other burger places around the country at that time. Equally amazing was the fact that he really does have a daughter named Wendy. I wonder how well those other guys would have done if they called their place "Kroc's"?

Then came 1978 and I was at Augie Busch's home in St. Louis at a party being hosted in the courtyard of his marvelous stables. I have a clear remembrance of two things from that particular outing. The first was how clinically clean the stables were that those famous Clydesdales lived in. Their stables were cleaner than many homes I have been in. Then I remember, as the smell of the barbecue wafted into the stables, I felt a sudden urge to count the horses to see if any of the stables were empty!

It was around this time that I began to realize that "fresh" really begins at home, so I started making burgers on the grill at home again. I remember a lot of charcoal fires and a lot of coaxing coals into the proper temperature so we could grill before all hope of daylight vanished.

Today burgers have been given a new level of sophistication with the new Gucci ketchup and fancy French mustards, but never forget that the best burger is the one that is a two-napkin burger.

As popular as burgers are it is, nevertheless, quite difficult to find a good juicy burger at any kind of a restaurant these days. Why do you suppose that is? Write me if you figure it out.

Well, they have always been with us and I suspect that they always will be. You know we really ought to give more respect to something that has been that much a part of our life. Make a better burger and do something meaningful for humanity!

To make a better burger, you must remember this: pack it tightly. It is just like making a snowball. You scoop up a handful of the stuff (about baseball size), and you pack it firmly by patting and rolling it in the cup of your hands. If you do this gingerly, the burger will fall apart and leave gaping fissures the size of the San Andreas Fault. All the juice will escape into the coals while it is cooking, and you will be left with a dry, crumbly mess. So, roll up your sleeves and get your hands right down into the thick of things.

Once you get it firmly packed into a nice ball, you can then flatten it into burger shape. Keep it thick and do it on a very hot flame so it sears on the outside and retains a juicy pinkness on the inside.

BURGERS!

BASIC BURGERS

All burgers start with good meat. There is a lot of concern about fat and cholesterol in red meat, and most people should chose as lean a cut of beef as they can in *most* situations. However, when making burgers on the grill, I prefer to use ground chuck since the fire will tend to cook off some of the fat. If you use meat that is too lean, it can come off the grill rather dry. The most basic burger on the grill is still a treat over anything that you might buy in a restaurant or fast food place provided you use fresh buns and dressings. The egg plays an important role in keeping the meat together so it does not crumble and fall apart.

1 lb. ground chuck
1 large egg
salt & pepper

Mix the egg and salt and pepper with the meat forming 4 round balls and flattening them into patties. Add additional ground pepper on the surface of the burger, apply to a hot grill, and cook to your liking.

BLUE BURGERS

The nice thing about burgers is that you can mix anything you want in them. Most blue cheese burgers in restaurants put the cheese on top of the meat, but in this recipe you put it inside. It is important to have a hot grill so the meat seals and cooks quickly and the cheese does not melt through onto the coals.

1 lb. ground chuck
1 large egg
2 Tbsp crumbled blue cheese – heaping
1 Tbsp Italian bread crumbs
1 tsp garlic powder
1 tsp black pepper
1 tsp salt
8 strips of bacon – cooked

Mix the ingredients together and form 4 balls that have been firmly packed and then flatten them into burgers. Criss cross the bacon on top of the burgers and serve on whole wheat buns with sliced tomatoes and onions.

GUIDO BURGERS

When you fold the cheese into the meat, it not only flavors the meat better but it also allows you to use less cheese on your burger, which thereby reduces your total fat intake. It is important, however, that you use a lot of hair cream to slick your hair back and that you put on one of those sleeveless T-shirts while you grill these things in your back yard.

2 large green peppers – sliced thick
4 slices of white onions
2 Tbsp olive oil
1 lb. ground chuck
1 large egg
3/4 Cup mozzarella cheese – shredded
1 tsp fennel seed
½ tsp garlic powder
½ tsp basil
1/4 tsp crushed red pepper
1 Tbsp Italian bread crumbs
salt & pepper
4 slices of tomato

Heat the olive oil in a sauté pan and cook the peppers with salt and pepper and garlic powder over medium heat for about 15 minutes—stir frequently. Add the onions and lower the heat until peppers become completely limp and soft. This may take 30 to 60 minutes, but they can be prepared as much as two days ahead of time.

Mix the remaining ingredients and form 4 round balls and flatten into patties. Cook on a hot grill. Serve on kaiser rolls with a slice of tomato on the bottom and warm peppers and onions on the top.

Serve with ice-cold soda and garnish with an assortment of olives, pepperoncinis and **Frank Sinatra** music.

KING LEO BURGERS

He rides a Harley Road King, his name is Leo, and he likes burgers about as much as any guy I know. I prefer to ride with guys who love to eat. In fact, our motto is, *"Live to Ride, Ride to Eat."* Fresh onions are always an important complement to any hamburger, and in this case they are the staple flavoring inside the ground meat. You can make these patties earlier in the day and refrigerate them until you are ready to throw them on the grill. This will enhance the flavor even more. You can use a whole grain or rye roll, as the flavors will complement each other well.

1 lb. ground chuck
1 large egg
3 slices Bermuda onion – diced
3 slices white onion – diced
1 Tbsp Worcestershire sauce
1 tsp salt
2 tsp coarse black pepper

2 Tbsp mayo
1 tsp horseradish
1/4 tsp paprika

iceberg lettuce
4 whole-wheat hamburger buns

Mix the ground meat, egg, onions, Worcestershire, salt and pepper into four round balls and then flatten into patties. Grill on a hot grill until cooked to your satisfaction. Mix the mayo, horseradish and paprika into a horsey sauce to spread on the buns and top with lettuce. These are tall burgers, so you need a drink that will stand up to them—make it a Coors Banquet—Leo would like that!

Serve with pickles, potato chips, and *Milwaukee Potato Salad*.

PUEBLO PAULY'S PEPPER BURGERS

The green peppers remain crunchy, so the grilled onions make a nice contrast on this burger. This burger is super without much in the way of dressings. I like a nice polish mustard, and it is imperative that you use bakery-fresh Jewish Rye with seeds instead of a bun. If you do not use the rye bread, we will track you down and recall this cookbook and you will be banished to canned food for the rest of your life.

1 ½ lbs. ground chuck *
1 large egg
1/3 cup green pepper – chopped
1 ½ tsp coarse grind black pepper
1 tsp garlic powder
1 tsp salt
2 Tbsp Romano cheese – grated
4 slices thick bacon
8 slices Bermuda onion
2 tsp butter
black pepper
balsamic vinegar

In a large mixing bowl, combine the ground chuck, egg, green peppers, black pepper, garlic powder, salt, and Romano cheese. Mix it well—getting your hands good and messy—and then form four large balls and flatten into big burgers. Put burgers on a plate, and return to the refrigerator to chill while you fix the onions and other items of the meal. Light the coals.

You should cut the bacon in half so you have 8 pieces. Fry 5 or 6 slices in a small fry pan, and fry the other 2 or 3 slices in a large cast iron skillet. Set the fried bacon on a piece of paper so it can drain.

Put the burgers on the hot coals and begin cooking them.

Add the butter, onions and a good measure of black pepper to the iron skillet and cook over medium heat until the onions begin to soften. Add a splash of vinegar, cover, and turn the heat off.

* If you are doing the burgers on a grill, you will want to use the ground chuck, but if they are being cooked in a broiler in the oven, you may wish to use ground round instead. A fire will take out more of the juices from the fat, so you need somewhat of a fattier meat so the burgers do not dry out on you. If you wish to make a cheeseburger, use a sharp New York state cheddar. *Uncle Jimmy's Italian Tomato Salad* is a winner with this burger. Go out for ice cream later in the night.

SOUTH OF THE BORDER BURGERS

Some like it hot! This burger will be a good stand in if you cannot get to ***Senor Miguel's*** for a Mondango Burrito, and nothing less than "2 alarm" will do. If the jalapenos are too much, you can cut back on the amount but be daring on your first try.

1 lb. ground chuck
1 large egg
1 Tbsp jalapeno peppers – diced *
3/4 Cup Monterey Jack cheese – shredded
1 Tbsp cilantro
½ tsp garlic powder
salt & pepper
1 ripe avocado
4 slices of tomatoes
iceberg lettuce
4 hamburger buns

Mix the ground meat, egg, peppers, monterey jack, cilantro, garlic and salt and pepper into four nice large round balls. Flatten into patties and grill on a hot grill until cooked to your liking.

Skin and pit the avocado and slice equally on each burger in a bun, topping with the fresh tomatoes and lettuce.

This is an ice-cold Coors Light and *Michigan Cole Slaw* combo.

* Be careful about getting the jalapeno juice on your bare hands and then putting your hands in the wrong place, i.e. eyes, lips, etc.

BIG DADDY BURGERS

Once you master all the burgers above, you are ready to take on the **BIG DADDY BURGER**, honest to God. All of the above ingredients mixed into one burger and heaped on the top of it! Since there will be so much fill, it is important that these become ½ pounders to accommodate all the fillings. Pack them flat so they are about 5 to 6 inches across. Really……try it!

GEE WHIZZERS AND BIG DEALS (*ENTREES*)

THE SOCIAL ASPECTS OF EATING

Dining should always be a class act. If you know how to cook—even modestly—you have the means of creating an attractive social drawing card. My oldest son is a gifted athlete and musician, and I used to think that he had the real social ticket. Upon reconsideration, however, it occurred to me that at some point in life, the notion of asking a girl to come over and shoot some hoops or play saxophone with you might limit your audience. On the other hand, while not everyone plays sax, everyone does eat! This is even truer if you can expand your portions beyond one or two, add a little flair and charm, and turn your cooking into a social event. You can impress dates, host dinner parties, and make new and lasting friends through the medium of food.

There is an old saw that says eating is a substitute for romance. I have heard this thesis advanced and discussed with good-natured levity on more than one occasion, but I would like to add another dimension to that discussion. There are those who would argue that romance might actually be a substitute for eating.

On one hand, it seems to me that eating may be clearly more essential, and in some cases, as enjoyable. But then why be exclusive here when we can easily strike an acceptable compromise that should make everyone happy. In truth, we may do well to agree that each serves as an interchangeable forerunner to the other!

It is quite easy to create a mood without having the finest of china or silver. One need not have an impressive penthouse apartment with a stunning view of the city to serve an impressive meal. A tasty meal simply presented on the plate and served with a little candlelight and some soft music can do wonders.

Yes, you protest, but the real problem is getting it to the table while it is still hot and presentable. That, indeed, is the hard part and in many cases, it is the stumbling block that keeps most of us from entertaining. It is the proverbial bucket of cold water tossed upon our raging fire of passion. It simply is too difficult, you say. Not so, if you manage it properly, and I am here to tell you that you can manage it easier than you think and even enjoy the process itself.

Let's do a Saturday dinner party. This can be an intimate dinner party for two or a gathering of many friends.

Begin the day around 10:00 A.M. by planning the meal with your partner. (Now, note that you just solved the problem of what to do. You have a "date" for the entire day that will prove to be fun and inexpensive.) Brew a pot of coffee and spend 30 minutes determining the menu. Once you agree on the menu, you should write out a list of ingredients. Then plan the shopping attack like you would a corporate merger and make an event of it. I always like to go to a farmer's or ethnic market to buy as many of the ingredients as possible. Elizabeth, New Jersey may not be the social epicenter of the universe, but a few hours in their outdoor market will transport you to Italy without the airfare. The Lexington Market in Baltimore, the Eastern Market, or the Maine Avenue Waterfront in Washington, D.C. offers those same mini-escapes. You can often catch lunch at a stand-up vendor's corner while you are in the middle of your shopping. These simple and carefree activities can guide the entire shopping experience into an easy and fun event.

It is helpful to try to return home early in the afternoon so you will have time to do some advance preparations and marinating if it is required. Try doing the preparations together with your other guests, if there are any. It is easy to divide duties among your guests so that some chop and dice and others peel and grind. You will need an assortment of bowls or Rubbermaid containers to store the items as they are being prepared, so be certain that you have the proper number and sizes of them handy. If you have some kind of easy munchies and something to drink while you do your preparation, it will lend to the social aspect of the dining experience. In any case, it can be fun and it does not take a lot of effort to make it so. As for the dirty kitchen after the feast, you can always refrigerate any left over food and just leave everything else where it is. **Yes, leave it.** Remember, you wanted to make this evening special, so don't mess it up by spending an hour in the glaring lights of a dirty kitchen doing K.P. That is a sure fire mood destroyer if there ever was one. Close the kitchen door, trim the candles, and enjoy the afterglow—you can always clean the kitchen in the morning.

PASTA PATTI

If ever there were a personal favorite, it would most likely be this recipe. This dish has become my signature piece, I think, for three reasons: It is quite simple to make, it makes an attractive presentation, and it is a ***Happy Heart*** item.

This is clearly a summer favorite when fresh tomatoes are available, but if you must do it during the winter, then you need to find some good reliable tomatoes with flavor that come close to the real thing. You need to give this dish some time to "flavor blend". The actual cooking time is quite short, so it helps to let the ingredients marinate together for a time so that all the flavors can properly unlock and wed with one and other.

1 lb. boneless chicken breasts
-or-
1 lb. large shrimp
4 links of sweet Italian sausage – sliced on the diagonal
1/4 cup olive oil
garlic powder
dash cayenne pepper
6-8 ripe tomatoes
4 spring onions
1/4 cup fresh basil
4 oz frozen peas
1/4 tsp crushed red pepper
1 lb. ziti (rigatoni or penne)
Pecorino Romano cheese for grating
salt & pepper

Place chicken or shrimp (sometimes I use half of each) in a Corning-type bowl and add olive oil, garlic, cayenne, salt & pepper and stir. Allow to set, covered, in refrigerator for 2 to 4 hours. If you are in a hurry, you can let it stand for 20 minutes and it still works.

Dice tomatoes into ½ to ¾ inch chunks. Dice spring onions and mix items together in a bowl with basil, crushed pepper, salt & pepper. Let stand for at least 30 minutes, or while the other items are being prepared.

In a pot of boiling and salted water, cook the pasta until al dente. It is important that it be firm since it is going to cook a little longer with the rest of the ingredients.

In a large hot sauté pan, cook the sausage slices until they are well browned. Dump in entire chicken/shrimp marinade and stir frequently for about 10 minutes. Add 2-3 Tbsp of tomato mix and cook an additional 2-3 minutes, turn the heat off, cover, and let stand while tending to the pasta.

When the pasta is finished cooking, add the peas to the hot water and drain immediately.

Add the pasta, peas, and 1 Tbsp of olive oil to the large sauté pan. Keep stirring until pasta takes on a glazed appearance—about 3 minutes. (If you want to break away from the ***Happy Heart*** method, you can now add a large heaping tablespoon of ricotta cheese at this time and cook for an additional minute or two.)

Place pasta mixture in a large pasta bowl, top with tomato mixture, and grate cheese over the top. Serve in individual pasta bowls.

If you serve Pellegrino water with lemon slices, *Nanny's Italian Lettuce Salad*, and Ferrara bread sticks, you have nearly a zero fat gram meal. Light a few candles and put some Jerry Vale on the stereo, and you will have a sure hit. Some of my finest dining memories center around this dish.

NOTES:

This recipe is designed for four people. If you want to make this a twosome, just cut portions in half or do the full portion and refrigerate the remainder for another day. It is a very good cold salad the next day.

You will need a very large pasta bowl for table service. If you do not own one, it would be useful to invest in one—you will make this dish often.

Safety note: Do not reuse marinade bowl until it has been washed in hot water. Chicken and seafood, when marinated, should never find their way back to the marinade bowl after they have been cooked. Incidentally, ***Patti*** is also the name of a little village in the northeast corner of Sicily.

PASTA CHAIRMAN OF THE BOARD

This is the "Chairman of the Board" because your guests will surely think that you got that big promotion and you are now in tall cotton. Warning: You may not want to serve this to anyone in authority over you, since you run the risk of having them think that you are already making too much money if you can afford to serve this kind of food.

1 lb. large shrimp
4 Tbsp olive oil
1 Tbsp sweet butter
½ tsp garlic powder
2 links sweet Italian sausage

8 spears fresh asparagus
4 large ripe tomatoes
1 Tbsp fresh chives – chopped
1 Tbsp fresh parsley – chopped
1 Tbsp ricotta cheese
1 lb. cut ziti or rigati
Fresh pecorino romano cheese for grating
salt & pepper

Sauté the peeled shrimp in 2 Tbsp of olive oil, the butter and the garlic powder until they are done, and then remove from pan and set aside.

Dice the tomatoes in a mixing bowl and add the chives, parsley and salt and pepper to taste. Stir and set aside.

Slice the sausages into 1-inch strips and sauté until properly cooked. You can now add the pasta to the boiling water and cook until al dente.

In the large sauté pan, add the remaining olive oil and the asparagus cut into 2 inch pieces and gently sauté until they become tender. Add half of the tomato mixture and the ricotta cheese and simmer for 5 minutes.

Drain the pasta and mix into the sauté pan along with the shrimp, sausage and asparagus. Sauté on medium heat for another 5 minutes and remove from pan. Toss remaining tomato mixture and serve with fresh grated cheese.

Start the meal with *Insalta Ronaldo* and a nice bottle of Barolo, and I guarantee that promotion you have been looking for.

SEAN'S FAVORITE PASTA

Shortly after my son got his own apartment, he began to develop an interest in cooking. At first he wanted me to fix things to send home, or he wanted me to come over and fix for him. In time, he graduated to calling for advice or ideas. The first cookbook I bought for him was an all-you-ever-wanted-to-know-about pasta book. For a time, I thought he was going to try every recipe in the book. The one he seems to like best involves tuna, and he has modified it from the book, and I have further modified it on him. It is nice to swap recipe ideas so when you pass this sleeper on, be sure to give my son a mention. This recipe will serve four normal people or two growing young men.

3 Tbsp olive oil
2 garlic gloves
1 12 ½ oz can Progresso tuna in olive oil
1 28 oz can Italian tomatoes (San Marzano)
1 Tbsp basil
1 tsp allspice
1 tsp capers
5 spring onions – diced to the stem
1 lb. ziti – rotini – or rigati
grating cheese

Peel and sliver the garlic. The garlic should be twice slivered so that no piece is larger than 1/8 inch across.

Pulse the can of tomatoes in food processor so tomatoes are broken into small chunks.

Heat the olive oil in a large sauté pan and gently cook the garlic for approximately 10 minutes. Add the tuna and break into smaller pieces stirring over medium heart.

Begin cooking pasta, since the entire remaining process only takes about 10 to 12 minutes. Add the tomatoes, basil, chopped onion and allspice to the tuna. Increase the heat until mixture begins to bubble vigorously. Turn heat off and cover pan.

Rinse capers and add to sauce just prior to serving.

Drain pasta when finished cooking, and serve in pasta bowls with mixture ladled over the top of the pasta. Grate generous amount of cheese on pasta and eat up!

If you do not eat all the sauce, give it to your neighbors! Fish does not keep well in tomato for more than a day.

SUMMER RIGATONI WITH RICOTTA

On those warm summer days, we tend to shy away from heavy meals and all too often we mistakenly cast pasta into that category. It is true that certain gravies require long cooking, but not all pasta sauces should be included in that. The next recipe is a summer favorite because it does not require long cooking times. It does, however, beg for fresh ingredients. Because the cooking time is short, it is not advisable to use dry spices. In this recipe, you make servings for four normal people or two sailors who have spent all day on the boat with nothing to eat. If you only eat half of this meal, you can refrigerate the combined leftovers and serve it as a cold salad the next day.

4-5 nice ripe garden tomatoes
1/4 cup olive oil
1/4 cup fresh basil – chopped
1 Tbsp spring onion – chopped
1 cup ricotta cheese *
1 cup Parmesan cheese – grated
1 lb. rigatoni
salt & pepper

Dice your tomatoes and set aside in a mixing bowl. Salt & pepper to taste. Heat the olive oil in a large sauté pan over medium heat. When you begin to cook the pasta in the boiling, salted water, you should also dump the tomatoes, basil and onion into the hot oil. Stir mixture until it begins to bubble, then cover and turn heat off, leaving pan on the stove. When pasta is finished cooking, remove it from the heat and at the same time, return the heat to the tomatoes and add the ricotta. Drain the pasta. Once the tomatoes and ricotta are heated through, you can dump the pasta in a large bowl, pour the tomato mixture over it, and toss with the grated cheese. What you have done is limit the cooking time of the tomatoes and brought everything together hot at the same time. Serve in deep bowls with bread sticks.

* You can use a light ricotta cheese for this recipe, and it will not affect the taste at all.

RONNIE'S RAGU

If you are thinking Ronnie isn't Italian, you didn't see the movie *"Moonstruck"*. Go rent it for after-dinner entertainment. Now, the recipe: This is not something that comes in a jar, and it is a staple of the Italian table in Tuscany. I am not a strong fan of veggies, so this recipe took a long time to make it on my "hit list". But, trust me, this is good stuff on a cold day, and it is one of the few recipes that warrants something other than a pasta that fits on a fork. Normally, I don't like doing the spin-the-fork-in-the-spoon thing, but this one calls for a broad, flat, long pasta to make it work right.

¼ cup olive oil
4 cloves garlic – sliced thin
1 cup onions – chopped fine
1 cup celery – chopped fine
¾ cup carrots – chopped fine
1 ½ lbs. of ground veal
¾ tsp salt
¾ tsp black pepper
½ tsp allspice
1 bay leaf
1 cup white wine – dry
1 can chicken broth
1 32 oz can of whole Italian tomatoes – pulsed
1 cup milk
2 Tbsp chives
1 pkg. fettuccine
Asiago cheese

Heat the olive oil over medium heat in a large, heavy stockpot (enamalized porcelain). Add the garlic and stir until it just begins to color. Stir the onions, celery and carrots into the olive oil. Cover and simmer for 10-15 minutes. Add the ground veal and salt & pepper, stirring until it becomes light brown. Add the chicken broth, white wine, tomatoes, bay leaf, and allspice. Cover and simmer for an additional hour. Add the milk, and simmer for another 15 minutes. Cook the fettuccine according to instructions, drain, and serve with a freshly grated asiago cheese. Sprinkle some chives over each plate for a nice visual.

By the way, this recipe only calls for 1 cup of white wine, so you can go ahead and drink the rest of the bottle while you are cooking—I do!

NAPOLITANO ITALIAN GRAVY

The Lombardo's, Martinangelo's and Pedicano's always called it *gravy*. Whenever I asked, I got a simple answer, "That's what it is." You make "brown" gravy for "American" dishes and then there is "Gravy"! Who can figure? This recipe is the mother lode. Once you learn to make this simple sauce or gravy, you can make all sorts of Italian dishes by simply altering accordingly. I have used this basic recipe and modified it to create 500 servings for our annual Boy Scout fundraiser, and I have also made it for two people. Word of caution: You want to make this so there will be leftovers, and if you do not make leftovers, you will miss out on the best. Good gravy is like fine wine and gracious women—they get better with age. You can keep this in the refrigerator up to one week and for as long as three months in the freezer.

1/3 cup olive oil
3 medium cloves of crushed fresh garlic
1 6 oz can tomato paste
2 28 oz cans tomato puree
2 28 oz cans of water
3 Tbsp basil
2 Tbsp oregano or marjoram

2 Tbsp crushed red pepper
4 bay leaves
3 cloves
salt & pepper

The beginning is the most important part of this recipe—it all hinges on the first 2 minutes of cooking. Peel and crush the garlic. In a small heavy stockpot, heat the olive oil—gently over medium high heat—until it begins to dance a little in the pot. Do not allow the oil to smoke at any time. Quickly add the garlic and immediately stir with a wooden spoon until garlic begins to look golden. Do not let the garlic stand still—you must stir constantly. When the garlic turns golden, it is unlocking all its flavor modules so you must now add your can of tomato paste. (Note: if you opened both ends of this little can you can push it out clean and quickly) The paste should sizzle—that is fine—but you need to keep moving it around and breaking it up with your wooden spoon until it, too, takes on a nice golden glow and is thoroughly mixed with the oil and garlic. This aroma is heavenly. I wish I could make a man's aftershave from this fragrance—"Eau d'sauce". This is the most important and most attentive step in the gravy. It should only take about 2 to 3 minutes to this point.

Now you need to add the 2 cans of tomato puree. If you fill each can about half to three quarters full of water from the tap and swish it around, you will recover the residue while adding the water. Add the remainder of the ingredients and salt and pepper to taste. Remember that tomato puree—unlike tomato sauce—has no salt in it, so you will need to season accordingly.

You should continue stirring frequently at this stage until the gravy begins to bubble slightly, at which time you reduce the heat to a simmer and continue to cook for at least 1 hour but not longer than 3 hours. If you need to be out running errands, it can cook by itself if it is not scorching. It is good to stir it once or twice an hour. You can also taste test it at the same time to see if it meets with your approval and needs salt.

The cloves will tend to soften the acidic nature of the tomato and are much better than using sugar. If you read your labels, you will know that this is a ***Happy Heart*** recipe because there is no fat in the gravy. Now read the pasta label and you will find no fat in the pasta!

This recipe makes a very nice light tomato sauce that can be used just as it is on any kind of pasta. It can be used as the base in lasagna or even on pizza. It should not be cooked down so as to produce a heavy or thick sauce. It is meant to be light. Once the gravy has cooked for an hour, you can add cooked meatballs, sausage, or even pork chops and allow it to simmer together for an additional 1 to 2 hours.

When you cook your pasta, it should be al dente. When you drain the pasta, you might want to ladle some gravy over the pasta while it sits in the pot. This will keep the pasta from sticking together. Never rinse the pasta. That removes the starch that makes the gravy stick to it. Serve the pasta in a bowl and pour generous portions of gravy over the pasta. Grate some fresh cheese on the pasta and garnish with a sprig of parsley. You may like to try a tablespoon of ricotta cheese dropped right on top of the pasta dish.

Lastly, you will want to be sure you have some good fresh Italian bread to eat with this and eventually sponge up the remaining gravy from your bowl. Bella, Bella!

Cheese should always be grated when it is needed—the finer the grate the quicker it will lose its full flavor.

INVESTMENT-GRADE ITALIAN GRAVY

There are those days when nothing will satisfy you but an extra hearty bowl of rigatoni and gravy. It has to have substance to it, it has to stick to your ribs, and it has to satisfy your caveperson instincts. That means it has to have nice big chucks of meat! In short, you want to feel like you got your money's worth. Good news fellow travelers! This recipe can be made with ground turkey, and you will never know the difference. Viva ***Happy Heart*!**

The Gravy

See recipe on preceding page

The Meat

1 Tbsp olive oil
1 clove garlic – crushed
2 lbs. ground turkey *or* ground round
1 Tbsp fennel seed
1/4 tsp rosemary
1 tsp oregano
salt & pepper

Heat the olive oil in a sauté pan and lightly cook the garlic over medium heat until garlic begins to turn golden. Add the ground meat and remaining ingredients and brown over medium heat. When meat is browned, reduce heat and cook on low heat for an additional 5 minutes.

Drain meat in a colander, add meat mixture to gravy, and simmer for 1 to 2 hours. Serve this gravy over hearty pasta like rigatoni or mostacolli, accompanied by a loaf of fresh Italian bread, a bottle of Chianti and fresh fruit for dessert.

RON'S RIGATONI & MEATBALLS

Every community that has an Italian population has at least one place that serves basic spaghetti and meatballs without pretense or high prices. Most often than not, it will be a place that has modest checkered table clothes, travel posters of Italy, and pictures of the Pope hanging on the walls. It is the kind of place that you tuck the napkin in your collar and do not feel out of place. This is a recipe to satisfy those urgings when you do not want to go out for a store-bought meal.

1 ½ lbs. meat loaf mix (beef, pork & veal)
1 large egg
1 cup Italian bread crumbs
1 Tbsp parsley
1 ½ tsp basil
1 tsp oregano
½ cup Parmesan cheese – grated
½ tsp garlic powder
1/3 cup milk
1 tsp salt
1 tsp pepper
1 Tbsp olive oil
Napolitano Italian Gravy
1 lb. rigatoni or ziti
Pecorino Romano cheese for grating

Mix together all of the items, except the olive oil, in a large bowl. Form golf-ball size meatballs by rolling the meat between your hands, being careful to pack the meat together.

Heat the olive oil in a large skillet and brown the meatballs by turning them often until all sides are well browned.

Make the *Napolitano Italian Gravy* and drop the meatballs into the gravy after they have been browned. Simmer the gravy and meatballs on low heat for at least 1 hour prior to serving. This recipe keeps well in the refrigerator and tastes better the next day.

Boil the pasta in salted water until al dente. Drain and serve with gravy and meatballs ladled over the pasta and the cheese freshly grated at the table.

Tuck a bib into your collar, break a fresh loaf of Italian bread, and eat to your heart's desire!

NANNY'S GIANT STUFFED SHELLS

I call this Nanny's Shells simply because I have memories of her getting up at the crack of dawn and working all day in the kitchen on certain big-affair-type meals. This is one of those meals. It cannot be done quickly, and it will never be a ***Happy Heart,*** so you may as well reconcile yourself to the fact that this will be a once-in-a-while meal. It is like going to visit that client in the ***Baca Grande, Colorado***—it is not easy to get to, but well worth it once you do. Simply finding the shells can be a challenge, since the giant-sized shells are not made by a lot of pasta companies. You must have the big guys, or you don't have stuffed shells!

2 – 1 lb. boxes giant shells (35-40 of them)

Sauce

1/4 cup olive oil
1 28 oz can tomato puree
1 Tbsp basil
1 Tbsp parsley
1 Tbsp rosemary

1 tsp garlic powder
1 tsp crushed red pepper
1 tsp allspice

Meat

1 lb. ground turkey
1 Tbsp fennel seed
salt & pepper

Filling

2 lbs. ricotta cheese
7 oz mozzarella cheese
3 eggs
1 cup loose, fresh basil – chopped
½ cup grated locatelli
½ cup fresh parsley – chopped
1/4 cup fresh chives – chopped
1 tsp black pepper

PREP NOTES:

I call for 2 boxes of shells, which will provide more than 35-40 shells, only so you can sort out the best 35-40 shells and save the rest for another time. You can, and should, make the sauce the day before. You can make this with or without the meat in the sauce.

Sauce

Sauté the ground turkey, the fennel seed, and salt and pepper to taste in a large pan until cooked thoroughly and set aside.

In a 3-½ quart saucepan, heat the olive oil and garlic powder until the oil begins to dance. Then add the can of tomato puree and 1 can of water. Add all spices and stir until sauce begins to bubble. Reduce heat and simmer for 30 minutes. Add meat and continue to simmer for an additional 30 minutes. Cool and refrigerate overnight for best results.

Filling

In a large mixing bowl, grate the mozzarella (packaged mozzarella comes in 8 oz sizes, but you should not use all of it), add the remaining ingredients, and mix thoroughly. A large wooden spoon or two medium hands will do the job quite well. Actually, it is kind of fun to mix it together with someone you are fond of. The key to this mix is fresh herbs. The herbs should be minced and waiting in mixing bowls for the preparation. Remember that your pizza wheel will mince perfectly for this job.

Shells

Heat a large pot of water to boiling and add salt to taste. Slide the shells—a few at a time—into the boiling water, and allow them to cook for about 5 to 6 minutes. Drain quickly and lay them out on the countertop so they do not stick to each other.

Preparation

With a tablespoon, you can fill the shells with the filling and place them in a Corning with an inch of sauce on the bottom. Cover the Corning and bake in a 325-degree oven for 45 minutes.

Since you are going feed a lot of people, why not throw in an *Antipasto Classico* and then offer an assortment of fresh fruits and gorgonzola cheese for dessert. Sounds good!

FOUR-STAR LASAGNA

My pal "Mondo" Arch Campbell was the world famous movie critic on Channel 4 in Washington, D.C. Arch awards about as many four-star ratings as he wins golf outings. In other words, a four-star rating is a rare and memorable event. This lasagna is a four-star. It has plot, holding power and substance, and you go away satisfied. This is not sissy stuff. It is made in a big blue turkey roaster and will feed the entire cast and crew.

The "Gravy"

You can use the recipe for Napolitano Italian Gravy, Investment-Grade Gravy, the Sauce in Nanny's Giant Stuffed Shells, or the following:

1/3 cup olive oil
1 tsp garlic powder
2 35 oz cans Italian tomatoes
1 Tbsp oregano
½ tsp allspice
½ tsp crushed red pepper
1 Tbsp chives
1 ½ lbs. lean ground beef or turkey
1 tsp garlic powder
1 Tbsp rosemary
salt & pepper
3 links Italian sausage
3 lbs. ricotta cheese
3 cups mozzarella – shredded
½ cup Romano – grated
5 large eggs
2 Tbsp basil
2 Tbsp parsley
1 tsp black pepper
1 ½ lbs. lasagna noodles

In a large saucepan, heat the olive oil and garlic over medium heat until hot. Run the tomatoes through the blender and add to the hot oil, along with the oregano, allspice, red peppers, chives, and salt and pepper to taste and simmer while you cook the meats.

In a large sauté pan, fry the ground meat, garlic powder, rosemary, and salt and pepper to taste until the meat is well-browned. Drain the oil from the meat and add the meat to the tomato sauce. In the same sauté pan, you can fry the sausage. Cut the links into thin diagonal slices and sauté on both sides until they are browned and cooked through. Remove and set aside in a bowl for later use.

In a large mixing bowl, combine the ricotta, eggs, romano, basil, parsley, and pepper. Blend together to an even consistency.

Shred the mozzarella into a third bowl and set aside.

In large pot of boiling salted water, cook the lasagna noodles for approximately 10 minutes, or according to the instructions on the package. When the noodles are finished cooking, add 1 tablespoon of olive oil to the water and immediately drain into a large colander.

Ladle a thin covering of sauce into the bottom of your large turkey roaster and then lay down a covering of lasagna noodles. Spoon a covering of cheese mixture over noodles and then add more sauce. Repeat this process on every layer and add the shredded mozzarella to every other layer. Every layer will have the sauce and ricotta, and every other layer will also have the mozzarella. In the middle layer, place the sausage, sauce, and mozzarella, but no ricotta. The top layer should have everything on it: sauce, ricotta, and mozzarella.

Bake the lasagna, with the cover on, in a pre-heated 350-degree oven for 30 minutes. Remove the cover and bake an additional 10 minutes. Allow to stand for 10 minutes before cutting.

You should have some of the gravy left over that you can ladle on the top of the lasagna, along with some freshly-grated parmesan cheese.

This recipe needs *Nanny's Simple Lettuce Salad*, lots of fresh Italian Bread, and a hearty Chianti wine. This is NOT a ***Happy Heart*** by any means, but your taste buds will overrule your head.

Keep your tax returns and supporting documents for at least four years. Most audits take place three years after you filed your return. The statute of limitations never expires if fraud is involved!

RYAN'S "GRATE" BAKED ZITI'S

At 15, my friend Ryan acquired the reputation of being a "grate" guy since I always asked him to grate my cheeses. The importance of freshly grated cheeses cannot be understated, and the job of grating three or four cheeses for a given recipe can be a yeoman's task. One of the handy features of this recipe is you can prepare everything ahead of time—up to the oven stage—and then just pop it in the oven 60 minutes before you serve it. This gives you time to do other things just prior to the meal, and that can be useful if you are entertaining.

1 lb. ground beef
½ tsp garlic powder
½ tsp black pepper
½ tsp salt
1 tsp parsley
1 tsp fennel seed
4 links sweet Italian sausage – sliced 1" thick
1/4 cup olive oil
½ tsp garlic powder
2 tsp tomato paste
1 28 oz can Italian tomatoes
1 Tbsp basil
2 tsp chives
1 tsp marjoram
1/4 tsp allspice
1/4 tsp crushed red pepper
1 lb. zitis
1 3/4 cups mozzarella – grated
1 cup fontina – grated
2/3 cup ricotta
½ cup Romano – grated
8-10 fresh basil – torn into small pieces

Brown the beef with the garlic powder, fennel seed, parsley, and salt & pepper and drain fat when cooked. Brown sausage slices in the same pan and set aside with ground meat.

In a saucepan, heat the olive oil and garlic powder and add tomato paste when hot. Stir. Run the tomatoes through a blender with one or two pulses and add to hot oil and paste. Stir in basil, chives, marjoram, allspice and red pepper, and bring to a slow boil. Turn off heat, add meats, and cover. Boil the zitis in salted water about 2/3 of the normal time. Drain when zitis are still very firm. Dump pasta into a large Corning and stir in sauce, cheeses, and basil, mixing well.

Bake in 350-degree oven for 60 minutes.

Remove from oven and allow to stand for 10 to 15 minutes before serving.

Check the holdings in your mutual funds to determine if stock overlap exists—many funds with the same objectives hold a lot of the stocks from the same companies.

CUGINO'S CHICKEN CACCIATORE

This dish is a must for an authentic Italian portfolio, and it is easy to recreate. ***Cugino's*** was a little unassuming place in Denver that had a lot of ethnic character and, at one time, did a memorable cacciatore. It was here that I first thought that this was a dish worth creating at home.

1 chicken + two pieces – cut up
4 cloves of garlic
4 links sweet Italian sausage
3 cups chicken stock
1 32 oz can Italian tomatoes
1 28 oz can crushed tomatoes
4 large slices white onion – halved
3 bay leaves
1 Tbsp basil
½ tsp rosemary
1 tsp crushed red pepper
1 large green bell pepper
1 large red bell pepper
1 Tbsp parsley
olive oil
salt & pepper

Wash the chicken and heat ¼ cup of the olive oil and garlic in a large stockpot. Salt & pepper the chicken parts to taste and sauté them for 5 minutes on each side.

Sauté the sausage until fully cooked and set aside.

In the stockpot, place the chicken and enough chicken stock and water to cover the chicken. Add the other ingredients—except the peppers and parsley—and simmer for 1 hour.

Remove the tops of the peppers and clean out the seeds. Cut the peppers in 2-inch strips and add to pot, along with the sausage and parsley. Simmer an additional 30 to 40 minutes.

Before serving, you can retrieve the chicken parts and remove the skin or you can leave it on. This is a ***Happy Heart*** winner either way. If you fix any kind of pasta to accompany it and some Ferrara breadsticks, you have a delightful low-fat meal.

There are two secrets to this recipe:

The sautéing and long cooking combination will cause the chicken to fall right off the bones, which makes it easy to eat so you can look cool through out the entire meal.

Adding the peppers during the last third of the cooking time allows adequate time to cook the flavor into the rest of the recipe and still retain some body in the peppers. If you keep some leftovers for a day or two—and this is a great item for that—you will notice that the peppers will fade somewhat on the next serving.

This meal really begs for a bottle of Chianti in a basket and a red-checkered tablecloth. You can buy disposable red-checkered paper table clothes in the supermarket for this type of occasion.

Incidentally, *Cugino* is Italian for "cousin" and since this is a large recipe, you can invite all of your cousins over for dinner and have plenty of food to feed them all.

TONI'S TIMPANO

I owe lots of credits for this dish. First, the movie. Stanley Tucci and the cast of *Big Night* are all my heroes—what a feast! From the first day I saw that movie, I wanted to make this dish, but I had to wait until I had a crowd big enough. Ray Bob's birthday provided that opportunity, and without Ray Bob kneading the dough and Toni (his wife) rolling it out for me, I would never have been able to do it. This recipe is a major project, but that is what wonderful food and dining should be all about.

The Dough

4 cups all purpose flour
4 large eggs
1 tsp salt
3 Tbsp olive oil
½ cup water

The Filling

8 cups *Investment-Grade Italian Gravy*
10 meat balls (slightly smaller than *Ron's Rigatoni & Meatball* size)
6 links cooked, sweet Italian sausage – cut into 2" pieces
6 hard-boiled eggs – quartered & halved
2 cups sharp provolone cheese – grated
2 cups of Genoa salami – cut in ½" cubes
1 cup Pecorino Romano – grated
3 lbs. penne rigati
2 Tbsp mascarpone cheese
4 large eggs – beaten

1 6-quart enameled washbasin

Make dough by hand. Put flour & salt together in a mound, create a crater in the center, and mix the eggs and water into the center until doughy. Knead by hand and set aside to rest for 5 minutes. Roll out into a 1/16" thick round, fold, and put in butter-greased washbasin. Assemble stuff in basin (cook penne only half the time). Bake for 1 hour at 350 degrees, remove from oven, cover with tin foil and bake an additional 30 minutes. Allow to stand at least 30 minutes before cutting. Cut the timpano like a cake, and ladle hot gravy over the wedges.

Timing is very important when you are making this dish—it takes a lot of time. I recommend making the gravy the night before, or even two days before. Give yourself lots of prep time, at least an hour, and then allow time for the Timpano to set before you cut it. If I am doing a dinner party with the expectation of eating around 7:00 p.m., I usually start the Timpano as early as 3:30.

In spite of the fact that this is a big dish all by itself, you need to make a big *Antipasto Classico* for starters and finish up with *Bananas Pisciotta* to make this a huge, blowout event. You could also serve some Manhattans—straight up—to complete the *Big Night* effect of the evening. Ask the ladies in attendance to see if they can find some of those elbow-length white gloves to wear with an exposed shoulder dress—wow!

Bring fresh flowers home once a month—even if you live alone most of the time.

POLLO DI PESCO

One afternoon I found myself sitting in ***Toots Shor's*** saloon across from Madison Square Garden with a friend of mine who is the best securities trial lawyer in the country. We had just finished a hearing before the New York Stock Exchange, and we were looking for conversation that would help ease our worried client's mind. What followed was a lively conversation about our roots and a discussion of the things we ate growing up. Dana Pescosolido began to tell us about a memorable chicken treatment that sounded quite good to me. I asked him to share that recipe, and here is my post-Martini recollection of his favorite.

2 Tbsp olive oil
3 large cloves garlic – minced
2 Tbsp onion – diced
4 boneless chicken breasts – cut into fork-size pieces
2 boneless chicken thighs – cut into fork-size pieces
½ cup white wine
1 35 oz can Italian tomatoes
1 15 oz can tomato sauce
1 Tbsp oregano
1/4 tsp crushed red pepper
1 Tbsp sugar
1 bay leaf
2 Tbsp fresh basil
15 large Sicilian-type green olives with pits
salt & pepper

Heat the olive oil in a heavy stockpot and cook the garlic and onions until the garlic begins to turn golden. Add the large chunks of chicken, and salt and pepper to taste. Stir often, allowing chicken to turn white on all sides. Add the white wine and cook vigorously for three or four minutes until it begins to reduce. Add can of Italian tomatoes, cover, and cook on medium for approximately 30 minutes, until tomatoes begin to break up. Add tomato sauce, oregano, red pepper, sugar, and bay leaf and simmer an additional 45 minutes over low heat. Add basil, olives, and salt and pepper to taste. Cover pot, raise heat to a hearty boil, and turn off immediately. Let pot stand on stove for 30 minutes.

You can use this recipe as a sauce over pasta or rice, or you can add a handful of very short pasta to the sauce and eat it like a stew or soup with nice Italian bread. Be careful of the olives, since they do have pits in them.

CAVILL'S CIOPPINO

The Italians have a marvelous tradition of a big fish dinner on Christmas Eve that usually includes anywhere from 7 to 12 different seafood dishes. Since Cioppino includes so many different seafoods, I have decided it can be a substitute when you are having less than 20 people over for dinner. It does not have to be Christmas to enjoy this hearty offering, but it is a festive dish, so it goes well with any celebration at any time of the year. In the San Francisco Bay area, I have seen people line up at fish houses to buy this delight to take home with them so they don't have to go through the work of making their own. That shortcut takes away all the fun of a relatively easy dish—provided you have, at least, a 14-quart stockpot! Invite at least three others to the table.

1/3 cup olive oil
1 medium white onion – diced fine
4 garlic cloves – minced
5 32 oz cans of Italian tomatoes – pulsed
2 cups good white wine
2 Tbsp basil

1 Tbsp oregano
2-3 Tbsp crushed red Pepper
1 tsp rosemary
3 bay leaves
1 lb. scallops
1 lb. large shrimp
1 lb. mussels
4 lobster tails – fresh or frozen
24 Cherrystone or Steamer clams
salt & pepper

In that large stockpot, place the olive oil and onion and heat over medium heat until the onion becomes translucent. Be careful not to burn it. Add the canned tomatoes, two 32oz cans of water, and the spices—including garlic—and cover. Bring to a rapid boil, turn off the heat, and allow to stand for 60 minutes. This recipe is done best if you make this part the day before and refrigerate overnight.

While the sauce is re-heating, you should add the 2 cups of wine. Clean the mussels and clams by scrubbing them in cold water. Peel the shrimp, but leave the lobster meat in the tail. Cook all the seafood, covered, on medium high heat for 10 – 15 minutes. Turn heat off and allow to stand in a covered pot for 5 minutes. Be sure that all clams and mussels have opened, and be careful to discard any that have not opened.

This is a genuine ***Happy Heart*** but most importantly, it is also a Happy Palate recipe.

Serve this meal in large bowls with *lots* of hard-crust Italian bread for soaking up the sauce. Don't forget to put an empty bowl in the middle of the table to collect the shells. This will be a fun meal, unless you invite a bunch of sissies for dinner!

Since this dish is very Italian, you might want to serve *Nanny's Simple*

Lettuce Salad at the end of the Cioppino dish, and then finish with a plate of cheeses and fruit.

You can drink a red or white wine with this dinner. The white is traditional because of the presence of seafood, but the strong marinara can handle a robust red like a Chianti Classico or an old vine Zinfandel.

Don't store coffee or coffee beans in the freezer. They will dry out and lose their flavor—instant cardboard!

VITO'S LINGUINI AND CLAMS

When you get the woolies for linguini and clams, there really is not much else that will satisfy that desire. I recall searching the streets of Philadelphia one night for just such a meal. After many blocks of walking—and a lobster at ***Bookbinders***—we still had a quest for linguini and clams. Arriving at the ***Il Gallo Negro*** at close to 11:00 p.m., we found a willing waiter—Giuseppe—and sat down to our second meal of the evening! Yes, it was worth it. People who do this meal have almost cult status with those who eat it. I never knew Old Man Vito's last name, but his Linguini and Clams were legend throughout his neighborhood, and more than 30 years later, I still remember eating them.

12 Cherrystone clams
½ stick sweet butter
1/4 cup olive oil
4 garlic cloves – crushed
1/4 tsp crushed red pepper
8 oz shucked clams & juice
1 tsp basil
2/3 cup parsley
black pepper
1 lb. linguini
Parmesan cheese – grated

Steam the Cherrystone clams in a large pot with about 1 to 1 ½ inches of salted water until all the clams open. Set aside.

In a large sauté pan, heat the butter, olive oil, garlic and peppers over medium heat, stirring frequently until garlic begins to brown. Add shucked clams and juice, basil, and parsley and simmer for 5 minutes. Turn off heat, cover pan, and leave on stovetop.

Boil the linguini in salted water until done—follow instructions on package.

Drain water from linguini and return linguini to cooking pot, add sauce from sauté pan, and toss thoroughly.

Serve in large bowls surrounded with the Cherrystone clams still in their shells, freshly grated cheese, and black pepper generously sprinkled over the serving.

Tuck a napkin in your collar, open a bottle of Chianti, put on the musical score from the **Godfather,** and enjoy!

TUXEDO CRABS

On the East Coast, we tend to associate our Chesapeake crabs with summer outings that call for bushels of steamed crabs served with ice-cold beer. Everyone really gets into the "crab pick'n" so that only a good swim in the pool really makes you clean again. It is no surprise that hard shell, steamed crabs are not served in restaurants with tablecloths. This recipe, on the other hand, is elegant and comes dressed for the occasion with the bow tie pasta. Be certain that the crabs are fresh and cleaned when you buy them. A good fish market will have the crabs alive when you buy them. Get them home very quickly so they do not spoil in your car.

1 Tbsp olive oil
1 Tbsp sweet butter
4-5 garlic cloves – slivered
10 soft shell crabs
2 links sweet Italian sausage – sliced
cayenne pepper
½ cup white onion – diced
4-5 tomatoes – diced

10 fresh asparagus – sliced
½ cup fresh basil
½ cup Pecorino Romano cheese – grated
1 lb. bow tie macaroni
salt & pepper

Cut the crabs in half down the middle so that one large pincher is on each side of the crab.

In a very large sauté pan, heat the oil, butter, and garlic over medium high heat until the garlic begins to turn golden. Add the crabs and sausage, and sprinkle a little cayenne, salt and pepper on the crabs. Cook until crabs turn reddish in color and are moderately crisp in texture.—approximately 10 minutes. Remove the crabs and set aside. Add the onions to the empty pan, and sauté about 5 – 6 minutes. Meanwhile, boil the bow ties in salted water until done.

Add the tomatoes and asparagus to the onions, cover and cook for 10 – 15 minutes—about the same cooking time as the bow ties. When the bow ties are done, drain and add them, the basil and the crabs to the tomato mixture and cook 5 more minutes. Dump the ingredients into a large bowl, mix in the grated cheese, and serve with a nice, crisp white wine. This is an elegant summer evening dinner that begs to be eaten out of doors with candles and tiki torches burning all about. Serve a nice, crisp Caesar salad and freshly baked Italian bread. Forget dessert—enjoy a nice cognac after dinner.

PESTO ROTINI WITH ARTICHOKES & OLIVES

Sometimes we forget that Italian food does not always have to be "red". In the south of Italy, you have a very warm tropical climate where olives and artichokes grow in abundance. This is a nice sauce that clings to all the spirals of the rotini and makes you think of white-washed, sun-drenched Sicilian villages and strains of Verdi or Pavarotti playing in the background.

2 cups basil – fresh
3 garlic cloves
2 Tbsp pignola (pine) nuts – toasted
1/3 cup parmesan cheese – grated
1/3 cup olive oil
8 oz artichoke hearts – diced
20 green & black olives – pitted and sliced
pinch crushed red pepper
salt & pepper
1 lb. rotini

Heat a non-stick frying pan over a medium high burner. Add the nuts, stirring constantly, until they begin to brown and you can smell the nutty flavor. In a food processor, combine the basil, garlic, pignola's, parmesan cheese, and olive oil to make the basic pesto sauce. Blend thoroughly. In a large bowl, fold in the artichoke hearts, olives, crushed red peppers, and a few twists of fresh pepper, along with the pesto sauce. This part of the recipe can actually be done 2-3 days ahead of time. Allow the mixture to stand at room temperature while the pasta boils.

Boil the pasta in salted water until al dente. Drain the rotini, and toss pesto mix, butter and pasta together in a large bowl and serve immediately with fresh Italian bread and a glass of chilled white wine.

After the pasta is eaten, serve *Nanny's Simple Italian Salad* and some sliced pears and coffee. ***Happy Heart*** and happy diners!

VEAL TOSCANO

Probably my very first real elegant dinner party involved my dearest friends in Denver. We had invited two couples for dinner that had very strong Italian heritages, and I wanted to do something extra special for them. I searched my cookbooks for days looking for something that was just for them. Unable to find that special recipe, I gave up and created my very first "private" recipe. Since it was a new creation, I named it after one of the dinner guests and in so doing, also began a tradition of naming my dishes after my friends.

1 oz porcini mushrooms
4 veal scaloppini – about the size of a man's hand – sliced thin
2 cloves garlic – peeled
1/4 cup fresh parsley– chopped
3 Tbsp basil or 1/3 cup fresh basil – chopped
4 pieces of prosciutto ham – sliced thin
8 slices Genoa salami
4 strips of fontina cheese
1/8 cup olive oil
2 cloves garlic – chopped
½ cup red wine
2 Tbsp arrowroot
salt & pepper

Place porcinis in 1 cup of water and bring to a quick boil. Let stand for 30 minutes in water.

If you begin the veal preparation as soon as you put the porcini in water, you should have about 15 minutes for the veal to sit before the porcini are ready. You can also prepare the veal early in the day a keep covered in the refrigerator for up to 8 hours. It does enhance the flavor and allows you a less messy final prep for your meal.

Lay the veal out flat and rub with the peeled garlic and salt & pepper to taste.

Sprinkle all but 1 Tbsp parsley and basil evenly over veal and then layer the prosciutto, Genoa and fontina cheese on the veal. Roll the layered veal and tie the ends with kitchen string.

Sauté the chopped garlic in the olive oil until garlic begins to turn golden (moderate high heat), add the veal rolls, and sauté, turning until all sides are browned. Add the porcini and its juice (through a strainer). Continue to cook 5 minutes.

Add the wine, remaining parsley, basil, and arrowroot, and cook an additional 5-6 minutes, stirring regularly until sauce thickens and browns. Salt & pepper to taste.

According to the U.S. Census Bureau, the life expectancy in the United States is 79 years for females and 76 years for males. Eat and drink appropriately!

MARA'S MAGIC

My best pal, Susan, called me in a panic, "The boss is coming to dinner, what do I do?"

"Call me", I said. I knew her boss, and since Mara was the most powerful woman at the world's greatest brewery, I figured it would not hurt to show off and keep the friendship growing. I had not met her fun-loving husband, Craig, but from what I had heard, I thought this looked like the makings of an entertaining evening. I had tried this recipe once or twice and knew it was easy to make, but thought it could use one more little tweaking, I hoped I would discover that 'something' when I made it this time. How do you take on an elegant dish for only the second or third time for an important dinner party? Pick an easy recipe, and this one is real easy.

2 lbs. medium raw shrimp
2 Tbsp sweet butter
1 tsp garlic powder
cayenne pepper
¾ cup asparagus tips – cut in 1-inch diagonals
1 large ripe tomato – pureed
1 cup heavy cream
1 cup Locatelli cheese – grated fine
1 # farfelles
¼ cup fresh chives – chopped
fresh black pepper

If you are good at multi-tasking, you can drop the pasta in a 3-quart pan of salted water at the same time you start the shrimp. It will all be finished in about 12 cooking minutes!

While you are peeling the shrimp, dicing the asparagus, grating the cheese, snipping the chives, and pureeing the tomato, you can turn the heat under your sauté pan to simmer, melt the butter, and add the garlic powder. Do not use fresh garlic—you only want a hint of the flavor.

Turn the heat to medium high; drop the shrimp in the pan, and dust with the cayenne pepper, to taste. If the asparagus is thick, add it now; otherwise, wait 5 minutes if they are early-season skinny. Add the tomato for the next five minutes of cooking, covering the pan. You now have 10 minutes of cooking time, and farfelles take 12 minutes. Remove the cover; add the cream and cheese, stirring until it bubbles. Turn off the heat, replace the cover, and allow it to stand while the pasta cooks.

Drain the pasta and dump in a large, deep bowl. Stir in the shrimp mixture and blend by hand.

Here comes, "Mara's magic": Grind some fresh black pepper on your clean, white, wide-shoulder pasta plates (If you don't have these, go buy them.) and ladle the pasta into the bowls, decorate with the fresh chives, and serve with great fanfare!

Sometimes, it is that last touch that makes the meal perfect. Thanks, Mara.

We had a couple loaves of crusty Italian bread, *Tomato & Mozzarella Salad*, and finished the dinner with *Banana's Pisciotta*—perfecto! Not even the famed Traveling Linguini Brothers could have improved on this one!

FARFELLES AND FRIENDS

It seems that most Italian recipes are really summer recipes, because everything is fresh during the summer. The fresh asparagus and chives really make this recipe and should not be substituted with frozen or dried products. This recipe makes for a good "day of shopping and night of eating" excursion. For a little variation on this theme, I sometimes use a one-pound ham steak and cube it in place of the shrimp.

1 lb. large shrimp (peeled)
1/3 cup olive oil
1 Tbsp sweet butter
1/4 cup shallots – diced fine
1 lb. fresh asparagus – sliced diagonally into 2" strips
3/4 cup white wine
3/4 cup chicken broth
1 1/4 cups heavy cream
½ tsp tarragon
1 lb. farfelles (bow ties)
1 Tbsp fresh chives – 1" cuts
salt & pepper

In a measuring cup, pour the wine, add the tarragon, and let stand while you prepare the other steps of this recipe.

In a large sauté pan, heat half the oil and sauté the shrimp over medium high heat, stirring often until shrimp turn pink. Remove the shrimp with a slotted spoon and set aside.

In a large saucepot, cook the farfelles in boiling salted water until al dente. These things should be done just about the time the remaining items are ready. Add the remaining oil and shallots and continue cooking until shallots become soft and translucent. Add the butter, asparagus, and wine and bring to a boil for 3—4 minutes. Stir in the chicken broth and cream, and reduce heat to a simmer. Simmer for an additional 5-6 minutes, return the shrimp, and simmer for an additional 2-3 minutes.

Drain the pasta and mix the farfelles and sauce in a large bowl. Add the fresh chives as you are tossing the pasta, and serve immediately. A nice, crisp dry white wine is a perfect companion to this dish.

You can double this recipe by simply expanding the recipe times two, and if you are feeding a large number of people, it will work. I also like to combine the shrimp and the ham for a unique taste.

PASTA ALLA STRASBOURG

We had spent a long day on the rented Harleys coming up from the Bodensee on our way back to England. Strasbourg is a wonderful cathedral town that used to beckon when we lived in Stuttgart and wanted French food for a change of pace. This time was 30 years later, and much had changed. I was weary and longed for something familiar. The man in the hotel told us there was a nice Italian place up the block. I looked at Bob and said, "*Italian food in France? Why not?*" This is how I remember it.

1/3 stick of sweet butter
2 Tbsp olive oil
2 cloves of garlic – crushed
paprika
black pepper
1/2 cup good, unflavored vodka (room temperature)
1 32 oz can whole Italian tomatoes – blended
1 tsp fresh parsley
½ tsp basil

1 tsp crushed red pepper
1 cup heavy cream
½ cup grated Pecorino Romano cheese
1 lb farfelles
salt to taste

In a large (14") sauté pan, melt the butter over medium low heat, add the oil and garlic. When the garlic turns a light color (3 or 4 minutes), add the paprika and pepper and cook for a minute or two. Kick up the heat to medium high and add the vodka. When it begins to bubble, set a match to it. When the flames are nearly out, drop the tomatoes, parsley, basil, and crushed red pepper into the pan. Cook for about another 3 to 4 minutes and salt to taste. Add the heavy cream and pecorino, stirring until the color becomes consistent. Turn off the heat and cover the pan. Set aside for a few minutes.

You can begin the pasta at the same time you put the butter in the pan. Cook according to package directions. Drain and dump into a large, deep serving bowl. Pour the sauce over the pasta and toss.

FREDO RONALDO

Who does not like an all' Alfredo sauce? There are just two things wrong with most all' alfredo's. The obvious is the impact it has on your arteries, and the second is all the tracks the linguini leaves on your shirt when you eat it. So after having a knee replaced and not eating for nearly two months ,I thought I could afford some fat grams. Then I thought of Fredo in the Godfather. He was a skinny, little guy, so I said, "Hey, I can do this and knock off some of the fat." Here is a slimmed-down version—you had better like it!

2 boneless chicken breasts – diced
½ lb. peeled shrimp
8 stalks of asparagus – sliced in 2" diagonals
Extra Virgin olive oil
paprika
1 Tbsp sweet butter
1 cup skim milk
1 cup parmesan cheese – grated
fresh chives
salt & pepper
1 lb. farfelles (bow ties)

Heat about a tablespoon of olive oil in a sauté pan at medium heat and add diced chicken. Season with paprika, salt and pepper to taste. Add the asparagus and sauté for about 5 minutes. Add the shrimp and continue cooking until the chicken is done and the shrimp turn pink.

Cook the farfelles until they are al dente and drain.

Melt the butter in the shrimp, add the milk, and blend in the grated cheese. Immediately add the farfelles, stirring to mix the sauce. Serve in big pasta bowls and sprinkle some freshly-cut chives over the pasta. Oh baby, this is good stuff! Make sure you have some really good Italian bread and a nice red wine, and you have the real thing........ *"I knew Fredo would break my heart."*

PENNE ALLA PROUD MARY

We were on our way to the Montreal Jazz Festival and stopped over in Kingston, New York and had dinner at the ***Mary P.*** on the waterfront. We ordered the *Penne Contina* and the *Chicken Gorgonzola* and found that they tasted better when we combined the dishes. As we sat outside eating on the banks of the river and I began to think about making this dish, I could not help but envision that imaginary side wheeler steaming by and the "big wheel keep on turning"—hence the name "Proud Mary" as a combination of the name of the restaurant and that great riverboat song.

1 lb. boneless chicken breast – diced
2 cups chicken broth
1 bay leaf
3/4 cup heavy cream
3/4 cup Gorgonzola cheese – crumbled
1/4 cup fontina cheese – grated
½ cup Pecorino Romano cheese – grated
4 Tbsp sweet butter
juice of 1 lemon
1 Tbsp pignola nuts
salt & pepper
1 lb. penne

In a small saucepot, bring 2 cups of water to a boil. Add the cubed chicken and bay leaf and cook on medium heat for about 20 minutes. Turn off the heat and let stand until later. Toast the pignola nuts in a dry pan over medium heat until they turn brown, and set aside.

Bring a large pot of salted water to a boil, add penne, and cook until al dente. Drain.

In a 2-quart sauce pot, stir in ½ cup of the chicken stock, the heavy cream, lemon juice, butter, and the three cheeses. Bring to a gentle boil—stirring frequently so as not to scorch to cream. Add the chicken cubes with a slotted spoon and cook for 5-6 minutes.

Toss the pasta, sauce, and pignola's in a large bowl and serve hot with nice bread sticks and a cold salad.

I have served both red and white wine with this meal. The red works because this is a sauce that has a lot of body and can use a bold wine to offset these powerful flavors.

PENNE WITH THREE CHEESES & PORCINI IROQUOIS

While on ***Mackinac Island***, we were eating at the Hotel Iroquois one evening and overheard the couple at the table next to us mention how disappointed they were with the Penne with Three Cheeses. As we observed their behavior, however, we determined they knew little of what it meant to have a developed palette, and concluded that they knew not of what they spoke. The next meal we ordered the Penne and found it to be exquisite. It was a reminder to me that not everyone's tastes are the same. My first day home, I recreated the following recipe.

1 lb. penne
3 Tbsp porcini mushrooms – diced
3 Tbsp olive oil
1/4 cup fresh tomato – diced
1/3 cup sweet butter
1 cup mozzarella cheese – shredded
1 cup fontina cheese – grated

1 cup asiago cheese – grated
1 cup heavy cream
2 Tbsp fresh chives – chopped
salt

In a small saucepan, place 1/4 cup of water and the porcini mushroom pieces. Bring the water to a boil and turn heat off. Allow the mushrooms to sit in this water for 30 minutes. The water will turn brown and take on the mushroom flavor.

Boil your penne is salted water until al dente. While the pasta is boiling, heat the olive oil in a large sauté pan and gently cook the diced tomatoes until they are well broken down.

Drain pasta and dump into large sauté pan with olive oil and tomato mixture. Add the butter, cheeses, heavy cream, porcini with water, and chives and stir over moderate heat until the cheese is well mixed and blended.

Serve immediately.

This recipe will serve four main courses or a number of appetizer-size portions.

Note: If you are a real cheese lover, you can make this a four-cheese pasta by adding 1/3 cup of fresh gorgonzola cheese at the same time you add the other cheeses to the pan.

OINKERS IN THE WOODS

Rule Number One is not to take any of this too seriously. Food and eating should be fun and entertaining, so boring names of recipes run contrary to that principle. The two main ingredients to this recipe are bacon (oinkers) and porcini (woods) mushrooms, and the pasta of choice should be a curly fusilli so the name seems right. Not to be fooled, however, this is a nice pasta dish that complements a fine bottle of white wine, candles, and soft music. Your companion to this meal will quickly see beyond your lighthearted humor and recognize your mature and sophisticated depth of taste. HONEST!

1 cup water
½ oz porcini mushrooms
3 strips thick bacon – diced
1 lb. fusilli
1 1/4 cups Pecorino Romano – grated
1/3 cup sweet butter
3/4 cup frozen peas
1 Tbsp chives
black pepper
salt

Heat the cup of water to a boil and add the porcini mushrooms – broken in pieces. Turn off heat and allow pan with mushrooms to sit on the stove for at least 20 minutes. The dried mushrooms need to be brought back to "life", and the soaking in hot water does this job.

Cook the bacon over medium high heat until the bacon is crisp, remove bacon with a slotted spoon, and set aside on a paper towel.

Cook the fusilli in boiling salted water until al dente. While the pasta is cooking, grate the cheese and set aside. Melt the butter over low heat.

When the pasta is cooked, add the peas to the water and then immediately drain. Place the pasta and peas in a large bowl and add the cheese, butter, chives, mushrooms, liquid from mushrooms, and a generous amount of freshly ground black pepper. Toss until well blended.

Serve *Crostini Olivio* as an appetizer, Oinkers in the Woods as a second course, and *Nanny's Simple Lettuce Salad* in that order, and you have an authentic Italian meal. Finish with some fresh fruit and soft mandolin music for the right Bella Vita!

SHRIMP DELLA SUSAN

If you have a friend who likes indoor picnics—sitting on the floor in front of the fireplace, like Susan—then this is a perfect dish. All you need is a bowl for the shrimp, a loaf of bread, and a glass of wine. I was thinking of doing a pesto sauce, but it was the middle of the winter and I couldn't get the traditional fresh ingredients for pesto. This is what came out of that quest.

1/3 cup of olive oil
6 cloves of garlic
1/2 cup spring onions
1 large tomato – quartered
2 lbs. large shrimp – peeled
1 tsp crushed red pepper
2 Tbsp sweet butter
1 cup white wine
fresh parsley
Pecorino Romano cheese
salt & pepper

Put the olive oil and the garlic in a blender and work it over real good. When you have it nice and fine, add the onions and tomato and pulse just enough to mix it up. Pour the mixture over the shrimp, adding the crushed red pepper and a twist of salt & pepper. Cover and let stand for about 20 minutes.

Melt the butter in a large sauté pan and add the shrimp mixture, stirring often until the shrimp begins to turn pink—about 5 minutes. Pour in the white wine; reduce the heat to medium, and cook for an additional 5-10 minutes.

Serve the shrimp in nice, large pasta bowls, along with crusty Italian bread for mopping up the sauce. If you want to be real Italian about it, serve a *Tomato & Mozzarella Salad* at the end of the meal.

Remember to chill a bottle of Sauvignon Blanc early in the afternoon.

CHICKEN CUTLETS ITALIANO

The biggest key to making good cutlets is good bread crumbs. If you buy them, you want to get *Italian* breadcrumbs, but you can make your own real easy if you have some French or Italian bread that has aged in a paper bag. Simply run the bread through your food processor and add some garlic powder, parsley, and fresh grated cheese. It will store in a baggie for a few weeks. The second key is getting all your prep and set up down right because you need to move quickly once you get to the frying stage. I find that two glass pie plates work well for the egg batter and breadcrumbs. Lastly, keep the heat on medium, and do not allow the oil to burn.

1 lb. boneless chicken breast
½ cup corn oil
2 cloves garlic – sliced
1 large egg
½ cup Italian bread crumbs
salt & pepper
juice of 1 lemon

Slice the chicken breasts into thin slices—approximately ½ inch thick—and rinse in cold water.

Beat one egg well and pour into open pie plate. Pour breadcrumbs into second pie plate.

Heat half of the corn oil in a large, non-stick sauté pan over medium heat, add the garlic, and stir until it is golden. Do not overheat. Add additional oil as you are cooking and the pan begins to dry out.

Dredge each piece of chicken in the egg, then the breadcrumbs, and then the salt and pepper and add to the pan and. Cook until they become golden—do not overcook.

Squeeze some lemon juice over the cutlets as you remove them from the hot pan.

You can serve these on Italian bread with fresh sliced garden tomatoes next to some rice. You can add a slice of provolone and some spaghetti sauce (gravy) and bake in the oven. Or you can eat them cold the next day. Wonderfully versatile and tasty.

Wiener schnitzel is made the same way, except you use veal cutlets instead of chicken breasts.

SAUSAGE & PEPPERS

You will not find a more fundamental or a more pleasing item than sausage and peppers. This is as basic to an Italian table as potatoes are to the Irish. You will find this item at every Italian wedding, anniversary, family reunion, and especially during the holidays. It is important that you find a source for good Italian sausage and fresh green peppers. You can use either the long, pale green Italian frying peppers (some markets call these Cuban peppers) or green bell peppers. The following recipe calls for 2 lbs. of sausage, which may or may not be consumed at one sitting. But they keep well in the frig for up to one week and may be added to your pasta sauce or frozen.

2 lbs fresh Italian sausage links *
olive oil
6 large green peppers
2 cloves garlic
salt & pepper

In a large heavy frying pan, sauté the sausage in a tsp of olive oil. Brown the sausage, remove from pan, and set aside. Cut the peppers into 2" strips from top to bottom. (Clean away seeds.) Peel & crush the garlic. Add 1 Tbsp olive oil to the frying pan, stir in the peppers, garlic, salt and pepper to taste, and sauté the peppers until they begin to blister—about 30 minutes on medium heat. At this point, you can return the sausage to the pan, cover, and continue to cook on the stovetop on medium low heat for another 30 minutes. If you do this, you will need to stir regularly to keep from burning. As an alternative to the frying pan, you can dump everything in a large covered Corning—or your turkey roaster—and bake it in a 400-degree oven for 1 hour and 30 minutes. It is important that the baking piece be covered—you do not want the sausage to dry out.

This recipe does very well between two slices of Italian bread or nestled in a hoagie roll with a slice of provolone. It can also be a meat dish that accompanies potatoes or pasta. You can make gravy and add the sausages to it. I like nice robust red **Italian Chianti** with a sausage sandwich.

* Italian sausage comes in varieties—sweet, hot and mild. I prefer the sweet, with maybe one or two links of hot thrown in to liven things up a little bit.

SAUSAGE, POTATOES & ONIONS

When my son acquired his first apartment, I gave him a handful of recipes that had few ingredients and were easy to prepare. This is one of those recipes. A few days after I gave it to him, he called me in a panic wanting to know why the sausage was "limp" and "mushy". He said he followed my instructions and cooked it in the oven at 50 degrees for an hour and a half.

50 degrees! Starting out can be intimidating, but it also can be fun if you have a sense of humor. Sean has since learned that 50 degrees is closer to the temperature of his refrigerator, and the lowest setting in his oven is 250 degrees. Practice is a good teacher after all.

1 lb. of Italian sausage links
2 large baking potatoes
1 medium white onion
1 Tbsp olive oil
salt & pepper

Wash the potatoes and leave the skins on. Slice the potato in 1/4 slices and arrange on the bottom of a large Corning. Salt and pepper to taste as you lay them out.

Next, slice the onion and arrange the onion slices on top of the potatoes.

Place the sausages on top of the onion, and drizzle the olive oil over the top of the mixture.

Bake in a preheated 375-degree for one hour with a top on the Corning ware. Remove the top and bake for an additional 30 minutes.

This is a simple meal that recalls the country cooking of Italy.

Call your Mother every weekend—She worries about you!

ITALIAN ZUCCHINI BOATS

When I lived in Denver, I came across this recipe because the zucchini seemed to prosper even in my dry, barren garden and was so abundant that nearly every possible way of preparing the stuff had been exhausted. This recipe requires a fairly large zucchini, but the cooking process eliminates any concerns about toughness. If you find a "zuch" that is 12 to 14 inches long and about 4 or 5 inches in diameter, you have a perfect boat looking at you.

1 very large zucchini
1 Tbsp olive oil
1 lb. ground round or lean beef
1 Tbsp fennel seed
1 tsp garlic powder
1 tsp basil *
1 15 oz can tomato sauce *
4 slices mozzarella cheese
salt & pepper

Par-boil the zucchini in boiling salted water for 5 minutes.

Remove from water, slice zucchini down the middle, and scoop the seeds from the cavity.

Place 2 Tbsp of the seeds in a sauté pan, along with the olive oil, ground meat, fennel seed, garlic, basil and salt and pepper. Sauté until browned thoroughly, add the tomato sauce, and cook an additional 10 minutes on moderate heat.

Salt & pepper the inside of the zucchini and place in a shallow baking dish with the scooped cavity side facing up. Using a slotted spoon, fill the cavity with the meat mixture and two slices of mozzarella cheese on the zucchini. Pour the remaining tomato meat sauce over the zucchini and bake in a pre-heated 350-degree oven for 30 minutes.

Serve hot from the oven with *Nanny's Simple Lettuce Salad*, garlic bread, and a hearty Chianti wine.

You can substitute the beef with ground turkey and eliminate the cheese and you have a ***Happy Heart*** entree that works well on any table.

* In the summer, I like to substitute the tomato sauce with 1 diced tomato and 1 blended tomato in the meat mixture. Add 3 large, torn basil leaves to the meat just before filling the zuch with the meat mixture.

COUNTRY FRITTATA

We appear to be living in a time that is calling us back to basics, traditions, and roots. It is curious that much of today's *"Nouveau Cuisine"* is actually turning out to be the things that our mothers and grandmothers did as a matter of course. The frittata found its way to the table when an assortment of ingredients began to stockpile and needed to be eaten—sort of a stew approach to refrigerator management—dump in whatever is laying around. This is not an omelet because the fillings outweigh the eggs. When the eggs dominate the filling, it is an omelet; and when the filling dominates, it is frittata.

1 link Italian sausage
-or-
8 slices pepperoni
1 Tbsp olive oil
1 medium russet potato – diced
4-5 large mushrooms – sliced
½ small zucchini – sliced

2 slices tomato – diced
1 slice white onion – diced
4 large eggs
3 Tbsp fresh parsley
1 Tbsp ricotta cheese
1 Tbsp Romano cheese – grated
1/8 tsp garlic powder
salt & pepper

Slice the sausage into small sections and sauté in an 8" non-stick omelet pan in olive oil over medium heat. (If you are using the pepperoni quarter the slices and do the same.) When the sausage is fully cooked, remove it from the pan with a slotted spoon and set aside. Add the potatoes to the oil and sauté for 5 to 8 minutes. Then add the mushrooms, zucchini, salt and pepper and continue to cook for and additional 5-6 minutes. Test the potatoes for doneness. When the potatoes are done, you should add the onion and stir for one minute to brown.

In a mixing bowl, blend the eggs, ricotta, parsley, garlic powder, and half of the diced tomatoes. Add the sausage and beaten eggs, cover, and cook over medium heat until firm—about 5 to 7 minutes.

Place a 10-inch dinner plate over the top of the pan and invert the pan so the frittata drops into the plate. Remove the pan and garnish the top with the remaining tomatoes. Quarter and serve hot. If you do not eat it all, you can refrigerate and eat cold at a later time.

MEX-ITALIANO MACS

I remember Uncle Ben buying a drive-in type restaurant in Denver and calling it the ***Mex-Italiano***. It looked like an old Conestoga Wagon, and the menu was made up of meatball subs, cheese steaks, tacos, burritos, and soppapias. A lot of people laughed about the strange combination of decor and menu, but Aunt Marge and Grandma Angie put out some tasty food, and in the long run, that is what matters when it comes to eating. This next recipe cannot quite tell if it is Mexican or Italian, hence the name. It is, however, easy to make and is a good use of that leftover chile that is lurking in the back of your refrigerator or freezer. This recipe is a lot like Uncle Ben's old restaurant—maybe a little strange, but certainly fun and definitely tasty.

1 lb. rotini or wheels
4 cups *Big Ron's Original Colorado Chile*
1 cup cheddar cheese – shredded
2 tsp chives

Cook the rotini or wheel pasta in salted boiling water until it is al dente, drain, and fill four bowls half full of pasta.

Meanwhile, heat the chile and ladle over the pasta in the individual bowls, topping with cheddar cheese and equal portions of the chives.

Serve hot with crusty French bread and a cold drink. If you serve with *Nanny's Simple Lettuce Salad*, you will have an easy and complete meal for four people.

Beneficiary designations override a last will and testament—be sure you keep your designations up to date to avoid the wrong person getting your insurance money.

ARIZONA HACIENDA PASTA SAUCE

My son, Sean, has a fondness for Arizona. Perhaps it was born out of a Christmas trip we did to the desert for skydiving a few years ago. In any case, we both enjoy the desert climate and mountains of Arizona, not to mention the wonderful flavors of the local cuisine from that region of the country. While being cooped up in my house for five days due to a 100-year blizzard, I came up with this sauce, which seems to bring the Southwestern flavor to an Italian dish. I tried it out on Sean, and it was his idea to call it Arizona Hacienda.

2 Tbsp olive oil
4-6 large red peppers – sliced
1 can of chicken broth
2 Tbsp slivered almonds
1 14 oz can of fine-diced tomatoes
1/2 cup heavy cream
1 tsp butter
1 lb. large shrimp
garlic powder
cayenne pepper
1 oz brandy
1 lb. zita rigati
Locatelli
chives

Heat the olive oil in a large pan over medium heat. Add the red pepper slices and sauté for 5 minutes, covering the pan. Add the chicken broth and heat to a mild boil for 15 – 20 minutes. In a separate dry pan, heat the almonds, toasting them lightly.

Place the peppers, broth and almonds in a blender and puree to a fine consistency. Add the cream and tomatoes to the blender, but do not blend—let them stand until the shrimp are cooked.

Heat the butter in the same pan and sauté the shrimp with liberal amounts of garlic powder and cayenne pepper. After 5 minutes, add the brandy and flame the shrimp for another 1 minute, or until the flames die out. Return the pepper sauce to the shrimp, stirring well, cover, and cook on low heat while pasta boils.

Serve sauce over the pasta by grating some fresh cheese and chives on the sauce.

MONGO'S GREEN CHILE

Mongo like beef! Mongo also likes spicy food, so when he invited me over for Monday Night Football, I offered to make green chile. I debated whether or not I should include this in the Soup section of the book, because you can either eat it in a bowl with a tortilla, or you can ladle it over anything Mexican to create the "smothered" version. This recipe takes a couple of days to make, so allow plenty of time. You can bypass the homemade chicken stock, but why would you when this recipe is so easy.

CHICKEN STOCK

chicken legs
chicken thighs
1 chicken bouillon cube
1 carrot
1 stalk of celery
½ white onion – quartered
water
parsley
salt & pepper

GREEN CHILE

pork chops
paprika
salt & pepper
corn oil
2 cloves of garlic – sliced
1 small onion – diced
6-8 peppers **
1 tomato
6 cups chicken stock
1 tsp cumin
¼ cup fresh cilantro

Chicken Stock:

Place the chicken parts in a medium stockpot and cover with water. Bring to a boil, skimming fat off the top. Boil vigorously for about 30 minutes. Add the bouillon, carrots, celery and onion and about a teaspoon of salt. Allow to simmer for an additional 3 hours. During the last 30 minutes, add about a ¼ cup of fresh parsley. No cover, just add water to maintain water level. The meat should fall off the bones, so help them out and toss the bones out—they have served their purpose. You can eat the chicken and veggies, if you like. I usually shred them into one of those nice little flour tortillas and turn it into a quick snack for the cook! By the way, this is also why I use quality parts and not the chicken leftovers, like a lot of stock recipes call for. Strain the broth through a strainer into a bowl to cool. Once it is cool, transfer to a Rubbermaid container and refrigerate until the next day.

Green Chile:

Pork chops are a higher grade of meat than most people use for green chile, so be sure you use the entire pork chop. Keep the fat and the bones in the stockpot for the initial process. Trim the meat off the pork chops and cut into 1-inch cubes. Dust the meat with salt, pepper, and paprika before cooking.

Heat the corn oil in a large stockpot, brown the garlic and onions for a few minutes, and then add the pork and pork bones. Stir the meat until it browns evenly, cover the stockpot, and cook on high simmer for about 30 minutes. This will create a nice liquid for later use.

Cut the tops and stems from the peppers and add them to the liquid in the stockpot. What kind of peppers? Poblanos or anaheims both work well—experiment and see what kind you like. I have tried Anaheims when I charred two of them and cooked the rest as they were—nice flavor. Add about 3 cups of the chicken stock to the pot, cover, and cook for about 45 minutes on medium simmer.

Remove the pork and bones from the stockpot with a slotted spoon and then blend the rest of the mixture in your food processor along with the tomato. Return the mixture to the stockpot, add the remaining chicken stock, the pork meat (including the bones), and the cumin. Cover and simmer for an additional hour to an hour and a half. Add the cilantro the last 30 minutes of cooking time.

When the chile is finished, fish out the bones and throw them away—or if your dog's name is Spike, feed them to him. They should have yielded all their flavor by now.

** Your choice of peppers is only limited to your geographic area and your grocer's inventory. I try to use fairly medium heat peppers as my mainstay, which would be a poblano or an anaheim in most cases. If you wish to ratchet up the heat factor, you can always add a jalapeno to the process, or for that matter, toss in a habanera if you want three alarms. Hot is good, but remember the flavor is what you want, and this recipe is bursting with flavor.

DEEP DISH SANTA FE PIE

Every now and then we find ourselves being called upon to bring a "covered dish" to an event, and for most of us, it is like being sent to the headmaster's office to be disciplined. Help is on the way, for here is a dish worth staying home with. Moreover, a special pottery piece (either bought or made) is worth it just for this offering. You will also find the corn bread topping to be an excellent, stand alone corn bread recipe.

The Pie

2 lbs. ground pork *
1 cup green pepper – chopped
1 15 oz can tomato sauce
2 Tbsp tomato paste
1 Tbsp cumin
1 Tbsp chile powder
1 Tbsp Worcestershire
1 tsp tabasco
½ tsp allspice
1 10 oz pkg. frozen corn
1 Tbsp corn meal
salt & pepper

The Ring on Top

1 cup flour
1 cup yellow corn meal
1 tsp sugar
2 tsp baking powder
1 1/2 cups milk
3 Tbsp sweet butter – melted
1 large egg – lightly beaten

2 Tbsp jalapeno peppers – chopped
½ cup Monterey Jack cheese – grated

In a large sauté pan, brown the pork and green peppers until the meat is no longer pink in color. Add 1 cup of water and the remaining ingredients, except the corn & corn meal, cover, and cook for an additional 20—25 minutes on medium heat. You can make the recipe to this point a day ahead of time. Simply refrigerate the meat mixture until the next step.

In a mixing bowl, sift the flour, corn meal, sugar, and baking powder together. Mix the milk, butter, and egg until consistent and then fold the monterey jack and jalapeno peppers into the mixture.

Mix the corn and corn meal into your meat mixture, ladle it into your baking dish, and top with a ring of the corn bread mix. Bake in a preheated oven at 425 degrees for 10 minutes and then finish baking at 350 for an additional 30 minutes until corn bread is firm. You should allow the dish to stand for about 10 minutes before you serve it. If you eat the whole thing on the first serving, you will not go wrong. The corn bread topping does not keep well in the refrigerator for any period of time.

Ground pork can be quite fat, so you should ask your butcher to grind you a boneless pork loin roast. If they don't do that, buy the roast, take it home, and cut it into small dime-size pieces. It takes some work, but the finished product will be worth it. If you do not use ground pork, then allow the meat to cook in the covered pan for at least 35 – 45 minutes, instead of 20.

If you want Mexican, serve up some of *Susie's Salsa* and some *Honest Guacamole Dip* while you sit on the deck with a pitcher of margaritas watching the sun set.

Buy quality, classic clothing—it is a good investment that will last forever. Always dress well!

TAOS ENCHILADA STACK

Enchiladas come in two variations. The traditional Mexican method is to roll a yellow corn tortilla with the stuffing inside of it so it forms a log-like item. In and around Santa Fe and Taos, the Indians made blue corn tortillas and stacked them with the filling in between the tortillas like you would a bunch of pancakes. Taos is one of those lovely little communities that have managed to continue living as if it were still the 19th century. In that part of the country, this enchilada could be made with either type of tortilla; but I like to mix the two together and think of it as a blend between the two native cultures.

The Chicken

1 lb. boneless chicken thighs
2 cups water
2 chicken bouillon cubes
1 Tbsp cumin seed
1 bay leaf
1 tsp cilantro

The Beans

1 cup black beans
2 cups water
3 chicken bouillon cubes
1 tsp salt

The Sauce

1 ancho chile
1 cup water
1 chicken bouillon cube
1 tsp corn oil
1 medium tomato – quartered

8 corn tortillas (4 yellow – 4 blue)
4 oz. Monterey Jack cheese – shredded
1 Tbsp *Honest Guacamole Dip*
4 sprigs fresh cilantro

Both the chicken and the beans can be prepared as much as a day ahead of time. If you do the chicken before the beans and the sauce, you can use the stock from the chicken as a substitute for the chicken bouillon cubes.

Wash the chicken and place the thighs in the water, along with the bouillon cubes, cumin and bay leaf. Bring the water to a vigorous boil; reduce heat to medium, and cover. In about 45 to 60 minutes, the chicken should be ready to shred with two forks. Set aside and use the stock accordingly, reserving 2 Tbsp of stock.

Rinse the black beans and soak for 6-8 hours. In a pot with the water, add the beans, chicken bouillon or stock, cilantro, and salt and bring to a boil. Reduce heat and simmer in a covered pot for approximately 1 hour, until beans become tender but not mushy. Set aside.
Remove the stems and seeds from the chiles, and in a small pot place the cup of water, 2 anchos and a bouillon cube, and bring to a boil. Cover, turn off heat, and allow to stand for 15 to 20 minutes. Pour the mixture into a blender, add the corn oil and tomatoes, and blend into a smooth mixture. Set aside.

If you have a cast iron frying pan, you should heat the pan over medium heat with a small amount of corn oil on the bottom of the pan. Place the corn tortillas in the pan and heat for a few moments to make them pliable.

Place the tortillas in a baking dish and layer some cheese, chicken, and black beans on the tortilla. Top with another tortilla and repeat the process, building a four-story stack. Spread some chicken and cheese on the top layer and spoon a couple of spoons of the chile sauce over everything.

Bake the two tortilla stacks in a preheated 350-degree oven for 15 to 20 minutes.

Ladle a spoonful of guacamole on the hot stack and serve with some of the black beans as a side dish. Some Mexican rice and a nice bottle of Chardonnay will round out this meal. A Linda Ronstadt CD could provide some pretty good entertainment to go with this meal.

This is not a quick meal, but it is one that works well with a good friend because it gives you the opportunity to work together. You can make up some appetizers, like *Crostini Olivo,* and open a nice bottle of wine and make an event of it. If you prepare the three main ingredients the day prior, you will save a lot of time, but you might also miss out on the real fun of creating together.

There are quite a number of peppers in the markets these days, both fresh and dried. Try different ones in your recipes until you find the tastes and amount of heat you like. Be daring!

STAY-AT-HOME CHICKEN FAJITAS

Fajitas have made quite a mark of popularity over the years. While they are quite common in many restaurants, it is sometimes nice to be able to fix the same meal in the comfort and ease of your own home. Next time you get an urge to have fajita's but do not feel like going through the bother of getting dressed up and going out, here is your answer.

1 lb. boneless chicken breast – cut in 3" thin strips
juice of 3 limes
1/4 tsp crushed red pepper
2 Tbsp corn oil
1 large Bermuda onion – sliced
1 large green pepper – sliced
salt & pepper
4 flour tortillas
2/3 cup *Colorado Red Salsa*
2/3 cup *Honest Guacamole Dip*
1 cup Monterey Jack – shredded
1 Tbsp jalapeno pepper – diced
1 cast iron frying pan

Marinate the chicken breasts in the lime juice and crushed red pepper for at least 4 hours. Heat the oil over medium high heat in the cast iron frying pan and sauté the chicken, onions and peppers together until the chicken is cooked—about 7 minutes. Salt & pepper to taste.

Warm the tortillas—wrapped in a damp towel—in a 300-degree oven for a few minutes.

Spread the chicken, onion, pepper mix on a tortilla and top with salsa, guacamole, jack cheese, and jalapeno peppers to taste. Roll up your sleeves and watch the juice run down your arm.

This is a nice informal meal that is easy to make and easy to eat, especially when it is served with some *Border Rice*, fresh corn on the cob, and a pitcher of home-made lemonade on the picnic table under that big old aspen tree in the back yard.

QUICHE LAREDO

Forget whatever you may have heard about real men don't eat quiche or for that matter, dead men don't wear plaid. This quiche is a real wrangler's favorite. I have it on good authority that before every cattle drive leaving the famed Lazy Big R Ranch overlooking the beautiful Rio Grande River, the boys would sit down to a hearty meal of quiche and tamales before the long ride. Sort of like a marathon runner's breakfast of pasta.

Crust

1 cup flour
1 stick sweet butter
4 oz cream cheese

Filling

1 cup baby shrimp
1 cup cheddar cheese – grated
½ cup Monterey Jack – grated
1 cup frozen corn

1 cup artichoke hearts – diced
3 Tbsp green chiles *
4 eggs – lightly beaten
1/3 cup heavy cream
½ tsp salt
1 tsp chives
black pepper

In a large mixing bowl, combine the flour, butter and cream cheese until it forms a ball and flakes into smaller pieces. In a pie plate or quiche dish, work the dough into a crust with your fingers, pressing it around the edges and the bottom of the plate. Refrigerate until ready to use.

Drain the shrimp, corn, and artichokes of any liquid. Whip eggs and cream together. Combine all ingredients in a bowl, fold, and pour into the pie shell.

In a preheated 425-degree oven, bake quiche for 15 minutes and then reduce heat to 375 degrees and bake for 1 additional hour, or until quiche sets up firm. There is a lot of moisture in this quiche so baking time will vary. Do not worry about removing it from the oven to check it—it will not spoil the end result. Poke a toothpick or a knife into the center of the quiche to test the texture. When it is finished, let it stand for 15 minutes before serving.

* If you are on a long cattle drive, you can substitute 1 Tbsp of diced fresh jalapeno peppers for the milder 3 Tbsp of green chiles, and that will dispel any notion of wimp food once and for all. *Wee Doggie, Pilgrim!*

SANTA FE CHICKEN BREASTS

One of my favorite restaurants in the Washington, D.C. area was *Houston's*. It was a favorite until they began to acquire 2-hour waits for lunch and dinner. If that were not enough, they removed my favorite **Chile Fries** and **Santa Fe Chicken Breasts** from their menu. Well, you can make both of them at home—just make up some French fries and top them with a ladle of *Big Ron's Original Colorado Chile*, some grated sharp cheddar, and some diced onions—*wee doggie*! Anyhow, here is the chicken breast that was on the menu and also disappeared, but is now re-designed for your dining pleasure.

4 chicken breasts – boneless
1/4 cup olive oil
8 cloves garlic
1 tsp rosemary
juice of 1 lemon
1 ½ cups *Colorado Red Salsa*
½ cup sharp cheddar cheese – shredded
1/4 cup spring onions – diced
salt & pepper

Marinate the chicken breasts in the olive oil, lemon juice, rosemary, garlic, and salt & pepper for 2 to 8 hours in a covered Corning dish. You may prepare these by grilling on an outdoor grill (best choice) or in the oven for 1 hour at 400 degrees. Discard garlic after cooking.

Be sure salsa is at room temperature and then cover hot chicken breasts with salsa, spring onions, and cheese (in that order). If the salsa is still cold from the refrigerator, you can nuke it by itself for 20 seconds or so to bring it to room temperature.

This is a genuine ***Happy Heart*** recipe if you have skinless breasts and hold the cheese.

FIESTA CHICKEN BREASTS

I recently visited my friends, Meg and Larry Luken, in San Antonio, Texas and I was taken by the friendly atmosphere of that city. It has been said that some cities have "heart" and others I know of have "soul". This city has "spirit", and it is best captured by *Fiesta*, easy-going, laid-back, but a treat to the senses. This chicken embodies that concept.

4 chicken breasts
3 oz crushed pineapple
3 oz sugar cane rum
1 Tbsp olive oil
2 Tbsp soy sauce
1 tsp chives
1/8 tsp crushed red pepper
garlic powder
Pecorino Romano cheese – grated
salt & pepper
corn tortilla chips

Combine the pineapple, rum, olive oil, soy sauce, chives and red pepper in a mixing bowl, stirring well until blended.

Wash the chicken breasts under cold water, pat dry, and place in a shallow Corning. Dust the tops of the chicken with the garlic powder and freshly ground salt and pepper. Ladle the marinade carefully over the chicken breasts, cover, and refrigerate 3-4 hours.

Preheat the oven to 450 degrees.

Crush a handful of tortilla chips over the top of the chicken breasts and grate a measure of cheese over the chicken.

Bake, uncovered, in the oven for 20 minutes. Reduce the heat to 400 degrees, cover the Corning, and continue baking for an additional 60 minutes. Remove the cover and increase the heat to 450 degrees and bake an additional 15 minutes. Be sure the chicken is brown but does not burn.

NOTE: The soy sauce is salty so that should influence the amount of salt you use. Do not eliminate the salt but be conscience of the amount. If you remove the skin and crush the chips finely, you will not miss the skin, and the recipe becomes a genuine ***Happy Heart*** item. I like to serve this with *Popeye's Spinach* and some *Border Town Rice* for a complete and healthy meal. Meg and Larry would like it that way.

NEW MEXICO CHICKEN ROAST

This is one of those real easy meals that can pretty much be done in one roaster. It is nothing more than a roasted chicken with a New Mexican flavor to it. I love the taste of poblano peppers, and this recipe will flavor most of your chicken with a subtle poblano flavor.

5-6 lb. roasting chicken
1 medium poblano pepper
½ cup Monterey & cheddar cheese – shredded
6 baking potatoes – quartered
3 garlic cloves – peeled
½ cup chicken broth
paprika
garlic powder
salt & pepper

Wash the chicken with cold water. Sprinkle the inside of the cavity with salt. Place one garlic clove inside cavity. Remove top of pepper, fill with grated cheese, and insert pepper into cavity. Talk about a big Chile Relleno!!

Place potatoes, other 2 garlic cloves, and chicken broth in bottom of roaster around the chicken. Season the entire roasting pan with salt, pepper, paprika, and garlic powder. Cover and place in a cold oven with temperature set on 450 degrees for 20 minutes—reduce heat to 325 degrees, and continue roasting for additional 2 ½ hours. Remove cover and roast for 20 to 30 minutes. Remove pepper from chicken prior to carving. Serve with potatoes.

Note: You may want to do *Chicken Roasted Garlic Potatoes* with this recipe.

TURKEY OLE

Just when you thought there were no more left over turkey recipes, here comes another one! But, I am here to tell you, this one is so good, you will want to roast a turkey for *Cinco de Mayo* just so you can have the left overs to make this recipe. This is no limp wrist Turkey Tetrazini or Turkey Pot Pie.

1 cup of chicken broth
2 10 ½ oz cans of cream of chicken soup
½ can of water
4 oz cans of chopped green chiles
1/3 cup onion – chopped fine
1 cup sour cream
1 tsp cilantro
½ tsp cumin
1 tsp granulated garlic
12 corn tortillas
2 cups (8oz) shredded sharp cheddar
3-4 cups cooked turkey – shredded

Preheat the oven to 350 degrees. In a 3-quart saucepan, combine the chicken broth, cream of chicken soup, water, sour cream, cilantro, cumin and garlic. Stir over medium heat until blended. Add the onion and chiles, stirring until smooth. Butter the bottom of a 9x9 Corning baking dish and ladle a serving spoon of sauce into the bottom of the dish. Lay down 4 tortillas, a layer of turkey, some cheese, and spoon the sauce over the top of the cheese. Repeat two more times. Finish the top with cheese and, finally, sauce.

Bake uncovered in 350-degree oven for 45 minutes. Allow to stand for 10 minutes before serving with a nice, cold Winterfest beer—yo, Mama, this is good! Viva la Thanksgiving!

Pair this up with *Nanny's Simple Lettuce Salad*, finish up with a plate of *The Big Sailor Chocolate Chip* cookies, and you will soon forget all the fuss over Thanksgiving dinner.

HIGH PLAINS PINTO BEANS & HAM HOCKS

Many years ago, I was driving across southeastern Colorado near Limon with a business colleague who had family in a small, dusty village on the Plain. We stopped to visit, and the people insisted that we sit down and eat some pinto beans before we went on our way. They served us a very simple dish with a coarse-grain, home-made bread that made a lasting impression on me. As we drove away, my friend pointed out to me that what was a simple meal to us, was very special to these people because it had meat in it—meat that they gave to us because we were guests in their home.

1 16 oz pkg. dried pinto beans
4 medium ham hocks
2 Tbsp cumin
1 tsp thyme
3 bay leaves
1 Tbsp jalapeno peppers – diced
2 cups chicken stock
1 large tomato – diced
salt & pepper

Soak the pinto beans in enough water to cover the beans by 2 inches for at least 8 hours, or overnight. Drain and rinse the beans and then place in a stockpot with all the rest of the ingredients—except the tomato—and enough water to cover about 3 inches above the beans. Bring liquid to a boil, reduce to a simmer, and cook for about 4 hours or longer until the ham hocks break apart with a fork. Replace any liquid that evaporates during the cooking process with water. Dice the tomato and salt & pepper to taste.

Serve in large bowls with a large tablespoon of tomato sprinkled on the top. If you do not have a coarse-grain bread to serve with this, you can serve corn bread or flour tortillas. Don't forget to have a couple of long neck Tecates on hand to round out this meal.

SANTA ROSA POSOLE

In the old South, you would want to eat Hoppin' John on New Year's Day to bring good luck in the coming year. If you are traveling old Route 66 in New Mexico and stop off in Santa Rosa, you would probably order this Posole and Pork, and it would make you so happy you wouldn't care what the New Year had in store! Some think this may have been what did Billy The Kid in. He ate his last Christmas meal nearby, and it probably included this dish. Make this recipe the day before and enjoy the aromas your kitchen will produce two days in a row. It takes a long time to cook, so be prepared to do other things while this delightful brew simmers on your stove.

1 Tbsp corn oil
1 medium yellow onion – diced
2 cloves garlic – diced
2 lbs. boneless pork spare ribs
1 14 oz chicken broth
1 lb. posole (hominy) *
3 – 4 oz cans Hatch chiles – medium hot
2 tomatoes – diced
3 baby carrots – diced
1 tsp oregano
1 Tbsp cumin
cilantro
salt & pepper

Cut the boneless ribs into large chucks (2"). Saute in a large stock pot with corn oil, onion & garlic over medium heat. Salt & pepper to taste. Add the chicken stock, cover, and simmer for 1 hour. Add the hominy, chiles, tomatoes, carrots, oregano, and cumin and cover with about 2 inches of water. Increase the heat and bring to a rapid boil, then reduce to a low boil for 1 hour. Check the water level and test the hominy. It can take up to 3 additional hours before they begin to open up and become tender. After 2

½ hours, chop a handful of the fresh cilantro fine and add to the pot, along with salt and pepper to taste.

Serve with warm flour tortillas and cold beer.

* You can buy canned hominy in the Mexican food section of most grocery stores. This will reduce the cooking time considerably. Add the canned hominy at the same place in the recipe along with the cilantro, and simmer for 20 minutes and serve. It is a lot quicker this way!

DAD'S BETTER-THAN-A-DINER MEAT LOAF

My father lived in a time when men rarely entered the kitchen for any other reason than to eat. There is a curious twist to this notion, however, in that these men were **able** to cook, unlike some younger people that I have encountered who simply choose not to cook. Many of them, however, did have their one dish specialty, and whenever that meal was prepared, they were the ones to prepare it. My paternal granddad was the T-Bone-steak-in-the-cast-iron-frying-pan-at-the-cabin guy, and I will remember that one for my entire life. My father was the meat loaf king! This, however, is not his recipe. His recipe he took to his grave, and that is part of the reason that prompted me to write mine down. Not even my mom knows how he did it. Well, Dad, here is Number Two Son's version.

3 lbs. lean ground beef
1/3 cup grated Parmesan cheese

½ small green pepper – diced
2 Tbsp white onion – diced
1 Tbsp Worcestershire sauce
2 tsp black pepper
1 tsp garlic powder
½ tsp rosemary
1 tsp salt
1 egg
1 15oz can tomato sauce

In a large mixing bowl, mix all of the ingredients except the tomato sauce. Add half of the can of tomato sauce in the final mixing stages.

Roll the mixture into a large ball and shape it into an oblong shape on top of your cutting board. Roll the cutting board to the side and remove the meat loaf. Place it in a large Corning if it is to bake alone. I like to prepare it in my large turkey roaster with quartered baking potatoes, celery, and carrots. In any case, once it is in the baking device, pour the remaining tomato sauce over the top of the meat loaf.

Bake in a preheated 425-degree oven for 15 minutes, reduce the heat to 375 degrees, and continue baking for and additional 1-½ hours.

If you added the vegetables, you have a complete meal. If you did not add the vegetables, you might like to cook some white rice to utilize the nice sauce in the bottom of the cooker.

This meat loaf makes excellent next-day cold sandwiches on rye bread with a slice of Bermuda onion, fresh tomato, lettuce and mayo.

MISSION HILLS PORCUPINE BALLS

I grew up in the Upper Peninsula of Michigan, and my folks had a cabin on the Whitefish Bay of the grand Lake Superior. Across the county road from our cabin was an area of mystery and legend called Mission Hills—a deep hardwood forest filled with bears, wolves and lots of other wildlife. Our Llewellyn Setter, Rickey, loved to chase the small animals, including the porcupines, until he would come home with his nose filled with quills from the chase. Every summer, he would repeat this adventure, and every summer, we would pull the quills out of his nose. After that, he would content himself with chasing chipmunks and squirrels for the rest of the summer. We thought the "Porky" to be a magnificent animal with that special armor he wore. When my mom made these Porcupine Balls, they always brought back memories of the cabin and those happy days. Those were special times in the life of a growing boy, and this recipe is a light sort of thing that is easy to make and growing boys of all ages seem to enjoy.

1 26 oz can tomato soup
1 Tbsp chives
2 Tbsp fresh parsley
½ tsp black pepper
1/8 tsp mint
1 ½ lbs. ground round
1 large egg
1 cup cooked rice
4 Tbsp Bermuda onion – diced fine
1/4 tsp garlic powder
salt & pepper

In a large 3-quart pot, place the can of tomato soup, one can of water, chives, 1 Tbsp parsley, black pepper and mint, and bring to a low boil over medium heat.

Mix the ground beef, egg, garlic powder, rice, onion, remaining parsley, salt and pepper to taste and make golf ball size balls from the mixture—pack tightly.

Drop the meatballs into the sauce, cover, and cook over medium heat for approximately 30 minutes. You can make this dish early in the day or even a full day before you serve it. It will keep peak flavor for up to three days.

The recipe will make about 14 to 16 porcupine balls.

The sauce is nice over mashed potatoes, potato pancakes, or rice and is accompanied well with cream corn.

NORTH COUNTRY STUFFED PEPPERS

Things that bake in the oven have all sorts of good qualities to them. It is harder to burn something in the oven than something on the stovetop. You also have an added bonus in that you can do something else while things bake. In most cases, you need an hour to bake so that gives you time to exercise, write a brief, or make love. When bell peppers are abundant in the summer, you can make this dish without too much fuss and still have time left to do other things while the daylight hours linger. It is Susan's Minnesota wild rice that gives it the North Country handle and a nice change to the typical white rice ingredient.

½ cup cooked wild rice
6 large green bell peppers
1 lb. ground round *
1 15 oz can tomato sauce

½ cup Romano cheese – grated
1/3 cup frozen corn
2 slices Bermuda onions – diced
1 Tbsp parsley
1 tsp marjoram
½ tsp garlic powder
1/8 tsp nutmeg
salt & pepper

Cook the rice in salted water until done but still firm, about 40 minutes.

Loosely mix the rice, ½ can tomato sauce and 1/4 cup romano with remaining ingredients, including salt and pepper to taste.

Remove the stem end of peppers and clean out seeds. Fill the peppers with mixture and top each pepper with remaining cheese.

Place peppers in shallow Corning with the ends up. Mix the remaining tomato sauce and ½ can of water and pour it over the peppers so it runs down into the corning.

Bake—uncovered—in a 350-degree oven for 1 hour and 15 minutes.

* The ground round can be substituted with ground turkey, and you get a full-scale ***Happy Heart*** recipe.

PIGS IN THE BLANKET

This a recipe that takes a little more time to prepare, but much of the preparation can be done ahead of time, and the quantity that you produce is perfect for a dinner party for four people. If you use this as a dinner party entrée, you can do all the prep work in the early afternoon, pop it in the oven an hour before dinner, and it will be a no fuss meal. Or you can spend more time on an appetizer like a *Crostini Olivio*. This recipe will make about 10 large "pigs" and they store well. I find that the flavor is actually better when you eat them again about two days later.

1 large head green cabbage
1 Tbsp caraway seed
½ cup rice
1 ½ lbs. ground pork
1 ½ lbs. ground lean beef
1 large egg
3 Tbsp Bermuda onion – chopped fine
1 tsp sage
1/4 tsp mint
1/3 cup fresh parsley – chopped
1/3 cup Parmesan – grated fine
15 oz can tomato sauce
oregano
salt & pepper

First, cook the rice in a separate pot. Cook the rice about 2 minutes less than you would normally do so the rice is still good and firm. Remove rice from heat, drain, and set aside so it cools down. You may have more rice than you need in the recipe since it only calls for 1 cup of cooked rice, but you will always find a use for the left overs. You can do this the day before if you like.

Cut the core end of the cabbage flat across, remove the core, and discard. Place bottom end down in a large pot of shallow water (approximately 1 to 1 ½ inches of water), add caraway seeds, and bring to a boil, steaming the cabbage for approximately 5 minutes. This should make it easy to peel away the leaves one at a time. This requires a little patience and may also require the cabbage to return to the steaming water to soften the leaves once they have been removed. It is important that the leaves be pliable and easy to roll, so they do not break or tear. If you over steam, they can come apart, and if you under steam, they may still be "brittle" and break. It is O.K. to move the cabbage in and out of the water. Do not be afraid to take it out too soon to check for softness—you can always return it to the water.

Meanwhile, mix the meats, egg, onion, sage, mint, parsley, grated cheese, one cup of the cooked rice, and salt and pepper to taste. Be generous with the pepper since the parsley and mint will soften the sharpness of the pepper.

Lay out the cabbage leaves on the counter and fill with the meat mixture, rolling the leaves so they overlap and tuck on both ends. Each leave should have a generous serving of meat that approximates 1/3 the size of the cabbage leaf.

Lay the rolls in a Corning so they are tight next to each other.

In a separate mixing bowl, combine the tomato sauce, 3/4 can of water, and a sprinkle of oregano and black pepper. Mix well and pour over the cabbage rolls. At this point, you can cover the Corning and refrigerate for up to 6 hours before cooking. This actually allows the flavors more time to blend together.

Bake with the cover on (aluminum foil will work if the Corning does not have a cover) in a 375-degree oven for 1 hour.

I like to serve this with rice cooked with some corn and chives in it, fresh homemade biscuits, and a nice, cold bottle of Chardonnay.

NOTE: The logging camps in the great northern wilderness had a dish called ***Pigs in the Blanket*** that was made with fried pork sausage links rolled in pancakes and topped with fresh maple syrup. Yummie—**Timber!!**

It is important to change your oil every 3,000 miles—you need your car to do your grocery shopping.

GRANDPA FRED'S T-BONES

I have a svelte friend who says the only way she breaks her diet is if it's worth it—can't do it for McDonald's. Well, here is one that is really bad, but it might turn your head. All the wrong things here: red meat, butter, and salt. I can remember to this very day my grandfather coming to our cabin on Lake Superior and cooking these steaks on our wood stove in a cast iron frying pan. The wood stove is optional, but the cast iron frying pan is an absolute must. This is a great meal after a day of skiing or hiking in the mountains.

2 large 1 ½" thick T-Bone steaks
2 Tbsp sweet butter
1 large white onion
8 large mushrooms
salt & pepper

Slice your onion into nice large rings, and slice the mushrooms into 1/4-inch slices. Place onions and mushrooms, along with 1 ½ Tbsp butter, in frying pan and turn your heat on medium. Sauté the mixture with a little ground black pepper. Do not start it on high—just let it reach the medium level. Once the onions are a nice golden color, you can remove the onions and mushrooms.

Place the remaining butter in the pan and add the steaks. Salt and pepper the steak side that is up, increase the heat to medium high, and cook on one side for about 5-6 minutes. Turn the steaks, salt and pepper the other side, and continue cooking for an additional 5-6 minutes. Steaks should be frying vigorously and browning deeply. Return the onions and mushrooms to the pan, turn off heat, and cover for 2-3 minutes, and serve.

You should serve *Uncle Jimmy's Italian Tomato Salad* and lots of fresh French bread to soak up all the juices. A cold bottle of beer will complement this meal perfectly. If you finish this meal with a slice of *Mom's Apple Pie* with a scoop of French Vanilla ice cream, you will have good cause to spend an extra hour chopping wood the next morning.

DANA'S DELIGHT

Dana is one of those "go fast gals" that rides a pearl-white Harley Road King as proficiently as any of the guys in our group. Since she is a ready-to-ride-at-a-moment's-notice kind of person, I knew her recipe would be both tasty and easy to prepare. You won't be disappointed with the ease of this summertime favorite, just be sure to allow enough time for it to marinate. Her husband, Steve, says this is so good you can eat it for breakfast.

lbs. flank steak *
¼ cup soy sauce
2/3 cup olive oil
2/3 cup spring onions – chopped
3 Tbsp honey
2 Tbsp white wine vinegar
1 ½ tsp garlic powder
1 ½ tsp ground ginger
1 oz Myer's Dark Rum

* If you buy the flank steak from a butcher, have them run it through the tenderizer twice. If you can't do that, just poke it with the tip of your knife or a fork in about 20 different places before you marinate it.

Pour all of the marinade items in a mixing bowl and whisk them together aggressively—you need to break down the honey. Put the meat in a flat container, like a 9x12 cake pan, and cover with the marinade. Refrigerate early in the morning, or late the night before you plan to eat it. You can turn it once when you come home from work, or around midday. If you don't get to turn it, don't worry—it should be well marinated. Grill on a medium hot grill for about 6-8 minutes per side.

Slice against the grain and serve with *Uncle Jimmy's Tomato Salad*, some crusty bread, and a very cold beer—*Yo, baby, crank up the Harley and head out on the highway!*

MARYLAND POT ROAST

Maryland is perhaps best know for her seafood and tobacco crop as far as agriculture is concerned. Maryland, however, is also a colonial state and boasts of a rich heritage of rugged outdoor individualism in her earlier days. Good basic food is part of that heritage, and there is nothing more basic and hearty, in my mind, than a good beef pot roast. This is a meal when a lower grade of meat will work quite well, since it is going to cook for so long. You also want the meat to give off lots of natural juices, so there should be some fat content in the meat itself.

3-4 lb. chuck pot roast
1 large onion
1 tsp Worcestershire sauce
juice of 1 lime
paprika
salt & pepper
1 Tbsp butter
1 tsp parsley
4 cups beef bouillon
1 cup baby carrots

Slice one onion into six slices. Place three slices of onion in the bottom of a deep turkey-type roaster and place the meat on top of the onions. Squeeze the juice of the lime over the meat, add the Worcestershire, dust with paprika, salt and pepper, and last three slices of onion. Cover and refrigerate for 8 to 24 hours.

Top the sliced onions with butter and place roaster in cold oven. Set heat to 450-degrees and roast for 30 minutes. Lower oven to 250 degrees, add bouillon, carrots, and parsley. Cover and roast for an additional 5 hours. Add water if necessary.

This recipe will make your house smell good all day long!

A hearty complement to this meal would be to throw in some redskin potatoes, a few stalks of celery, and corn on the cob for the last 5 hours of roasting. Think about it. You will want to serve whole-grain bread fresh from the bakery and some freshly-brewed ice tea. Add a spinach salad, and you have a complete farmhouse meal.

BRAISED SHORT RIBS OF BEEF

One evening after a grueling day with the I.R.S. and an audit of my income tax return, I came home with slightly less than a positive frame of mind. I hunted around in the refrigerator, found some short ribs, and made this dish. As I began to chop away at the carrots and celery, I found that most of my frustrations went away. I cannot guarantee it will solve your problems, but it may allow you to forget them for a little while, and that is always worthwhile in my book.

3 lbs. short ribs of beef
1/3 cup olive oil
2 cloves garlic – minced
1 medium carrot – minced fine
1 stalk of celery – minced fine
1 small onion – minced fine
1 cup white wine
1/3 cup Polish or Dijon mustard

1 Tbsp parsley
1 tsp sage
1 tsp thyme
1 Tbsp butter
salt & pepper

In a large Corning dish, you will heat the olive oil and garlic over medium heat. When the garlic is golden, you can add the beef ribs and brown them on all sides. Remove the ribs and set aside.

In the drippings, add the carrot, celery, onion, and butter and sauté until they begin to soften and the onion turns golden.

In a mixing bowl, whisk the remaining ingredients, along with the minced vegetables, into a sauce. Return the ribs to the Corning, and pour the sauce over them. Cover and bake in a 350-degree oven for 3 hours.

Remove the ribs from the Corning when they have finished baking, and use a slotted spoon to transfer the vegetable mixture to a food processor to be pureed. This will separate the oil and provide a nice marinade to spoon over the ribs and rice.

These ribs go well with wild rice, a Caesar Salad, and a crisp white wine.

NEW ENGLAND BOILED DINNER

In the early spring, boating on the Chesapeake is a special time when the air is cool and the waters not crowded. A day on the Bay at that time of the year is a lot like the waters of New England. One April, day Josh and I spent a couple of hours on the water taking on bow spray that left us both wet and chilled to the bone. We had a good day of it, though, because we spotted a loon on ***Herring Bay*** and came home to a couple of big bowls of New England Boiled Dinner.

ham left over from Easter dinner with bone in it
1 bottle of Killian's beer
1 tsp black & white peppercorns
2 bay leaves
½ head of cabbage – quartered
1 link of kielbasa
4-5 small white potatoes
4 small redskin potatoes
4-5 carrots
6-8 Cherrystone clams
***salt**

In a large stockpot, heat 1 gallon of water, the ham bone, the beer, the peppercorns, and the bay leaves to a rapid boil, then lower heat to low, cover, and cook for 1-½ hours.

Add the cabbage and cook for an additional 30 minutes

Add the kielbasa, potatoes, and carrots and cook an additional 30 minutes.

Wash the clams very thoroughly, raise the heat to a boil, and drop the clams into the pot. Cover and cook an additional 10 minutes, or until all clams open. Turn heat off and let stand covered for 5 more minutes. Serve in large soup bowls.

If the ham bone has a liberal amount of meat on, you only need one link of kielbasa, but if the bone has been picked over, add a few more links if you choose.

This is a simple, yet nourishing, meal that is as down home Americana as you can get. It will easily feed four adults and provide leftovers that can be eaten over the next three or four days. Serve with homemade bread and Sousa March or Boston Pops music.

* You will probably need some salt, depending on how salty the ham is. You should wait until the meal is completely cooked and then taste for salt needs. You may need very little.

PATTI'S PERFECT PORK CHOPS

Much of the joy of cooking is being able to share recipes and know that the shared recipe was a crowd pleaser. This next recipe is just one of those winners. I gave this one to my friend, Patti, and she has had so many successes with it, I decided to name it after her on the belief that she has probably fed it to more people than I have. The secret to this recipe is a long marinade and good pork chops—thick pork chops—at least 1 1/2 inches thick.

4 large, thick pork chops
½ cup Extra Virgin olive oil
½ cup crushed pineapple with juice
½ cup soy sauce
1 tsp powdered garlic
6—8 spring onions

½ tsp allspice
1/2 tsp dry mustard
Pecorino Romano cheese
ground black pepper

Dice the onions and mix in a bowl with the oil, soy sauce, pineapple, allspice, mustard, and garlic powder. Arrange the pork chops in a shallow Corning dish and pour the marinade over the chops. Grate a layer of pecorino and black pepper over the pork chops, cover, and refrigerate at least 6 hours, or as long as overnight.

Grill the chops on the barbecue grill over medium high heat for about 6 – 8 minutes per side until the outside is well browned.

Patti likes to serve a simple ziti with tomatoes, garlic and basil as a side dish. You can also serve fried cabbage or a wild rice and mushroom dish, but whatever you do, people will ask for more pork chops. This is a ***Happy Heart*** entree so you could eat two if you like.

This dish goes well with some *Goo Goots* or *Mixed Trading* and *Nanny's Simple Lettuce Salad* for an easy dinner on the patio.

CAROLINA PORK CHOPS

This is an old recipe that is as simple, yet tasty, as they come. I first thought it too common to include, but then realized that this is a common cookbook. I have been making this dish for years, but found an interesting twist after eating in Charleston and Savannah. I found a delightful use of spring onion tops to give an old standard a new lift. It seemed that everything I ate in those two cities had diced spring onion greens on the top of it, and it was all quite tasty.

4 pork loin chops
1 tsp olive oil
garlic powder
paprika
black pepper
salt
juice of ½ lemon
2 cans cream of mushroom soup
2 cans milk
1 can water
2 Tbsp spring onion greens – diced

Dust the pork chops with the garlic powder, paprika, black pepper and salt, and sauté in the olive oil in a hot, non-stick pan until chops brown on both sides—approximately 2-3 minutes on each side. Do not be afraid to use lots of pepper.

Squeeze a little lemon over the browned chops. Add the soup, milk and water, mix together, and bring to a slight boil. Reduce the heat and simmer for 30 to 40 minutes in a covered pan. This tenderizes the chops and seals the flavor in the meat.

You should serve this recipe with rice, mashed potatoes, or egg noodles, so you can soak up that great gravy.

Sprinkle a teaspoon of the onion greens over the plate just before you serve it.

Serve with a flavored ice tea and *Phoenix Corn Bread.*

LINDA'S LOINS

For years, I always did my pork tenderloins in a very traditional manner. If I did them in the house, I would butterfly and stuff them for roasting in the oven. My favorite way has been to marinate them and grill them on a wood fire. One day it occurred to me that a quick alternative might be to do them on top of the stove, but I had never done them before, so I threw a dinner party to experiment. I thought a gourmet friend would be attending to assist me in this experiment, but she opted to move to Carmel-by-the-sea instead—go figure. Nonetheless, we conferred by phone so here is Linda's recommendation.

¾ oz porcini mushrooms
1 pork tenderloin – cut in 2-inch diagonal slices
1 Tbsp olive oil
1 cup red wine – Vino Rosso
1 Tbsp dijon mustard
1 Tbsp no-fat sour cream
2 Tbsp flour
½ cup of water
salt & pepper

Pik-Nik shoestring potatoes
½ pound campanelle pasta

Reconstitute the porcini mushrooms in ½ cup hot water by soaking for 20 minutes.

Prepare the pasta in 3 quarts of boiling, salted water. Start the pasta when you finish sautéing the pork, but before you add the wine, sour cream, mustard and water. Drain and set aside when finished boiling.

Heat the olive oil, salt and pepper the pork to taste, and sauté on each side for about 4-5 minutes. Remove the pork from the pan and deglaze the pan by adding the wine, mustard, sour cream, and mushrooms with mushroom water. Whisk the flour into the water until all the lumps are gone, and slowly add to the pan. Return the pork to the pan, cover, and cook over medium heat for 15 minutes.

Place a layer of shoestrings on the plate and top with the pasta. Set two medallions of pork next to the pasta and ladle a generous serving of sauce over both items. Oh, baby, this is good stuff!

Serve a *Tomato and Mozzarella* salad as a starter, and be sure to call a special long-distance friend in the middle of the meal and tell them what a good thing they are missing!

ROXIE'S CHOICE

Roxanne won a famous Italian restaurant cook off with this sauce in a chicken recipe. I think I finally found my match when it comes to cooking and eating. In her generosity, she gave me the sauce recipe, which I have modified slightly, as an alternative to the previous pork tenderloin recipe. It is out of this world!

1 pork tenderloin – cut in 2-inch diagonal slices
1 Tbsp olive oil
½ pound Italian sausage (sweet), – crumbled
2Tbsp olive oil
2 Tbsp flour
1 cup chicken broth
1 cup white wine
¾ cup heavy cream or half & half
1 Tbsp fresh chives – chopped
1/2 cup Parmesan Reggiano – grated
salt & pepper
1 lb. bow ties

Prepare the sauce in a saucepan by cooking the sausage and olive oil over medium heat until well browned. Drain, break up and set aside. Clean the saucepan and heat the chicken broth. Add flour and heavy cream by whisking it into mix, bring to a boil, and cook vigorously for about 5 minutes, adding wine slowly to maintain consistency. Be careful not to burn the sauce. Blend in sausage, chives, cheese, salt and pepper to taste. Set aside. Cook the bow ties according to package directions. They should be done about the same time the pork is finished. In a separate sauté pan, cook the tenderloin in olive oil about 4 to 5 minutes on each side. Remove the pork, deglaze the pan, and return the pork and sauce to the same pan. Cover and simmer for 10 minutes.

Drain the pasta; arrange the medallions on a large plate next to the farfelles with lots of sauce ladled over the pasta and pork.

MIXED GRILL SUPREME

Grilling is a real American pastime, and food done on the grill out-of-doors is everyone's favorite. The *Mixed Grill* is a solution to not knowing what to grill, because this one covers all the bases—at least all the white meat bases. The key to this recipe is marinating everything ahead of time—way ahead of time.

Brats

4 bratwursts
24 oz beer
1 yellow onion – sliced

Breasts

4 boneless chicken breasts
1/4 cup olive oil
2 Tbsp soy sauce
1/3 cup orange juice
2 tsp chives – fresh
1/4 tsp garlic powder
2 Tbsp Parmesan cheese – grated

Barnyard

4 boneless pork loins
1/4 cup olive oil
1/4 cup sugar cane rum
½ cup black cherry juice *

Boil the brats and onions in the beer for approximately 20 minutes prior to grilling.

Marinate the chicken and pork in the marinade for 8 to 12 hours prior to grilling.

Put all three items on a hot grill. and baste the chicken and pork with the marinade until done. Serve on hoagie buns so you can eat it in your hands, or slice it on the diagonal and put it on a plate and eat it with a knife and fork and a linen napkin.

This one is easy and will guarantee results because it gives you great variety.

* Buy a can of pitted black cherries and drain the juice. Use the cherries to spoon over frozen yogurt, topped with hot fudge sauce, for a nifty dessert.

STUTTGART BATAVIA & CURRIED RICE

Near Stuttgart, Germany there was a little restaurant that looked like the inside of someone's home, and they served a dish called Batavia. It may very well have been the first gourmet meal of my life. Growing up in Escanaba, Michigan we did not exactly have any culinary landmarks that I was aware of. Here is an example of food imprinting: A good twenty years had passed between when I last ate this meal and when I re-created the recipe and ate it again. Not one bit of the magic was lost. Try to say that about a bond deal or a leveraged buy out.

2 Tbsp olive oil
4 Tbsp sweet butter
2 veal scaloppinis
2 pork scaloppinis
2 beef scaloppinis
4 garlic cloves
4 oz white mushrooms

1 cup white wine
1/3 cup evaporated milk
2 tsp parsley
1 tsp arrowroot
1/8 tsp sage
3-4 dashes of Maggi
2 pineapple rings
1 banana
all-purpose flour
salt & pepper
1 cup rice
4 spring onions
3 chicken bouillon cubes
1 tsp curry powder

Your scaloppini, or medallions of meat, should be sized in portions so that each diner gets a nice portion of each kind of meat on their plate.

The prep process in this meal is probably the most important part of the meal. You will want to have things laid out so that everything comes together at the same time, and the rice does not stand and become sticky.

Slice your mushrooms, peel your garlic and half it, dice your onions, and place them in separate containers.

In a large sauté pan, heat the olive oil and 2 Tbsp of sweet butter. Add the garlic, and cook over medium heat for a few minutes until it begins to sizzle. Add the mushrooms and some black pepper, and cook until they brown slightly.

In a saucepot, boil 2 cups of water and the 3 chicken bouillon cubes. When the bullion has dissolved, add the rice and the curry powder, lower the heat, and cook until it is done.

In the meantime, remove the mushrooms from the pan with a slotted spoon and set aside.

Salt & pepper the meat and brown it in the drippings with the garlic, turning so both sides brown. Add the wine, and cook over medium heat for 5-10 minutes.

In a bowl, mix the evaporated milk, arrowroot, sage and parsley until it is well blended and pour over the meat. Return half of the mushrooms to the pan and shake 4 or 5 dashes of Maggi into the sauce. Cover and simmer for 15 minutes.

When the rice finishes cooking, drain it and mix the remaining mushrooms and diced onions into the rice.

In a clean saucepan, melt remaining butter over medium heat. Cut the banana in the middle and then down the center, making four pieces. Flour the banana and the pineapple and fry them in the butter until a light crust develops.

Serve with a mound of rice on one side of the plate, and arrange the meat in a fan format with a ladle of sauce over the meat on the other side. Place the pineapple over the pork and a banana slice over the veal and beef. You will notice that the garlic is still in the sauce. The pieces are large enough that you can easily remove them if you wish—matter of personal choice.

I like to serve fresh asparagus as a side veggie. You can simply steam it and add butter at the end, and it makes a fine complement to this meal.

A *Tomato and Mozzarella Salad* is a wonderful opener.

Your choice of wine can be a fine red like a Chateau nuef du Pape or a nice white like a Pouilly Fume. This is one of those meals that will stand tall with either wine choice.

Breadsticks make a light choice for the bread, and you can forget dessert because of all the butter in the meal. If you have Jackie Gleason's "Music for Lovers", be sure to put it on the stereo.

EASTERN SHORE CRAB CAKES

In my mind, there are probably two places that create the best crab cakes, and these two places are as diverse as you can imagine. ***The Robert Morris Inn*** in Oxford, Maryland was built in 1710 and is steeped in U.S. Revolutionary War history. This is one of those places that boaters dream of—a small, quiet historic village with a four-star restaurant. The other place is ***Stoney's*** on Broome's Island, north and west of Solomon's Island, Maryland. My good friend, Pat Fitzgerald, introduced me to Stoney's—a modern facility with a friendly dock that serves its crab cake on a styrofoam plate with a plastic fork. What do they have in common besides a welcome haven to a weary boat and crew? Pure delicious Chesapeake crab meat—no filler. Here is my very simple and impressive rendition of that famous crab cake.

1 lb. lump crab meat
½ cup grated parmesan cheese
½ cup Italian bread crumbs
1/4 cup Hellmann's mayo
1 large egg
1 Tbsp German or Polish mustard
1 Tbsp port wine – or – sherry
1 Tbsp chopped parsley
juice of ½ lime
black pepper

Combine the grated cheese and the breadcrumbs into a measuring cup and set aside.

Combine remaining ingredients in a mixing bowl and add about 2/3 of the breadcrumb/cheese mixture. Blend well with a fork. Shape the mixture into about six large patties, and dip the patties in the remaining bread crumb mixture. Slide into a 375-degree deep fat fryer for about 3 to 4 minutes of cooking. Or use a frying pan on medium heat for 3 minutes on each side.

You can eat these on a bun with lettuce and tomato, potato chips, and a pickle slice as casual fare for a picnic in the back yard. If you serve them without the bun but with a few *Real French—Fried* and *Uncle Jimmy's Italian Tomato Salad,* along with a nice white Sauvignon Blanc, you will have a fine meal.

SOUTH COUNTY CRAB CAKES

There are essentially two fundamental methods of doing crab cakes. One method relies on a fair amount of filler and, in most cases, this does not do a lot for the flavor of the crab cake. I must admit, however, that I have had some crab cakes that use filler, and they actually tasted fairly good. Unfortunately, that is not usually the case because most of the filler is in the form of green peppers or other strong-tasting items that detract from the delicacy of the crabmeat. The real issue seems to be the availability of crabmeat. In the southern part of Anne Arundel County, we have a lot of crabbers so the crabmeat is plentiful. This recipe does use a little more "filler", but it is subtle and enhances the crabmeat. This is a dinner for four recipe since it will easily make six to eight crab cakes.

2 lbs. lump crab meat
3 eggs – lightly beaten
4 Tbsp fresh ricotta cheese
6-8 spring onions – diced
1 cup bread cumbs
1 tsp parsley
1 tsp paprika

1/4 tsp cayenne pepper
juice of 1 lemon
1/3 cup corn oil

Check the crabmeat for shells. Fold all of the ingredients, except the corn oil, into a nice mixture. Form the mixture into balls and flatten into patties. Pack them tightly. Place on a large plate and separate with waxed paper.

Refrigerate the cakes for at least one hour.

While the crab cakes are refrigerating, this will give you time to do other things, so you will not have a last minute rush on bringing the dinner to the table.

Heat part of the oil in a heavy, non-stick-surface frying pan. Sprinkle each side of the crab cake with a little breadcrumb just before placing in hot oil. Sauté each side on medium heat for approximately 3-4 minutes—or until golden brown. Add oil as needed.

As an alternative, you can broil them in the oven for 5 minutes on each side.

ANYTIME SALMON PATTIES

The truly nice feature of this recipe is you can make them at anytime of the year because the salmon comes from a can. This is an easy meal to make and can come from your pantry to your table in less than 30 minutes. Some things do quite well out of a can, and this is one of those items. I find this to be a good substitute for crab cakes or even a complement to them if you have a large gathering.

1 14 3/4 oz can pink salmon
1 egg – lightly beaten

1 Tbsp sour cream – heaping
1 slice onion – diced
14 saltine crackers – crushed
1 tsp parsley
juice of 1 lemon
1/3 cup corn oil

Place the saltines in a baggie and roll over them with a rolling pin until they are crushed to a fine consistency. If you do not have a rolling pin, use a large pickle bottle.

Blend all but the corn oil together in a mixing bowl, make 4 even balls, and pack them into patties. If you have time, you can refrigerate them for up to 3 hours before cooking.

Heat half of the oil in a heavy, non-stick frying pan over medium high heat. Cook the patties two at a time for approximately 3-4 minutes on each side. Add additional oil as needed and repeat for the last two patties.

Serve with sliced tomatoes, *Michigan Cole Slaw,* and freshly baked bread.

Bottled herbs and spices will lose their potency if kept too long. Dispose of them after six months in your cupboard—do it!

CHESAPEAKE SOFT SHELLS CON ROMANO

If you have ever spent any amount of time near the Chesapeake Bay, you have eaten crabs in one form or another. These "beautiful swimmers" are at their absolute best in their soft-shell form. These things are easy to fix—the most critical part is getting **FRESH** crabs. You should have no problem buying them fresh, but the problem will be keeping them fresh. Go to the fish house and buy the crabs live if you can. Have the fishmonger clean them for you. Remove the eyes and the "mustard" from the body cavity. Do not ride around with them in your car for a couple of hours and think you can cook them the same day! Go right home, because those crabs in your car without refrigeration will turn bad real quickly. If you do not cook them the same day, you can freeze them, but why freeze them if you eat them? The simple fact here is that the sweetness you find in the fresh crab quickly becomes rancor in the stale one. Seafood does not age like beef!

8 soft shell crabs – cleaned
1/4 cup olive oil
2 Tbsp sweet butter
8 cloves garlic – halved
2 large eggs
½ tsp Tabasco
1 cup Pecorino Romano cheese – grated
2/3 cup all-purpose flour
2 Tbsp fresh chives – chopped
black pepper
sea salt

Whip the eggs and Tabasco into a fine consistency and pour into a shallow baking dish. Place the crabs in the dish to soak in the egg mixture. If you wish to eliminate eggs in your diet, a ½ cup skim milk will accomplish the same purpose.

In a large sauté pan, heat the oil and butter over medium heat, and poach the garlic until it turns golden brown.

Combine the romano, flour, chives, and freshly ground salt and pepper in a large plate for dredging. Turn the crabs in the egg mix and shake off excess, dredge in cheese/flour and place into hot sauté pan. You should be able to prepare four crabs at a time. Sauté for approximately 3—4 minutes on each side and serve.

I recently served this to a group of adults and youngsters with homemade French fries and sliced tomatoes. It was a hit with all!

CAMPFIRE RAINBOW TROUT

Sometimes the memory of where and how we ate something is as strong as the memory of the taste of the thing we ate. When fish is fresh from the stream, it brings with it memories that will never die. I recall, even today, when I fix trout—no matter where I do it—I find myself going back to an early morning alongside a riverbank in the wilds of northern Michigan. If you want to catch good trout, you have to get them early in the day or as the sun sets. Early in the day, you can smell the dew on the moss, and you can hear the sun's rays moving gently across the water. It is a sort of sacred time to be in the woods with your fishing pole early in the morning angling for your breakfast. The secret to this recipe is fresh fish and a cast iron skillet. Now, you can cook it anywhere, but it will still be called "Campfire" because that is the origin of all good fish. You want to buy fresh trout with the head still on and a nice clear look in the fish's eye. Have the fish cleaned and boned at the fish market, and the rest is easy.

2 strips of bacon
1 2 lb. Rainbow

flour
salt & pepper

Cut the bacon into 1-inch strips and cook in the cast iron skillet over medium heat until done.

Remove the bacon from the skillet with a slotted spoon, being sure that the bacon fat remains in the pan. If you are making spinach, you can put the bacon in the spinach, otherwise save it for salad toppings.

Salt & pepper the inside of the Trout and then sprinkle with flour on both sides of the fish.

Fry the trout in the bacon fat over medium heat until both sides of the fish are well browned.

You could not ask for a simpler or more satisfying meal. If you fix *Popeye's Spinach* and a baked potato, you have a nice ***Happy Heart*** meal that is delicious and easy.

Remember not to overheat the cast iron pan. You should start it on medium heat and allow it to warm slowly to achieve best results.

GRILLED RAINBOW TROUT

This is one of those recipes that are so simple it is almost embarrassing to include it in this type of collection. The hardest part about this meal is going to the store to get the trout. Firing up the grill is the next hardest part. You can do this in the oven, but it is really best to do it on the grill. You get more mileage out of doing this on the grill. For some reason or another, it seems more macho to cook over a fire, and that covers the fact that this is so easy.

2 large Rainbow fillets
3 Tbsp olive oil
2 tsp rosemary
2 tsp chives
salt & pepper

You need to make a little tin foil pan to cook these things in. The edges should be rounded, and you should poke some fork holes in the bottom to allow maximum heat penetration.

Mix the olive oil, rosemary, and chives together and drizzle over the fish. Add salt and pepper. The fish should be on the foil, and you need to allow it to stand with the oil mixture for at least 10 minutes—while the grill heats.

When the grill gets good and hot, put the fish and foil on the grill, close the lid, and cook for about 10 minutes on high heat.

If you want to squeeze some lemon on the fish prior to eating, you may. You might find it quite tasty just as it is.

This is a bona fide ***Happy Heart*** choice that goes well with *Nanny's Simple Lettuce Salad* and some rice. Enjoy a Pellegrino with fresh lemon, and you have zero fat for the entire meal.

GRILLED SALMON STEAK

The countryside around Seattle is so ruggedly beautiful that it demands simplicity. The salmon is one of God's finest creations in its demonstration of determination. You cannot eat salmon without being struck by basic values of hard work and commitment. Whenever I have salmon, I reflect on my time in Seattle and the majesty of this fine fish and hope that I can renew that quiet determination that is so vital to finding balance and harmony.

2 large salmon steaks
3 Tbsp Country mustard
1 Tbsp olive oil
½ tsp tarragon
juice of 1 lemon
black pepper

Mix the mustard, olive oil, tarragon and lemon juice until blended. Make a foil pan for the fish, and poke random holes in the foil with a fork. Poke the fish with the fork to make a few holes in it. Grind fresh black pepper on the fish and then brush the mustard mix over the top of the steak.

Place on preheated hot grill, close the lid, and cook for 15 to 20 minutes, or until done.

The portions are designed for two, so candles and a good white wine will make the evening.

A *Tomato and Mozzarella Salad* and steamed asparagus will give you a very complete meal. ***Happy Heart*** awards take first place in the entire meal.

Everybody should have a Last Will and Testament—even single guys. It is important.

CINDY'S MARINATED SHRIMP

There is an old saying that says, "*Behind every good grill man, there is a good marinade woman*". If you liked *David's Grilled Chicken*, you are sure to like his wife's marinated shrimp. Cindy worked for me a few years back and has been kind enough to continue to look after me by inviting me to dinner on a regular basis, so I could lift some of David and Cindy's recipes. Once again, this is a transcription of a recipe she gave me a few years ago that may have changed with my use, but it, nevertheless, remains and becomes passed on as Cindy's Marinade.

18 jumbo shrimp – peeled
½ cup soy sauce
1/3 cup Extra Virgin olive oil
2 Tbsp white wine vinegar
1 Tbsp honey
2 cloves garlic
1 tsp ground ginger
1 tsp dry mustard

Whisk together all of the ingredients, except the shrimp, in a mixing bowl. Arrange the shrimp in a shallow Corning, pour the marinade over them, cover, and refrigerate for 8 hours.

Skewer the shrimp on metal skewers and grill over hot coals until shrimp are pink and cooked. This is a ***Happy Heart*** item, so be certain that you DO NOT use the marinade on the shrimp after they are cooked. Fish and poultry bacteria grow in a marinade and can be dangerous if the marinade is not cooked. That could make your heart very unhappy—or dead!

I like to serve this dish in the summer with *Uncle Jimmy's Italian Tomato Salad*, fresh corn on the cob, and some fresh home-made French fries.

This marinade also works well on pork and beef items to be grilled on the barbecue.

CRAB TOWN MUFFINS

One of the joys of living in the Washington, D.C. region, is the proximity of the Chesapeake Bay and the pleasures of the water. One can find an assortment of little "crab towns"—villages that for generations have made their living on the abundance of the Blue Crab. Many of these little villages can be reached easily by automobile, but some are best accessed by water. I have fond memories of watching a sunset from a little pier while eating some crab specialty or just "pick'n" crabs, as the locals say of eating these juicy morsels. When you make up a serving of *Big Deale Hot Crab Dip,* you want to make extra, or save some to build this meal the next day and relish a day "on the Bay" wherever you may be.

2 English muffins – split in half
1 ½ cups *Big Deale Hot Crab Dip*
4 slices fresh ripe tomato
4 slices sharp cheddar cheese
paprika for garnish

Toast the English muffins and lightly butter them. Put one slice of tomato on the muffin, mound the crab mix on the tomato, and add the cheese. Sprinkle some paprika. Place muffins in broiler and broil until cheese begins to bubble and turn brown. Serve hot.

This makes a nice lunch when served with a relish tray of olives, pickles, and peppers. A handful of chips and a glass of iced tea will round out your lunch for two very nicely.

Always be certain that your VHF radio is working before you leave the dock, even if you do not plan to be gone long or far.

SUNDAY'S CHICKEN FEAST

This country has a rich history of chicken on Sunday. In the South, they fry it and eat it on the lawn. In the North, they boil it and fix dumplings with it. The West barbecues it, and the folks in the East stuff it. Chicken should be Carl Ichan's favorite, because it accepts mergers so well. Chicken is a friendly substance—it takes on all kinds of flavorings quite well. For this reason, chicken is ideal for any kind of marinating. Here is a recipe that requires some time to marinate, so it goes well on weekends when you have that kind of time.

4 chicken breasts – with bones and skin
1/3 cup olive oil
1/4 cup Romano cheese – grated
1 Tbsp soy sauce
1 Tbsp rosemary
1 Tbsp cilantro
½ tsp garlic powder
1/4 tsp red cayenne pepper
juice of 1 lemon

Wash the chicken breasts in cold water and allow them to soak in cold water while you mix the marinade. This is an important part of preparing the chicken, so do not pass it by. Any time you use chicken, you should wash and soak it in cold water to wake up the flavors. In a glass measuring cup, you can mix together the remaining ingredients. Mix well so they are well blended. Arrange the chicken in a shallow Corning and pour the marinade over the chicken. Cover and refrigerate for at least 4 or as long as 8 hours.

In a preheated 450-degree oven, put the chicken without the cover in, and bake for 15 minutes. Remove from oven, squeeze lemon juice, and sprinkle grated cheese over breasts. Return to oven. Lower heat to 325 degrees and bake an additional 1-½ hours.

In the summer, this is great with *Mom's Potato Salad* and *Michigan Cole Slaw*.

In the winter, a baked potato and some green beans make a nice combination.

DAVID'S GRILLED CHICKEN

It is always a joy to break bread with others who also enjoy the art of fine food preparation and are willing to share the process with others. David Dressel is one of those people. He details every aspect of the preparation and involves his guests in the delivery, so you can go home and recreate it. David is a master on the grill, and to him I owe this technique.

Prepare your grill by removing the lava rock from one side of your gas grill and placing a two-inch deep metal pan filled with water on the grates. Soak a handful of wood chips in a container of water—just covering the top of the chips—for 30 minutes. You can use any kind of store-bought wood chips, but I tend to like apple wood or cherry wood chips for this recipe. This recipe turns your gas grill into a wood cooker! It also enhances your charcoal-fired grill, so it is a classic win-win deal.

4 chicken breasts – with or without the bones
2 Tbsp olive oil
1 Tbsp rosemary
1 tsp garlic powder
salt & pepper

Wash the chicken breasts in cold water and place in a non-porous container.

Sprinkle olive oil, rosemary, garlic powder, and salt & pepper over chicken breasts. Cover and place in refrigerator for at least 30 minutes (while wood chips soak). You can do this in the morning before you go to work, and it will be perfect for dinner in the evening.

Tear off 12 inches of aluminum foil, place soaked wood chips on one end, and roll foil so it becomes like a big hot dog. Do not close the ends of the foil. Bend about two inches of each end of the foil "log" upward, and place in middle of lava rock in grill.

Heat grill on high heat, until water begins to boil and foil "log" begins to emit smoke from each end. Reduce grill heat to medium for cooking the chicken.

Place chicken on grill above the water pan and cook with lid closed until done. This should not take much more than 30 minutes. The steam from the water pan mixes with the smoke vapors from the foil "log" to create a convection smoker that will give you a crisp outer texture with a succulent moist and lightly-smoked flavor in the interior.

After 30 minutes, move chicken from the water side to the lava rock side and allow 10-15 minutes for browning.

This is definitely a ***Happy Heart*** entree if you have remove the skin.

GINA'S PEACHY POLLO

Gina Schewe was the bundle of energy that ran the Pro-Am Golf Classic and the ***Rally Round the Redskins*** fundraisers for the ***Ronald McDonald House*** in Washington, D.C. When I told our committee that I was looking for new recipes for my collection, she volunteered this offering. True to her "get it done" attitude, it was in my mail two days later and in my oven a few days after that. I like recipes from busy people, because I know that they face the same problems as I do. This recipe requires a little bit of attending, but the rest of it is simple and straightforward. In her recipe, she fixed the broccoli on top of the chicken, but I prefer to steam it and serve it with rice as a side dish.

4 chicken breasts – skinned with bone in
6 Tbsp sweet butter
2 Tbsp paprika
3 cloves garlic – crushed
1 cup sour cream
1/3 cup light mayo
6 canned peach halves
1/3 cup Romano cheese – grated
salt & pepper

Wash the chicken in cold water and pat dry.

Melt the butter and stir in the paprika and garlic.

Coat the chicken with the melted butter mixture and salt and pepper to taste. Place in a covered Corning and bake for 35 minutes at 425 degrees.

Blend together the sour cream and mayo. Remove the chicken from the oven, coat with 2/3 of the sour cream/mayo blend, and return to the oven. Reduce heat to 375 degrees and continue baking for an additional 25 minutes. Remove from oven.

Place peach halves on top of each chicken breast, coat with remaining sour cream/mayo blend, and top with grated cheese.

On the middle rack of your oven, return the Corning without the lid and broil 6 to 10 minutes until cheese turns light brown.

This dish serves well with rice so you can absorb the nice sauce from the chicken. You can serve with a dry white wine and a pan of *Phoenix Corn Bread,* found later in this collection.

SHERRY'S CALIFORNIA CHIX

When planning our 30th high school reunion, I had the occasion to spend some time on the phone with a classmate who is now living in Palos Verdes. I had not had any dealings with her since we graduated, but there was still a connection. As we visited across the continent, our conversation eventually turned to eating and our mutual regard for cooking. This recipe came from that conversation. It reaffirmed my belief that both new acquaintances, as well as old friendships, are warmed by a good meal. This is a very easy recipe, but it demands *fresh* everything—especially the herbs—to be truly California.

5-6 lb. roasting chicken
2 whole knuckles garlic
8-10 sprigs parsley
6-8 sprigs sage
6-8 sprigs rosemary
6-8 sprigs thyme

4-6 sprigs marjoram
6-7 new potatoes – halved
8-10 spring onions – diced
1 cup California white wine
olive oil
salt & pepper

Wash and soak the chicken in cold water in the refrigerator for an hour prior to preparation. Salt the cavity of the chicken, and place two sprigs of each herb plus two garlic cloves in the cavity. Put two sprigs of herbs under the chicken in middle of a large roasting pan.

Surround chicken with halved potatoes, spring onions that have been diced nearly to the tops, and peeled garlic cloves. Add white wine to roaster, chop remaining herbs, and sprinkle over potatoes. Rub chicken with olive oil and salt and pepper entire roaster with freshly ground salt and pepper.

Place open roaster in center of 400-degree oven and roast for 30 minutes. Reduce heat to 325 degrees—cover—and continue to roast for 2 to 2 ½ hours or until chicken is done. Turn the potatoes and baste the chicken with juices at least twice during the roasting. This will insure the herb flavorings transfer to the chicken. Add small amounts of water, if necessary.

Serve with hot crusty bread that has been rubbed with the garlic from the roaster for dipping in the delicious juices. A fresh garden salad and ice-cold glasses of the remaining white wine make for a perfect California dinner. Put on some old Simon and Garfunkel, and you have a complete evening!

Note: The key with the fresh herbs is that you use lots of them.

Check the pressure on your motorcycle tires at least once a month—optimum pressure is a huge safety issue.

MOVING DAY CHICKEN

It should have come as no surprise that settlement had to be rescheduled at least three times before it finally became a reality. Nonetheless, caught me off guard. I had packed most of my kitchen by the time I made this recipe. I had no herbs or spices in the kitchen, so this had to be a real simple—make do with what you have—creation. I looked in my refrigerator, and there were four lonely chicken breasts, and that was it. My pantry, liquor cabinet, and garden supplied the rest.

4 chicken breasts
1 8 ½ oz can pineapple slices
2 Tbsp Cointreau
1 Tbsp fresh chives
salt & pepper

Wash the chicken breasts in cold water.

In a large Corning dish, place each chicken breast side by side. Grind some fresh salt and pepper on the chicken breasts and lay one pineapple ring on top of each breast. Pour the juice over the chicken and add the Cointreau and chopped chives. Marinate in the refrigerator for 4 to 6 hours.

Preheat the oven to 375-degrees and bake the chicken in the covered Corning for 1 hour and 15 minutes. Remove the lid, baste the chicken with the juices and bake an additional 30 minutes. Serve with some French bread, green beans, and potato pancakes for an easy minimum-ingredient meal.

Whenever a recipe calls for chicken, always wash in cold water prior to cooking for best flavor

JACK'S FRIED CHICKEN

When you go to Kansas City, you have to eat beef, right? Well, yes, but you also need to make a visit to Stroud's and have the pan-fried chicken. I never passed within 100 miles of K.C. without stopping for the night. I would call my old friend, Jack Fette, who was a retired NFL zebra and loved to eat as much as any man I have known. We usually went early to beat the rush and ordered a platter of chicken breasts with cottage fried potatoes and gravy with "dead" beans. "Dead" beans are those green beans that have been cooking for 6 to 8 hours—yes, *hours*. The real secret to this chicken is the cast iron frying pan, and if you do not own one, go out and buy one. The other secret is the lard. In our age of health awareness, this is a mortal sin. But canola oil does not give you the flavor, and flavor is what this is all about. Forget the arteries and run a couple of miles after dinner. Besides, Jack came up just shy of 80 and did it all with gusto! He went into the "end zone" standing up, and you can't ask for more than that.

1 12" cast iron frying pan
2 chicken breasts – with bone & skin
2 chicken wings
1 quart buttermilk
½ cup flour
½" lard in frying pan
paprika
salt & pepper

Wash the chicken and soak in cold water for at least 30 minutes. Then soak the chicken in the buttermilk for an additional 30 minutes. Grind fresh salt and pepper over chicken parts and dust with flour, paprika and salt and pepper.

Fry in hot lard for 20 to 25 minutes, turning often. (Make sure the lard is fresh.) Shake off excess grease and serve immediately.

I like to serve this with homemade lemonade, *Michigan Cole Slaw,* and *Grilled Roasted Redskin Potatoes.*

CHICKEN POTTERY PIE

This is not a traditional potpie in the *Marie Callendar's* sense, because it does not have a traditional crust. This is an item, however, that will justify the piece of pottery you acquired for use in the *Deep Dish Santa Fe Pie* described in this collection. A great cold-weather recipe to serve after a day of riding your motorcycle through the autumn colors.

The Filling

4 cups boneless chicken – cooked (2 breasts & 2 thighs)
½ cup cooked ham – diced
3 cups chicken broth
½ stick sweet butter
1/4 lb. mushrooms – sliced
3/4 cup heavy cream
1/4 cup flour
1 10 oz pkg. frozen peas & carrots
6 small pearl onions
½ tsp thyme
salt & pepper

The Topping

1 3/4 cups flour
2 tsp baking powder
½ tsp baking soda
½ tsp salt
½ tsp sugar
1 Tbsp Tarragon
4 Tbsp sweet butter – melted
1/4 cup skim milk
2/3 cup sour cream

Topping

In a mixing bowl, combine the flour, baking powder, baking soda, salt, sugar, tarragon and melted butter. Blend together and add sour cream and milk, mixing into dough. On a floured surface, roll out the dough into a ½ inch thick "donut" circle with a hole in the middle. Set aside.

Filling

Dice the chicken and ham and set aside in a mixing bowl.

Prepare the chicken broth by dropping 3-4 chicken bouillon cubes into 3 cups of boiling water.

In a large sauté pan, melt 1 Tbsp butter and sauté the mushrooms until they turn a uniform gray color. Add the rest of the butter and the peeled pearl onions. Cook, stirring regularly, for an additional 2-3 minutes on medium high heat. Add the flour and broth and cook an additional 5 minutes until it is well mixed. At this point, you can add the cream and increase the heat until a boil begins. Immediately place the peas & carrots, chicken, ham, thyme, salt and pepper in the pan and continue cooking until peas & carrots are well heated and mixed. About 10 minutes.

Place the hot mixture in your pottery casserole, and place the ring on top of the mixture.

Bake in a pre-heated 425-degree oven for 15 to 20 minutes and serve piping hot.

If the topping is too cumbersome, or if you do not have an adequate piece of pottery to bake this deep dish in, you can use one Pillsbury piecrust on top of a standard pie dish and bake in a 375-degree oven for 45 minutes.

RIB STICKIN' CHICKEN & DUMPLINGS

There are those nice crisp autumn days that are perfect for sitting in the stands cheering on your favorite football team that beg for this kind of food eaten from a big bowl in front of the fireplace. There are also those times when you need to fix something for a sick friend to help nurse them back to health. This is an easy recipe that takes a little time, but is basically fool proof. Dumplings can be tricky, so use Bisquick and never worry about it.

1 2-3 lb. whole frying chicken
3 chicken bouillon cubes
3-4 large carrots – diced
3-4 ribs of celery – diced
4 bay leaves
2 Tbsp parsley
1 Tbsp chives
salt & pepper

Dumplings

2 cups Bisquick
1/4 cup Parmesan cheese – grated
2/3 cup milk or buttermilk
1 Tbsp chives

Wash the chicken in cold water. Remove neck and organs if they are present. Place chicken in deep pot with enough water to cover the chicken with 2 ½ to 3 inches of water. Add salt, bouillon, and bay leaves, and bring water to a boil. Reduce heat to simmer and cook for 1-½ hours.

Take the chicken out of the pot and remove the skin, bones, and any grizzle. (They should fall off the bone with little persuasion.) Set chicken aside.

Add the carrots, celery, parsley, chives, and salt and pepper to taste. Continue to cook on medium heat for an additional 20 minutes.

In a mixing bowl, combine the Bisquick, cheese, milk and chives and mix into a firm consistency.

Drop the dumpling batter, a spoon at a time, into the boiling broth, reduce heat to a moderate level, and cook for 10 minutes without a cover. Cover pot and cook an additional 10 minutes. Return the chicken to the stockpot, turn off the heat, and let stand for 10 minutes prior to serving.

SAIGON FIRE DRAGON CHICKEN

Southeast Asian cooking is a marvelous blend of cultures and tastes, but the taste I like most from that region is **HOT** ! The French influence was found in many fine restaurants, but the "street kitchens" reflected the Thai contributions and produced heat that would make Mexican food look tame. If this recipe is too hot for you, I would suggest cutting in half the amount of garlic, ginger, cilantro, and red peppers, and you will have a subtle Hunan-type creation. Incidentally, for those who may have forgotten, Uncle Ho renamed the place Ho Chi Minh City.

1 lb. boneless chicken breast or thigh
1/4 cup olive oil
3/4 cup celery – diced
1 cup green pepper – diced

1 cup mushrooms – sliced
6-7 spring onions – sliced diagonally
1 Tbsp garlic powder
1 Tbsp whole red pepper
1 Tbsp cilantro
1/3 cup soy sauce
1/4 tsp ginger
½ cup pea pods
1 cup bean sprouts

Dice the chicken into small chunks and sauté with olive oil on medium high heat for a few minutes. Add the celery, green peppers, mushrooms, and spring onions and stir a few times. Now, add the garlic powder, red pepper, and cilantro and stir until chicken is fully cooked. Add the soy sauce, ginger, pea pods, and bean sprouts. Cook for two or three minutes more, and serve over white rice with Chinese noodles. If you want to do this in true street fashion, serve it in a hand-size bowl and eat it with your two forefingers and thumb.

This may not be the most authentic list of ingredients, but it is alright to Americanize your dishes to suit your tastes and to accommodate the availability of ingredients.

ST. JAMES PARISH ROUX

Ya cain't do real Louisiana fixin's without knowing how to make a genuine cajun roux. This stuff is the glue for many great old-fashioned recipes. It is real simple to make. What it requires is time and patience more than anything else. You will notice there are a number of ways of making a roux in the following recipes—they are all valid. The one constant is the flour. You can use oil or butter, or a combination of the two. You can start the blending in a cold pan or a hot one. You can use a roux in seafood, you can use it in stew, and you can use it in soups. You can make it dark or light, but if you want the old fashion way of doing it, here is the recipe that can't be beat. Don't mess around with anything less than a well-seasoned cast iron frying pan.

1/3 cup lard
1/3 cup flour
10" cast iron frying pan

In your cast iron frying pan, heat the lard on low heat to melt it into a liquid base. To this base, whisk in the flour, a little at a time, stirring out the lumps. Once the lumps are gone, turn the heat up to medium. Keep stirring the mixture until it turns brown—this might take a half an hour, so be prepared with something to drink and snack on while you are working. Also, please understand that the measurements are approximate—you will learn to use more or less ingredients the more times you make a roux. The darker the roux becomes, the more intense the flavor will be.

Simple?

Right on, but don't be fooled into thinking that because it is simple, it can be fast. Nothing on the Bayou happens quickly!

Individual stocks should always have a pre-set "stop-loss" order in place.

T-N-T JUMBO GUMBO

The first thing you will notice about this recipe is that the okra is missing. Right! I don't like okra, so I substitute corn for the okra, but you can suit yourself. You have to eat it. Secondly, don't let the fish guy talk you into medium shrimp—too small, and they take too long to clean. Go for the Jumbo! Roger & Susie have two lovely daughters, Tausha & Tiffany (T&T), so we decided to name this after them since they helped in the kitchen, ate the first run of this dish, and really liked it!!

1 stick sweet butter
1 green pepper – diced
1 medium yellow onion – diced
3 stalks of celery – diced
5 cloves of garlic – chopped
1 tsp black pepper
1 tsp cayenne pepper
1 Tbsp basil
½ tsp thyme
1/8 tsp Tabasco
1/2 cup roux (see below)
2 chicken bouillon cubes
1 tsp Old Bay seasoning
1 Tbsp white vinegar
1 cup frozen corn
2 lbs. large shrimp – peeled and cleaned
2 cups white rice

The roux is easy – it just takes time. Heat ½ cup of corn oil in an iron skillet. When it is good and hot (medium heat), whisk in ½ cup of flour, lower temperature to medium low, and stir constantly until it turns copper red in color. Set aside until later.

In a medium stockpot, melt the butter over medium heat and sauté the garlic, peppers, onions and celery until they become soft. Add 8 cups water, the roux, and all of the remaining items except the shrimp, corn and rice. Cover and simmer for 2 hours. Add the shrimp and corn, and cook for an additional 10 minutes.

Cook the rice during the last 30 minutes of prep time.

Serve the gumbo in bowls with the rice ladled over the top.

BIG DADDY'S SHRIMP ETOUFFEE

This is one dish that you want to prepare *only* for a close friend, not someone you have just met and are fixing dinner for the first time. This is traditionally a fairly elegant entrée, so you will find it served in the finer New Orleans restaurants. But believe me when I tell you that this recipe is so good, you will want to lick the plate clean! Licking the plate is not something you do with somebody you just met, or in a nice restaurant for that matter. Trust me on this—I *gua-rone-tee* it!

1/4 cup – plus 2 Tbsp – corn oil
2 cloves garlic – minced
1 stick of sweet butter
6-8 scallions – diced
1 rib celery – diced
2 tsp jalapeno pepper – diced
1 large fresh tomato – diced
1 Tbsp paprika

1 Tbsp parsley
3 Tbsp flour
1 lb. jumbo shrimp
2 Tbsp vodka
salt & pepper

Heat half the corn oil in a large skillet at medium heat and sauté the garlic for a minute or two. Add 3/4 of butter, scallions, celery, jalapeno, tomato, and paprika and continue to cook for about 8 minutes with the lid on. Drain the pan into your food processor, and blend the mixture until it becomes smooth and consistent. Set aside. In the same pan, heat the other half of the corn oil and remaining butter, adding flour and stirring so as not to burn. The longer you cook the roux, the darker it will become. Make your own call on this. When the roux is finished, add it to the other mixture you blended and set aside.

Place the 2 Tbsp corn oil in the same pan (no need to clean in between events) and sauté the shrimp with a little black pepper for 3 minutes. Add the vodka to create a flame. Sauté until shrimp turn pink, about 5 minutes more. Return the roux to the pan and thin with about 2–3 cups of water. You want to have some sauce come out of this recipe, so don't skimp on the water. (The roux will be strong.) Cover and simmer for 5 more minutes.

Cook some white rice and serve a ladle of it on top of the shrimp, or under it—you pick. A nice, thick country bread will soak up that sauce and slide down with a crisp white wine.

MASON-DIXON LINE JAMBALAYA

I know that when you think of jambalaya, you tend to think of New Orleans. So this is my disclaimer by naming this Mason-Dixon Line Jambalaya. One evening, I fixed *Warehouse Mussels* and put a lot more crushed red pepper in the recipe. While we were eating it, I said, "This sauce would make a great base for a Jambalaya." My partner said, "*What is Jambalaya?*" "*I don't know,*" I said. "*I think it has sausage and chicken and stuff in it.*" You know what is great about cooking? You do not have to file a prospectus with the S.E.C. before you can do it! Here is my version of jambalaya.

3 chicken bouillon cubes
1 ½ cups cooked rice
1 boneless chicken breast – skin removed
1 Tbsp olive oil
1 - 6" link kielbasa
4 cups *Warehouse Mussel Sauce* *
½ cup green pepper – chopped
½ tsp crushed red pepper
½ cup frozen corn

In 2 ½ cups of boiling water, dissolve the chicken bouillon cubes, remove ½ cup of the broth, and set aside to use in sauce mixture later. Then cook the rice in remaining broth it until it is done. Set aside.

Dice the chicken into bite-size pieces and cook in a large sauté pan with the olive oil. Slice the kielbasa into ½ inch slices and then cut the slices in half. Add to the chicken and brown. Add all remaining ingredients—except the corn—and cook over low heat for 30 to 40 minutes. Stir corn in, and cook an additional 5 minutes. Serve immediately with a ladle of rice on top of the jambalaya.

This is a ***Happy Heart*** meal that is not a budget buster.

* The *Warehouse Mussels Sauce* recipe is contained in the Appetizer section. If you have 5 or 6 mussels left over, they will add a nice touch to the jambalaya. Remove them from their shells and discard the shells, leaving the mussel meat in the sauce.

NOTE: You can cut down your prep time if you make the sauce/chicken/kielbasa mixture ahead of time and store it in the refrigerator for a couple of days. For meal day, you can add the rice, green peppers, corn, and chicken broth and only cook 15 minutes on moderate heat. The red sauce will have done an excellent job of flavor blending, and that reduces your cooking time.

NEW ORLEANS RED BEANS & RICE

This is a pretty standard recipe, but nonetheless one that you need in your Louisiana collection. This is one of those staples that you can use as a main course or as a party dish when you are invited out. If you do this at home, you need to stock up on a lot of classical jazz from guys like Davis, Brubeck, Monk, and even Goodman.

3 quarts water
2 cups red beans – dry
1 rib celery – chopped
2 chicken bouillon cubes
2 bay leaves
2 garlic cloves – sliced thin

½ cup ham – cubed
½ cup green pepper – diced
1 Tbsp jalapeno – diced
1 link kielbasa – sliced & halved
1 tsp Tabasco
1 tsp cilantro
½ cup rice
2 Tbsp spring onion – chopped
salt

Soak the beans in water, overnight, or for at least 6 hours. Drain and rinse before cooking.

Heat the water, red beans, celery, bouillon cubes, bay leaves and garlic to a rapid boil, cover, and reduce to a simmer. Cook for1 hour.

Add the ham, peppers, and jalapeno and cook an additional 30 minutes with a cover.

Add the kielbasa, Tabasco, and cilantro and simmer a final 30 minutes.

In a separate pot, cook the rice in salted water and drain.

Serve the beans in a soup dish with a ladle of rice and a splash of onions over the top. Keep the Tabasco handy, in case you want to turn up the heat while you listen to Pete Fountain belt out *China Boy* on the stereo!

ZYDECO PORK CHOPS

My first exposure to Zydeco music came in the form of a *Boozoo Chavis* concert from a friend of mine who is a government attorney in Washington, D.C. Joel may work for the government by day, but his heart is in New Orleans and the music of that city that is peculiar to the Zydeco culture. Zydeco is a strange blend of the happy Cajun influence—which in itself is a curious mix of northern French Canadian and southern Bayou cultures—and the soulful blues of the Black Island peoples. The recipe is a curious blend, as well, that will set your mouth to singing once you try it.

6 pork loin chops
1/4 cup soy sauce
1 can crushed pineapple
1/4 tsp cayenne pepper
1 cup leeks – chopped
1 cup Italian peppers – chopped
½ cup mushrooms – sliced
2 Tbsp garlic – crushed
1 Tbsp mint
1 Tbsp parsley
1 Tbsp jalapeno pepper – chopped
2 cups dry white wine

Marinate the pork chops in the soy sauce and pineapple for 1 to 6 hours.

Sauté the pork chops with the cayenne pepper in a hot pan until the chops turn gray in color. Add the leeks, peppers, mushrooms and garlic and continue to cook until chops brown. Stir in the soy/pineapple marinade, mint, parsley, jalapenos, and wine, and cover can cook over medium heat for approximately 30 minutes.

This dish blends well with rice cooked in chicken broth and served with flat bread. This serving will provide a nice base for a dinner party of four.

PIZZAS AND BREADS

RED SAUCE

Most pizza, as we know it, has a red sauce as the basic component. When I was in college, I worked in a place called ***The Pizzeria,*** and we were the hottest spot in that college town. We would make everything fresh every day and hand toss our crusts. We generally made our sauce the same way, but I also learned that there are any number of ways to make the sauce. Some people use crushed tomatoes, while others prefer a tomato sauce or puree. Either way you make it, I think it helps to pre-cook the sauce to create a better flavor blend. In this recipe, you will make enough sauce for a number of pizzas, but you can store it in the refrigerator or freezer and use it for a long time

1 8 oz can tomato sauce
1 tsp Herbs Pour Pizza *
dash garlic powder
½ tsp sugar
salt & pepper

Combine all items in a small sauce pan, bring to a light boil, and remove from heat.

* equal parts of oregano, marjoram, thyme & basil

PESTO SAUCE

There is no magic to a good pesto, other than fresh ingredients. The recipes for this classic are all pretty much the same; it is simply a matter of doing it. It is very important that all the items be absolutely fresh—including the nuts—so this is a must-do for the summer when the basil is in full bloom. If you are out of pignola (pine nuts), you can substitute nice walnuts with equally pleasing results.

3 cups fresh basil
3 cloves garlic
3 Tbsp pignola nuts
3/4 cup Extra Virgin olive oil
2/3 cup Parmesan cheese
1/3 cup Pecorino Romano cheese

Put all ingredients in a blender and puree into a smooth consistent blend. Refrigerate.

A CRUST FOR ALL REASONS

Pizza crust is the easiest of all bread products, because it is not important to have the dough rise. Some recipes do not even use yeast. There are three basic pizza dough recipes that follow. IF you want a thick crust, use yeast, allow the dough to rise, and roll out a thick portion. Use semolina flour if you want a crisp and or thin crust. Experiment!!

SOFT CRUST

1 ½ cups all-purpose flour
½ pkg. yeast
½ cup hot water (120 degrees)
1 Tbsp olive oil
1 tsp sugar
½ tsp salt

Dissolve the yeast in the hot water. Combine the flour, sugar and salt. Add the water and olive oil in small amounts, and mix well with your hands or in a mixer. You should knead the dough for about 3 to 5 minutes. Set aside in an oiled and covered bowl, allowing it to rise for 45 to 60 minutes. Punch down and cut into balls. On a floured surface, roll dough into a round or rectangular shape. Dust the pan or surface with corn meal before baking.

CRISP CRUST

2 cups all-purpose flour
1 cup semolina flour
1 ½ tsp salt
1 1/4 cups warm water (105 degrees)

Mix the flours and salt together. Pour the water into the flour in small amounts at a time. Mix by hand or in a mixer for 3 to 5 minutes.

Flour the surface of your counter top, and roll the dough into the desired shape.

Dust the pan or pizza stone with corn meal before baking.

THIN CRUST

2 cups all-purpose flour
½ cup semolina flour
1 pkg. yeast
1 tsp salt
1 Tbsp olive oil
1 1/4 cups warm water (105 degrees)

Mix flours and salt together in a mixing bowl. Add the yeast to the warm water to activate the yeast. Pour the water and oil into the flour and mix for 3 to 5 minutes until elastic. Place in an oiled bowl and cover for 1 hour so it can rise.

Punch down the dough and cut into equal balls. Flour a work surface and roll the dough into desired shapes. Dust the pan or pizza stone with corn meal prior to baking.

GARY'S CHOICE

Whenever we go to ***Ann's Restaurant*** in Hale's Corners for pizza, my brother always orders it with all these things on it.

4 Tbsp red sauce
1 16 oz ball of mozzarella cheese – shredded
3/4 lb. Bob Evans hot sausage
1 tsp fennel seed
24 slices of pepperoni
1/3 cup mushrooms – sliced
1 tsp butter

1/4 cup green peppers – diced
1/4 cup black olives – sliced

Sauté the sausage with the fennel seed. Set aside until needed. Sauté the mushrooms lightly in the butter. Set aside.

Roll out the dough into a large 17" x 12" bakers pan. Top with red sauce, cheese, and remaining ingredients. Bake in a 450-degree oven for 12 to 14 minutes.

SICILIAN SAUSAGE BREAD

This bread takes a little time to make, but it is a wonderful holiday or special event offering. It helps to have a lot of people around, because this recipe makes four loaves, and it is unbeatable when it first comes out of the oven.

Filling

1 Tbsp olive oil
1 lb. hot Italian sausage
1 cup Sicilian olives – chopped
1 lb. mozzarella – shredded
1 cup parmesan cheese – grated
4 Tbsp fresh basil – chopped
4 pepperoncinis – chopped

Dough

½ cup lukewarm water
2 tsp sugar
¼ oz yeast

4 cups flour
1 Tbsp salt
3/4 cup warm water
1 egg – beaten

Sauté the sausage in the olive oil over medium heat, stirring frequently to break the sausage down into small crumbs. When finished cooking, pour off the oil and set aside to cool.

Meanwhile, cut the olives off the pits and into small pieces. Combine in a mixing bowl with cheeses, basil and pepperoncinis, and refrigerate overnight.

In a large mixing bowl, put the warm water, sugar and yeast and allow to stand for 5 minutes. Meanwhile, stir the flour/salt/yeast water and an additional 3/4 cup of warm water together and knead for 8 to 10 minutes. Put dough in bowl that has been oiled with olive oil, cover it with a clean dishtowel, and place in a warm location for 1 hour. Dough should double in size.

Cut the dough into 4 equal size pieces and roll into a 10x12 rectangle.

Spread the filling onto the dough and allow a ½ inch border all around the dough. Roll the dough like a log and finish with seam side down. Tuck the ends closed, and seal the seams and ends with the beaten egg.

Bake in a pre-heated 350-degree oven for 25 to 30 minutes until loaves turn golden. Allow to cool for a few minutes, and serve warm with hot Italian gravy for dipping.

If you want to make extras, you can put them together and freeze them instead of baking them. Then when you want a little snack, you can remove them from the freezer, pop them in the oven, and bake for 45 minutes.

Red Wine that has been re-corked can be kept in the refrigerator up to one week—longer than that and it becomes cooking wine.

PHOENIX CORN BREAD

Corn bread is a very American offering, and it differs from one region of the country to the other. I have a leaning toward the Southwest and remember well a trip to ***The Point*** in Phoenix a few years ago. It was late winter, so our lunches on the sun-drenched patios and evening walks under the orange trees were an especially welcome balm to our Eastern blues. This corn bread salutes the American Indian influence on the Southwest.

2 cups yellow cornmeal
2 cups flour
6 Tbsp sugar
2 Tbsp baking powder
1 Tbsp cilantro
1 ½ cups milk
6 Tbsp sweet butter – melted
2 large eggs – lightly beaten
1 cup Monterey Jack – shredded
1 10 oz pkg. corn
3 Tbsp jalapeno peppers – diced

In a mixing bowl, sift the cornmeal, flour, sugar, baking powder, and cilantro together.

Blend in the milk, butter, and eggs, and mix to a consistent batter.

Fold in the monterey jack, jalapenos, and corn.

Batter can be baked in a cake pan, muffin tins, corn bread molds, or dropped on a cookie sheet. However, the cast iron frying pan way is best. In a cold oven, place a 10" cast iron frying pan that has the fat of two strips of bacon in it. Heat to 450 degrees. When the oven is hot, remove the pan and immediately spoon the mixture into the hot pan. Return to the oven and bake for 20 minutes. Remove the pan, turn it upside down, and the bread will drop out—serve hot!

RUTH'S ENGLISH MUFFIN BREAD

Ruth Benedict had been a good friend for a number of years. I had only known Ruth since she was widowed, but it seems to me that she was a perfect example of someone who has adjusted her cooking style to account for a change in the number of people at her table. Ruth was 86 years young when she gave me this recipe and every bit as full of life as she must have when she was a young cub reporter covering Capitol Hill many years ago. At 80, she rode through Yellowstone on the back of her nephew's motorcycle—that is young!

2 pkgs. dry yeast
6 cups white flour
1 Tbsp sugar
2 tsp salt
2 cups milk
1/4 tsp baking powder
½ cup water
cornmeal
butter

Heat milk and water over medium heat until quite warm—do not boil.

In a large mixing bowl, place dry ingredients and add liquid, beating into a stiff batter.

Butter two bread pans and sprinkle some corn meal into the pans. Add the batter, cover, and let rise in a warm place for 45 minutes.

Bake in pre-heated 400-degree oven for 25 minutes and serve immediately.

This bread is great with some marmalade and tea.

HONEY BANANA NUT COINTREAU BREAD

I am serious! Every time I make this and bring it to the office, it is gone before lunchtime. This is an easy bread to make, and it uses honey and Cointreau for the sweetness instead of sugar.

The bread comes out moist and stays that way for days—if the loaf lasts that long. You can use any kind of nuts, including pecans, walnuts, hazelnuts and almonds. If your sister ever lived in the South and sent you bags of pecans for Christmas, here is a good place to use them up. Those pecans do keep in the freezer almost indefinitely.

You can mix the ingredients by hand or use an electric mixer, as I do.

2 cups flour
½ cup hazel nuts – chopped
1 tsp baking soda
½ tsp salt
3/4 cup honey
½ cup sweet butter
½ cup skim milk
3 ripe bananas
2 eggs
1 oz Cointreau
1 tsp vanilla
1 Tbsp sugar

Grease the inside of a loaf pan with butter, and preheat oven to 375 degrees.

In a mixing bowl, whisk together the flour, nuts, baking soda and salt. Set aside.

In another mixing bowl, blend together the honey, butter, eggs, bananas, milk, Cointreau, sugar and vanilla. When you have an even consistency, blend in the flour mix until it becomes smooth.

Pour the mixture into the baking pan and bake for 55 to 60 minutes. When a toothpick inserted in the top of the loaf comes out dry, it is done.

A nice bottle of Sauvignon Blanc makes this bread a nice happy hour treat.

MANLY VEGGIES

HEALTH ISSUES

If you want to retain that competitive edge—or if you just want to live longer—it might be a good idea if you ate right. Sounds just like your mother, doesn't it? Sure, except remember that I am one of us—Type A Entrepreneur, remember?

Another real good reason to do your own cooking is that you can control what you eat when you cook it yourself.

I stated in the beginning that this was not a health book, but there are some basic concerns that we all share when we compete in this stress-filled society.

Let's hit the big one first. Fat and cholesterol are the topics on everybody's minds and hips today. It should be. I have tried every imaginable means of controlling my weight, and only one works and works without pain. Control the fat intake. Read the labels. In six months time, I lost 40 pounds by limiting fat intake and engaging in modest exercise three times a week. I ate as much as I wanted—I just ate low or no-fat items. Forget calories and count fat grams. Your "normal" intake of fat grams may range between 40 to 60 grams a day, but you can live on 10 to 20 grams of fat a day, and you will lose weight. A large bag of potato chips, on the other hand, will contain as much as 60 grams of fat—three days worth of fat. Enough said!

What are the other big offenders?

Milk: Drink and cook with skim milk. You can get used to the taste. Zero fat.

Butter: Do not substitute margarine for butter. It does not taste the same, and in most cases, it has more bad fat grams than butter. Use less butter and eliminate it whenever possible. Good bread tastes quite fine without butter.

Eggs: No question that it contributes to cholesterol, so you should not eat them for breakfast *everyday*. If you treat yourself to eggs once a month for breakfast, you will live through it. Cereal in the morning with fruit will do wonders for the rest of your day.

Oils: If you only use olive oil and canola oil (Puritan), your heart will last much longer. Run from LARD and any saturated fat oil like the tropical oils. Palm and coconut are bad! Shun fried foods like the plague! (Unless we are talking a few *special* recipes in this book!)

There are many more issues concerning healthy eating, but I am not qualified to cover them properly. Let me conclude with one last reminder: It cannot hurt to eat fresh and natural foods. All the healthy old people that I know have eaten natural foods most of their lives. I am not talking about organic. I am talking about an apple instead of a bag of Cheetos. Think about the chemicals and preservatives we find in most of the "quick" food items, and it will change your mind about factory-made food. My point is that it does not take that much more energy to cook from scratch, and it can be very much healthier. My fine sister and her husband often eat nothing but steamed vegetables for dinner during the week. And she looks fabulous, baby! It takes no longer than most T.V. dinners, and provides many more nutrients. A big baked potato with corn and green peppers on it makes for an excellent zero-fat meal. Try it.

If you young Turks want to be a master of the universe, and if you old dogs want to run with the fast cats, it takes some effort. You can pour yourself into those tight little workout suits and sweat buckets, but if you are eating and drinking the wrong stuff, it is going to take much more work to keep that edge. You can help yourself if you eat right. Eating right is going to include more veggies, so here are a few that might not be the healthiest you have ever eaten, but will get you started thinking about doing the right thing.

READ THE LABELS!

TWO-DAY CABIN BAKED BEANS

It is real easy to buy baked beans in a can or a jar in the supermarket, or even as take out from many delis. So why go through all the trouble to make your own? First of all, beans take a long time, but require little effort once they hit the oven. Secondly, home baked are appreciably different from the bottled and canned stuff, so your guests will most likely be impressed that you did these from "scratch". My mother used to bake these things in an old bean crock in a cast iron wood stove at our cabin when I was growing up. A round bean crock is best for baking the real thing, but a deep Corning can be a distant second choice when you have no other alternative. If you cannot find a bean crock in your local stores, call **L.L. Bean**.

This is a large recipe suitable for a group picnic. And now that you have a bean recipe, why not organize a picnic. This country needs more picnics with people playing softball and volleyball with lots of watermelon and lemonade.

5 cups Great Northern beans – dried
1 cup molasses
1 cup ketchup
1 cup water
½ lb. salt pork
4 slices of thick bacon – cooked
1 large ripe tomato – diced
5 spring onions
1 Tbsp cilantro
1 Tbsp Worcestershire
1 Tbsp brown sugar
1 tsp dry mustard
½ tsp garlic powder
½ tsp Tabasco

Day One: In a large sauce pan filled with water, bring the beans to a boil for 2 minutes, cover and let stand 1 hour. Repeat, then simmer for 1 hour, and drain the beans. Add fresh water and soak the beans overnight. Cover at least two inches over the beans—they will soak it up. Drain and rinse the beans with fresh water. Restore about a cup of fresh water to the beans.

Day Two: Drain and rinse the beans with fresh water, restoring about a cup of water to the beans. Mix the remaining ingredients into your bean crock, and cover the crock. Place the crock in a preheated 400-degree oven for 15 minutes, reduce the heat to 275 degrees, and continue to bake for an additional 6 to 8 hours. You may wish to check the crock after 2 or 3 hours and then again after 5 or 6 hours to be sure there is sufficient liquid in the crock. You can add water if it is needed.

This recipe requires a lot of prep work with all the boiling and rinsing of the beans, but by following this method, you will also reduce the amount of gas the beans bring to the party.

Never use a paper towel on your motorcycle windshield—the windshield is made out of plastic, and paper will scratch it and make it difficult to see through.

MIXED TRADING

(*Black Beans & Wild Rice*)

On Wall Street when the analysts can't quite figure out what is happening to the market or a particular security, they will tell you it experienced "mixed trading". They can't quite decide what it is all about. This is one of those dishes that I created when I had friends coming for dinner, and I went to the pantry and frig to see what I had. I threw a bunch of things together, not quite certain if I wanted to make a soup or a veggie dish. This is a simple dish that can be made ahead of time and reheated or even eaten cold a few days later.

1 cup black beans
2 cups chicken stock
1 bay leaf
½ cup Wild & Long Grain rice
1 cup chicken stock
1 rib celery – diced
1 center-cut slice of ham – cut into 1" cubes
1/3 cup frozen corn
salt

Optional Topping

Durkee's French-fried onion rings
cheddar cheese – grated

Soak the beans overnight in cold water. Wash and rinse the beans. Boil the rinsed beans in chicken stock (or 2 cups water and 3 bouillon cubes) with bay leaf, celery, and ham cubes. Reduce heat and simmer until beans are done—1 to 2 hours.

Cook rice with remaining cup of chicken stock in covered pot over medium heat until done—50 to 60 minutes.

Mix together the beans, rice, and corn in an uncovered Corning dish and top with onion rings and cheese to taste. Bake in a 350 degree oven for 30 minutes.

This dish makes a nice accompaniment to *MIXED GRILL SUPREME* and is clearly a ***Happy Heart*** without the cheese and onion rings.

POTATOES

You have got to love potatoes, because they are so versatile, they store well, and they cost so little. One of the neat memories of my childhood was my grandmother's potato bin. It was this dark room in the basement that had a little door about three feet off the ground and must have held 30 bushels of potatoes. As I look back, I am fascinated by the fact that they stocked up the way they did in those days. They would go out to the farm and buy their annual potato harvest in the autumn, and then have them all year round. What follows is just a sampling of the many ways to prepare potatoes.

BAKED

The key to a good baked potato is a nice crisp exterior. Do not bake them in foil. Wash the potatoes in cold water, grind some fresh salt over the skins while still wet, and bake in a preheated 400-degree oven for approximately 1 hour. Oven temperature can vary according to whether or not you are baking something else at the same time. You can test doneness by pinching the potato with your fingers. If the potato gives in, it is done—if it is resistant to your squeeze, you need to bake longer. You can slice this potato length wise, salt and pepper it to taste, and eat it just as it is for a *Happy Heart* item that is loaded with vitamins and no fat. A baked potato is a great meal in itself, or an accompaniment to any main course you have made.

TWICE-BAKED

Wash your russet potatoes in cold water, and salt and pepper the skins while they are wet. Bake in a 400-degree oven for 1 hour. Remove the potatoes and slice in half, lengthwise. Scoop out the potatoes with a spoon, and put scoopings in a bowl. Add a tablespoon of sour cream and a tablespoon of butter per potato. Sprinkle a dash of chives, salt and pepper and mix together until smooth. Return the mixture to the hollow potato skins and top with a dash of paprika. Broil for 5 minutes.

BUTTERED PARSLEY NEW POTATOES

Both new potatoes and redskins can be done this way. Boil the potatoes with their skins on for 30 minutes. Drain water, add butter and cut up fresh parsley. Mix together and serve. Easy and tasty!

REAL FRENCH-FRIED

Good French-fried potatoes are not hard to make. It is nice to have a deep fryer, but a good cast iron frying pan or any other sturdy pan will work. The key is to keep the oil hot and the potatoes fresh. I leave the skin on, and slice the fries nice and thick with a big knife. Use Idaho or baker—type potatoes—white or redskin potatoes do not work well, because their flavor is too sweet.

Fry them in Crisco oil or lard until they turn golden brown. Then place them in a bowl that is lined with paper toweling and sprinkle with liberal amounts of salt as they come out of the hot oil. A dash of vinegar will make you think you are at the Board Walk on the Jersey Shore. The lard is a real bad number for your arteries, but hot damn they are good that way!

OLD-FASHIONED MASHED

How many times do I hear people say when they are eating mashed potatoes that they taste so good and they don't understand why they don't make them more often? They are easy to make, and they do not take that long. I think that the key is to allow them to cook sufficiently and then blend them in an electric mixer of some kind. I will forego measurements in favor of ingredients because you really need to blend them to you own liking.

Idaho, russet or baker potatoes – cubed
milk
sweet butter
black pepper
Romano cheese – grated
chives
salt

Boil the potatoes in salted water until they are well cooked—soft to the fork. Drain the potatoes and save a little of the water. You can use this water to thicken your gravy. Put the potatoes in the mixer; add a chunk of butter, and some milk, a little at a time, while the mixer is running. Keep adding small amounts of butter and milk until the potatoes reach desired consistency. When the consistency gets close, add the pepper, chives and cheese. Serve warm and save the leftovers for Potato Pancakes.

GARLIC MASHED POTATOES

We were skiing in Vail over the Christmas holidays, we had dinner at Louie's Jazz Club, and a couple of us had garlic mashed potatoes, which we shared. They were so good, we made reservations to come back the next night just so we could have those potatoes again. They are so easy to make and so yummy to eat.

4—6 Idaho potatoes – cubed
8 cloves of garlic – unpeeled
olive oil
sweet butter
half & half
salt & pepper

Break the garlic away from the head and snip the tops off. Place in a small ovenproof dish and drizzle with olive oil. Bake in 250-degree oven for 1 ½ to 2 hours. Set aside to cool.

Boil the potatoes in salted water until fairly soft—about 25 to 30 minutes. Drain potatoes and put in bowl or mixer. Squeeze garlic from husk into bowl, add 1 tablespoon butter, about 1/3 cup of half and half, and grind fresh pepper to taste. Mash, adding additional half and half if needed. Serve hot and serve with a few lumps so everyone will know they didn't come out of a package.

CHICKEN ROASTED GARLIC MASHED

These mashed potatoes are real knockouts. They are wonderfully easy and mucho tasty. You fix them in the same roaster as your chicken or pork loin.

4-6 redskin potatoes – cubed
1 head of garlic – peeled
1 cup chicken broth
1/4 cup half & half
1 Tbsp sweet butter
3-4 spring onions
salt & pepper

Place the large cubes of potatoes and peeled garlic in the roasting pan with the chicken. Add the chicken broth, season the chicken and potatoes with salt and pepper, cover, and roast the chicken according to normal instructions. When the chicken is done, remove the chicken and remove the potatoes and garlic with a large spoon and transfer to your mixer. Add the butter and half & half and mix to desired consistency. When the potatoes reach proper consistency, diced the spring onions into the last blend of the potatoes. Serve immediately.

The potatoes will have a brownish color to them from the chicken drippings. You will capture some of those drippings with your transfer spoon, which is why you will need less half and half or other liquids.

BAY COUNTRY POTATO & CHEDDAR PIE

This is a great autumn or winter buffet item, because it tastes equally good fresh from the oven or at room temperature. Because it is good at room temperature, it is easy to make earlier in the day. That gives you more time to do other last-minutes things when preparing for large group. I first made this recipe for a Christmas Open House buffet and got a lot of compliments from my guests.

1 pie crust
6-8 medium potatoes – cut into ¼" slices
1 cup sharp cheddar cheese – grated
2 cups buttermilk
4 Tbsp flour
1 egg – beaten
1 bunch spring onions – diced to the junction
salt & pepper

Boil the potatoes in salted water for 6-8 minutes. Rinse and drain immediately. Dust the bottom of a 9" pie plate with flour or corn meal and place the piecrust in the plate. Mix the buttermilk, flour and egg together with salt and pepper to taste. Arrange the potato slices in rows, pour buttermilk mixture over each row, and sprinkle with cheese. Add spring onions in between each row until the pie plate is full and all of the potatoes have been used. Top the pie with a final sprinkling of cheese.

Cover the pie with foil and bake in a 400-degree oven for 1 hour. Remove foil and bake an additional 15 minutes at 400 degrees, or until the top turns golden brown. Serve direct from the oven or at room temperature. You can refrigerate for up to five days and serve at room temperature or microwaved (3-4 minutes). It is great for buffets, because it can be made ahead of time and served either direct from the oven or at room temperature.

BIG FRANK'S PAN FRIED

I think my grandmother fried potatoes for my grandpa every morning. I can remember waking up in the morning to the smell of potatoes frying, and that was even better than the smell of fresh coffee brewing. Oftentimes, my grandmother would use leftover boiled potatoes for pan fries, but you can slice up fresh bakers and achieve the same results. The important aspect of this recipe is to keep the oil in the pan and use a non-stick pan.

2 baker potatoes – sliced
2-4 slices yellow onion
corn oil
salt
black pepper
1 tsp parsley

Heat the oil in the pan and add the potatoes when the oil is hot. Stir for a few minutes, add the onion, salt liberally, and grind lots of fresh pepper on potatoes and onions. Add oil if potatoes begin to dry out. Fry until both sides become dark golden brown. Add parsley the last two minutes of cooking and serve with eggs, fish, or pork chops.

POTATO PANCAKES

This is a good use of left over mashed potatoes, but you can also start from scratch when you are in the mood.

3-4 large Idaho potatoes
1/3 cup cream
1 Tbsp sweet butter
3 large eggs
3 Tbsp flour
1 Tbsp chives
1 cup frozen corn – thawed
½ tsp coarse black pepper

Peel and cube the potatoes and cook them for 20 minutes in boiling salted water. Drain and mash with cream and butter until smooth. Add eggs, flour and chives and continue to mash into smooth mixture. Stir in corn and pepper and ladle batter into hot corn or peanut oil. Cook on each side until golden brown.

GRILLED ROASTED REDSKINS

When you are doing your summer grilling, these potatoes are a nice complement to chicken, steaks, and chops. They are easy to do and lend a nice touch to your meal.

4-6 medium red skin potatoes
1/4 cup olive oil
1 tsp chives
salt & pepper

Cut the potatoes in half and cook in boiling salted water for 5 minutes. Drain from water, place in a large bowl, and drizzle olive oil, chives, and freshly ground salt and pepper over potatoes. Allow to stand at room temperature for 30 minutes. Stir occasionally to spread oil over all potatoes.

Place on a hot grill and cook for approximately 20 minutes, turning so they cook evenly.

SCALLOPED

These potatoes complement a baked ham and can become a full meal if you add chunks of ham and asparagus to this recipe.

5-6 large baking potatoes
6-8 spring onions – diced
1 ½ cups milk
½ stick sweet butter
2 Tbsp flour
2 Tbsp sour cream – heaping
1 ½ tsp salt
3/4 tsp black pepper

Peel the potatoes, slice down the middle, and then again into slices. Put potatoes in a large shallow Corning dish with a cover.

In a small saucepan, heat the milk, butter, flour and sour cream, stirring frequently until mixture becomes smooth. Pour over potatoes, add salt and pepper, and cover and bake for 45 minutes in a 400-degree oven. Remove cover and bake an additional 10 to 15 minutes. Serve hot.

WONDER FRIES

These potatoes really are a wonder, because since they are baked and not fried, they are so easy and contain no fat. When I serve these, people cannot tell that they are not fried because they are crispy and tasty. A complement to any main course and a welcome addition to the breakfast table since they carry no fat.

2 large baker potatoes
Old Bay seasoning

Wash the potatoes in cold water and cut up into 1-inch cubes.

Arrange the potatoes in a metal baking pan, being careful not to have more than one layer of potatoes. Sprinkle some Old Bay on top of the potatoes and bake 35 to 40 minutes in a 400-degree oven. You may want to turn the potatoes once while they are baking.

If you are unable to find Old Bay, you can dust with fresh pepper, salt, and a little cayenne pepper.

Interest income from U.S. Government obligations (bonds) is not taxable on your State income tax return.

BORDER TOWN RICE

If you are making anything with a Southwestern flavor, you will need to do this rice to accompany the main dish. If you like the taste of this rice, you might consider experimenting by adding meats or poultry and turning it into a main dish casserole.

1 cup white rice
1 slice of Bermuda onion – diced
1 Tbsp green peppers – diced
¼ cup green peas
1 tsp cilantro
2 cups chicken stock
½ cup tomatoes – diced
1 Tbsp corn oil

Boil the rice in the chicken stock according to directions. You won't need salt because the chicken stock will provide that. Drain rice and set aside. Heat the corn oil in a large sauté pan. Cook the onion and peppers until onion begins to turn golden. Add the rice, peas, tomatoes and cilantro and stir, cooking for an additional 3 – 4 minutes.

This is a traditional Mexican favorite, but if you want to be different, try serving this as a side dish to your meatloaf, braised short ribs, or any number of fish recipes. Serve hot.

POPEYE'S SPINACH

It really is a pretty nice dish and so simple to fix. This particular spinach has a little more than just the spinach, so it has some additional flavor. I think that the key to good spinach is buying it fresh from the produce counter. Canned spinach is strictly for the comic strips, and even the frozen stuff comes up weak when you are eating it as a side dish.

a basketball-size portion of fresh spinach
1 cup water
1 chicken bouillon cube
2 garlic cloves
2 pats of sweet butter
salt

Wash the spinach. (Check for bugs) Heat the water with garlic, bouillon cube and salt until the water boils and the bouillon cube dissolves. Add the butter and spinach and cover the pot. Allow to stand on the heat for 2 minutes, then turn the heat off. Stir the spinach, cover, and let stand for a few minutes before serving.

BRAISED SPINACH

This is so easy, anybody can do it. You can even turn it into a flambé' if you so desire.

a basketball-size portion of fresh spinach
1 cup water
2 garlic cloves – crushed
2 Tbsp of sweet butter
2 Tbsp olive oil
salt

Bring the salted water to a boil, drop the spinach into the water, and cover for 15 seconds. Drain.

Heat the oil, butter and garlic in a large sauté pan over medium high heat. Pat the spinach into a large disk, drop in the pan, and sauté on each side for about 2 minutes. Serve hot. Want to start a fire? Toss in one ounce of brandy just after you add the spinach, light, and sauté it that way.....Holy smokes we have a dandy bunch of spinach!

ZUCCHINI RUSTICA

This is an easy, but tasty, recipe for zucchini. Simply slice into ½ inch thick slices and fry the zucchini in butter and olive oil over medium heat. Grind some fresh salt and pepper on the zuchs as they cook, top with freshly grated Parmesan cheese, and serve as a side to any dish.

ZUCCHINI DINGHIES

Earlier, you read the recipe for *Italian Zucchini Boats* that called for large zucchinis. This is a recipe that will make use of the much smaller and more common 6 to 8 inch variety. It also makes use of that small amount of left over rice that you did not throw away when you made *New Orleans Beans and Rice* or *Mission Hill's Porcupine Balls.*

3 zucchinis
1/3 cup cooked rice
1 Tbsp butter
2 Tbsp Bermuda onion – diced fine
½ cup cheddar cheese – shredded
½ cup fontina cheese – shredded

Square off the ends of the zucchinis and boil them in salted water for 3 to 4 minutes. Remove from water, slice in half—from end to end—and scoop out insides. Discard insides. Heat the butter and rice until butter is melted and mixed with the rice. Spoon rice in the bottom of the hollow, sprinkle a few onions over rice, and top with cheeses. Pack into hollow so the cheese does not fall out.

Bake in a 375-degree oven until cheese begins to bubble. Remove from oven and serve immediately.

GOO-GOOTS

This is a purely phonetic rendering of a phrase that I do not know how to spell. When I lived in Denver, I had a dear friend by the name of Jerry Galasso who would good-naturedly refer to various friends as ***"Goo-Goots"***. When I would inquire, he would say, "You know, zuchs, tomatoes and stuff cooked together". The reference meant an "earthy" or "common" person in a complimentary way. This recipe is exactly that—a blend of basic things that complement each other and are welcome in any setting.

2 green zucchinis
1 yellow zucchini
1 small Bermuda onion
1 small green pepper
8 asparagus spears
1 Tbsp olive oil
2 medium ripe tomatoes – quartered
2 Tbsp grated Parmesan cheese
salt & pepper

Slice the zuchs, onion, green pepper and asparagus and sauté in a large pan with olive oil for a few minutes over medium heat. When onions begin to become flexible, add the tomatoes and salt and pepper to taste. Use liberal amounts of pepper. Continue to cook until tomatoes break down. Sprinkle with cheese and serve hot. You can use this recipe to accompany the most elegant to the most basic of entrees.

This recipe makes a large serving, so you may wish to invite some friends over, put a pork loin on the barbecue along with some marinated chicken breasts, and make a party for the neighborhood.

TEXAS RODEO CREAM CORN

All the respectable Texas BBQ joints offer cream corn as a side dish. This is also a Southern standard with that nice *Holiday Ham* you will find a little later in this book. In the summer, you can scrape the kernels straight off the cob, but for a year-round treatment, just pick up a bag of frozen corn.

3 slices bacon
32 oz bag frozen corn
cup buttermilk
1 tsp sugar
Tbsp flour
½ stick sweet butter
Tbsp spring onions – diced
salt & pepper

In a cast iron frying pan, cook the bacon until it is crisp. Drain the fat, but do not clean the pan (you want the flavor). Crumble the bacon and set aside.

Place ½ of the corn, the buttermilk, sugar, flour, and butter in your food processor and blend until smooth.

Place the mixture in the frying pan, add the whole corn kernels and bring to a quick boil. Reduce heat to medium and simmer for 5 minutes.

Transfer the cream corn to a serving dish and sprinkle the bacon bits and spring onion over the top. Serve with ribs and white bread.

Don't forget the cold, long-neck bottle of Lone Star beer.

DESSERTS

You will quickly notice that this is not the largest section of this book. There are a few reasons for the lack of substance, and each of those reasons deserves a little bit of attention.

Desserts are often not easy to make in that they require more precision in preparation. You may recall that I like to hand measure ingredients, and in most cases, desserts do not lend themselves to that style of creation.

It is difficult to find any kind of dessert that is a ***Happy Heart*** item, except for the boring things that most people do not want.

I have often wondered why you would forego a larger or additional serving of the entree (if it were really good) just to eat a piece of cake. It is nice to put a cap on the meal, but that can be done quite effectively with fresh fruit, cheeses and a cup of espresso.

Lastly, since this book centers on cooking for small numbers in a romantic setting, why would you even want to eat dessert? It seems to me that if the meal was good and the presentation effective, you might come up with more interesting things to do after the main course.

If, even after all this coaxing to forget about serving dessert, you still find it necessary to serve it; I suggest that you find a good bakery and buy some fresh canolis.

THE BIG SAILOR CHOCOLATE CHIP

Time for uncensored honesty! *Everybody* likes a chocolate chip cookie. Next to the burger, this is probably one of the most American things we eat. Chocolate chip vendors are everywhere we go. They greet us as we disembark from subways and airplanes, and they are found in Manhattan, New York and Manhattan, Kansas. This is an easy recipe that can be made with or without the Grand Marnier without additional altering of the recipe.

2 1/4 cups white flour
3/4 cup sugar
3/4 cup brown sugar
1 tsp baking soda
1 tsp salt
2 sticks sweet butter
½ cup Grand Marnier liqueur
2 large eggs
1 tsp vanilla
2 cups semi-sweet chocolate chips
1 cup walnuts – chopped

In a mixing bowl, combine flour, sugars, baking soda, salt, and set aside.

In another mixing bowl (or your mixer if you wish), blend the butter, Grand Mariner, eggs, and vanilla into a smooth mixture. Add the flour mix until blended and then add chips and nuts.

Drop heaping tablespoons of mixture onto a cookie sheet and bake in a preheated 375-degree oven until golden brown (about 10 minutes) This will make large cookies worthy of a master of the universe to carry to work to tantalize their co-workers.

Suggested drink: Milk in a frosted mug!

MOM'S APPLE PIE

This is an old standard that I actually got from my mother, and she got it from her mother. Remember, basics are back, and this is one of the lowest sugar content recipes that I have seen. You can make your own crust, but Pillsbury already did it so I use theirs. I can remember as a young boy that my grandmother always had one of these in the pantry and one in the oven. I have fond memories of "helping" her make these pies. She would save the apple peels and sprinkle them with sugar and cinnamon and let me eat them while she made the pies. Simple pleasure.

8-9 Granny Smith green apples
2 Pillsbury pie crusts
½ cup sugar
2 oz chopped walnuts
1 tsp arrowroot
1 tsp cinnamon
2 pats sweet butter
juice of ½ lemon
flour
nutmeg

Peel, core and slice the apples and put them in a large mixing bowl. Add the sugar, walnuts, arrowroot, cinnamon, and lemon juice. Mix well.

Dust the bottom of the pie plate with a little flour, lay the crust in the plate, and add the apple mixture. Be sure the apples are well heaped, because they will shrink with baking. Top with the two pats of sweet butter and then place the top crust on the pie. Crimp the edges and poke four fork holes in the top of the crust.

Sprinkle sugar and a dusting of nutmeg on the crust.

Bake the pie in a preheated 400-degree oven for 50 minutes.

THE HOME PLACE PECAN PIE

MidField Plantation is a land grant estate in southern Virginia that has been in the Cooke family since colonial times. It is from this heritage that I acquired this recipe. It is, however, because of my sister's insistence on giving me fresh pecans for Christmas every year that necessitated that I learn to do something with all those nuts. So, here is a recipe that will take you to a genuine Southern plantation in a place that time has almost forgotten.

1 cup sugar
3 eggs
2/3 cup Karo syrup (Lite)
1/4 cup sweet butter
1 ½ cups pecans (½ chopped-½ whole)
2 Tbsp chocolate chips
1 tsp vanilla
1 Pillsbury pie crust

Melt the butter over low heat and set aside.

Beat the 3 eggs until foamy. Fold in the sugar, syrup, melted butter, vanilla, chips and pecans. The big ones will rise to the top.

Dust a pie plate with a little flour and place one crust in the plate. Add the filling to the crust and crimp the edges.

Bake on the middle rack of a preheated 450-degree oven for 5 minutes, reduce heat to 350 degrees, and bake an additional 40 minutes. Remove from oven and allow to set for 30 minutes before serving.

This pie does very well all by itself, but a nice scoop of ice cream next to the pie wedge is almost heavenly. Not ***Happy Heart*** material, but oh so good anyhow.

DOUG'S PEACHY COBBLER

What do you do when somebody drops a case of fresh picked Western Slope peaches on your desk? Doug did that to me, and after I tossed a couple of them into the blender with some ice cream to make a peach smoothie, I knew I had to go for a big time recipe that I could take to the office. Cobbler means exactly that—it is "cobbled" together, so any way you make it will be fine with me. Here was my creation, and it made a hit everyplace it went.

4-5 large Colorado tree-ripened peaches – sliced (or 12-14 grocery store normal size)
1/8 cup raw sugar *
1 Tbsp sweet butter
Tbsp corn starch
1 cup cold water
½ cup pecans – halved
¼ cup Chambord
2 ½ cups Bisquick
1½ cups buttermilk

In a small saucepan, melt the butter. In a bowl, pour the cold water and cornstarch, stirring constantly to eliminate the lumps. Once the lumps are gone, add it to the melted butter and Chambord and cook over medium high heat until it begins to thicken. Set aside.

You can slice the peaches with the skins on, or peel them off, whichever suits your fancy. Fill the inside of a Corning or pottery bowl with the sliced peaches. Sprinkle the sugar over the peaches; add the pecans, the cornstarch and the Chambord. Stir and toss.

In a separate bowl, mix the Bisquick with the buttermilk just enough to make a smooth mixture. Do not over mix; otherwise the dough will become stiff

Spoon the buttermilk Bisquick mix over the peaches, dust with a little raw sugar, and bake in a 350-degree oven for 45 minutes.

Serve hot with ice cream, or at room temperature. Either way, people will love it!

***If** the peaches are summer tree-ripe sweet, you could eliminate the sugar altogether.

Always check your tire pressure when the tires are cold—but check your transmission fluid when the engine is hot.

FLAMING DESSERTS

When I created **Veal Toscano,** I needed a dessert to go with it. "Uncle Ben" always enjoyed bananas and was so frequently seen eating one that it eventually became his trademark. Since I named the veal after Jigs, it was fitting that the bananas be named after Ben.

A few years ago, I was at the Montreal Jazz Festival with an old friend and his 21-year-old son. One evening, as we sat over dinner in Old Montreal discussing food preparation, I was pleased to see the interest young Joel Pelsue had in preparing flaming desserts.

This really is a simple item to prepare if you have a fondue set. If you are going to make this and other tableside creations, you should invest in a single portable gas burner. You can find them at most specialty cooking outlets. If you didn't plan ahead to have a tableside burner, then you substitute some canned heat—Sterno—and a rack to set the pan on. The fondue stand can get you through this until you can find the proper equipment.

In all of my flaming recipes, I use only fruit-based liqueur, and that eliminates the harshness that some people complain about when you have used brandies, vodkas, and kirshwasser for the igniter. The last three will give you a much bigger flame and work well for flaming meats and seafood; however, I prefer the more mellow flame of a fruit liqueur after dinner. The fruit liqueur will not leave as harsh a bite on your palate like the other three will. It will burn with a nice, blue, gentle flame instead of a three alarm raging inferno that the higher-proof alcohols give you.

BANANAS PISCIOTTA

This is such an easy recipe it is almost embarrassing in its simplicity. The key in this dessert is to get the sauté pan hot before attempting the presentation. Remember that this is pure entertainment, so take time to set it up properly. Have all your items lined up and your work surface organized ahead of time. I always fix this right on the table so it is important to have the table clean and all of your ingredients within easy reach.

You should have a portable gas burner. If you don't own one, go out and buy it! You will also need two large tablespoons for serving.

Ben always seemed to have a half-eaten banana in his hand, so I thought it fitting to name my best dessert after a good friend.

sweet butter
4 large firm bananas
Chambord
Cointreau
2 pints gourmet frozen yogurt or ice cream
2 oz slivered almonds
powdered sugar

Set a 7-inch sauté pan on top of your burner. Allow the pan to heat while you slice the bananas length wise and then in half to create 16 banana slices. You can serve the ice cream in 4 bowls, and each person will get 4 banana slices in their bowl.

Place a pat of butter in the pan, along with six bananas. When the butter begins to sizzle, add two or three ounces each of Chambord and Cointreau. Hold the pan in your left hand, slightly tilted toward the flame. If the flame does not jump into the pan, then place a tablespoon in your right hand and gently fan the flame toward the open pan. It should ignite with a subtle blue flame. Keep the pan over the heat to assist in the burning. DO NOT add more liqueur to the pan when it is burning. You do not want to create a Molontov Cocktail! If the pan is not hot, the flame will extinguish soon. Allow it to burn for a few minutes, keeping the flame stoked. You can spoon the flaming bananas over the ice cream while they are still flaming for a nice affect. Sprinkle the almonds and a teaspoon of powdered sugar over the ice cream and eat promptly.

Repeat the process again and you will serve four people.

HOLIDAYS

TURKEY

It is too bad we do not eat more turkey. It is an excellent low-fat, high-protein meat, and it is not that difficult to fix. The hardest part of preparing a turkey is the time required to cook it, but when you consider how many wonderfully-easy second meals you get from one bird, you will find that the *average* prep time is quite low. Most people want to use a fresh bird if at all possible. Some think that a 15 # bird is just about ideal. It certainly does not require that much cooking time, unless you want to slow cook it at 225-degrees overnight. If you slow cook it, you need to start the oven at 425-degrees for 15 minutes and then turn it down to 225-degrees. I would also advise cooking it breast side down. The dark meat is moister and will naturally baste the white meat below it when it is upside down in the pan.

As for basting, I prefer to do the turkey in a large enough roaster that you can put the top on it and not touch the turkey while it cooks. If you can't find a roaster big enough, then make an aluminum foil tent over the bird, and don't open the door while it roasts.

Be sure you remove all the extra "parts" from the cavity of the bird and thoroughly wash the inside and outside in cold water.

Salt and pepper the inside of the bird and pack the stuffing into the cavities in front and back of the bird. Roast the neck and giblets in the pan, because they flavor the gravy.

Rub the outside of the bird with Extra Virgin olive oil and then liberally salt and pepper the outside of the bird. Sprinkle some garlic powder and a touch of paprika over the skin and place in a pre-heated 450-degree oven for 15 minutes. Reduce the heat to 325 degrees and roast for approximately 20 minutes per pound.

The best way to tell when it is done is to stick a meat thermometer in the thigh, but you are able to test doneness if the legs and wings move easily. You can always error on the long side if the bird has a lot of juice in the pan while it is roasting. Add a cup of chicken stock to the pan to provide additional basting juices.

If you remove the cover for the last 45 – 50 minutes, the skin will brown nicely. You can baste once about midway through this process.

Allow the bird to stand on the counter for 15 to 20 minutes before carving. It is not a problem if it sits for an hour while you are eating, but be sure you bone and refrigerate it soon after dinner to prevent food poisoning!

HOLIDAY TURKEY STUFFING

The most difficult part of stuffing a bird is the time it takes to prepare all the ingredients that go into the stuffing on a day that is already impacted with so many things to do. You can do the sausage and mushrooms the night before, but I find it is just as easy to get up early and allocate an hour to the stuffing. It is helpful to get out all your mixing bowls, sauté pans, and ingredients and line them up on your preparation surface ahead of time. This recipe will fill the front and back of a 20—lb. turkey, so you can invite a lot of friends for dinner. If you have a smaller bird, you can reduce the quantities, or you can mound the stuffing at the end of the turkey roaster and have lots of leftovers.

1 lb pork sausage
8 oz mushrooms
1 pkg. bread stuffing for 7—lb. bird
1 pkg. corn bread stuffing for 7-lb. bird
1 stick sweet butter
1 Granny Smith apple – cored and diced
1 cup celery hearts – diced w/ tops
½ cup Bermuda onion – diced
2 oz slivered almonds
1/4 cup fresh parsley
1/3 cup Parmesan cheese – grated
2 Tbsp sage
1 Tbsp rosemary
1 Tbsp thyme

1 cup water w/2 chicken bouillon cubes
½ cup fresh orange juice
3 large eggs
olive oil
garlic powder
chives
salt & pepper

Set a small saucepan on the back of the stove with the stick of sweet butter in it and melt slowly. Turn heat off and let stand until later.

Sauté the sausage until brown, and set aside. Sauté the sliced mushrooms in olive oil, garlic salt and chives, and set aside. Heat the cup of water with the bouillon cubes until they dissolve, and set aside.

In a large mixing bowl, combine all the remaining ingredients, adding the chicken broth and orange juice with a liberal amount of salt and black pepper. Sprinkle salt and pepper in the cavity, and stuff the bird.

This is a messy job, and the only way I know how to do this, is to roll up your sleeves and get your hands into it. It will make a mess, but it can all be cleaned up once the bird is in the oven.

It is important that once the bird is stuffed, it goes in the oven and is roasted immediately. Do not stuff the bird ahead of time.

WILD RICE STUFFING OR SIDE DISH

This is a tasty stuffing for your holiday bird, but it also can be a hit as a separate side dish. The recipe calls for a lot of wild rice, so do your shopping to find a good buy because this stuff can be expensive, unless you are willing to take a ride to **St. Ignace, Michigan,** in which case I know where you can buy it for $2.00 a pound.

2 cups wild rice
½ cup long grain brown rice
3 cups water
3 cups chicken broth
1 cup baked ham – diced
1 cup butter beans
½ cup frozen corn
2 Tbsp sweet butter
1 leek – diced
1 celery rib – diced
2 Tbsp almonds – slivered

It is a good idea to sift through the rice to make sure no foreign objects are in there. Cook the rice in the water and chicken stock until the rice is done. That will vary so just keep testing it after 35 minutes. If all the liquid boils away, add more water.

If you are going to stuff the bird, mix all the rest of the ingredients with the rice, fill the inside of the turkey, and roast according to instructions.

If you are not going to use this as a stuffing, then mix all the ingredients—except the almonds—in a covered Corning and bake in 325-degree oven for 45 minutes. Sprinkle the almonds over stuffing, and serve hot or at room temperature on a buffet.

CORKY'S HOLIDAY MEAT PIE

Traditions are fun. I have enjoyed one that originated with my maternal grandmother and was passed to me by my mother during the holidays. One of the great things about the season from mid-November through the first of January, is the wonderful aromas that come from our kitchens. When you come in from the brisk cold air into a kitchen that is warm with goodies in the oven, you know that the world is in order. This pie is one of those contributions to that time of the year. It is also so rich, that you will long remember it and may not get an urging for it until the next holiday season!

2 Pillsbury pie crusts
3 medium potatoes
2 lbs. ground pork
3/4 lb. ground veal or ground round
3 large slices white onion – chopped fine
1 egg – beaten
1 ½ tsp black pepper
1 tsp allspice
1 tsp parsley
1/4 tsp thyme
½ tsp cinnamon
salt

If you wish to make your own pie crust, any recipe will do, but it is much easier to use the store-bought version. (Brush it with an egg wash before baking, and nobody will know.) Dice the potatoes and boil them until they are ready for mashing. Mash to a thick consistency and set aside to cool. You can use a little milk and butter if you like, but keep it thick.

My mom used to pre-cook the meat to remove some of the fat, but if you use very lean meat, that will not be necessary. I buy a boneless pork loin roast and grind it myself.

Mix the meats, egg, onion, mashed potatoes, and seasonings in a large bowl until they are well blended and form a large solid mass.

Dust the pie plate with a little corn meal, and lay the piecrust in the plate. Take the meat mixture in one large mass, pack it fully in the pie plate, and form it into the shell. Top with the top crust, crimp, and place four sets of fork holes in the crust.

Bake in a preheated 375-degree oven for 1 1/2 hours. Serve hot or at room temperature.

CAVILL'S CIOPPINO

The Italians have a marvelous tradition of a big fish dinner on Christmas Eve that usually includes anywhere from 7 to 12 different seafood dishes. Since Cioppino includes so many different seafoods. I have decided it can be a substitute when you are having less than twenty people over for dinner. It does not have to be Christmas to enjoy this hearty offering, but it is a festive dish, so it goes well with any celebration at any time of the year. In the San Francisco Bay area, I have seen people line up at fish houses to buy this delight to take home with them so they don't have to go through the work of making their own. That shortcut takes away all the fun of a relatively easy dish—provided you have, at least, a 14-quart stockpot! Invite at least three others to the table.

1/3 cup olive oil
1 medium white onion – diced fine
4 garlic cloves – minced
5 32 oz cans of Italian tomatoes – pulsed
2 cups good white wine
2 Tbsp basil
1 Tbsp oregano

2-3 Tbsp crushed red pepper
1 tsp rosemary
3 bay leaves
1 lb. scallops
1 lb. large shrimp
1 lb. mussels
4 lobster tails – fresh or frozen
24 Cherrystone or Steamer clams
salt & pepper

In that large stockpot, place the olive oil and onion and heat over medium heat until the onion becomes translucent. Be careful not to burn it. Add the canned tomatoes, two 32 oz cans of water, and the spices—including the garlic—and cover. Bring to a rapid boil, turn off the heat, and allow to stand for 60 minutes. This recipe is done best if you make this part the day before, and refrigerate overnight.

While the sauce is re-heating, you should add the 2 cups of wine. Clean the mussels and clams by scrubbing them in cold water. Peel the shrimp, but leave the lobster meat in the tail. Cook all the seafood, covered, on medium high heat for 10 – 15 minutes. Turn heat off and allow to stand in a covered pot for 5 minutes. Be sure that all clams and mussels have opened, and be careful to discard any that have not.

This is a genuine ***Happy Heart*** but most importantly, it is also a happy palate recipe.

Serve this meal in large bowls with *lots* of hard crust Italian bread for soaking up the sauce. Don't forget to put an empty bowl in the middle of the table to collect the shells. This will be a fun meal, unless you invited a bunch of sissies for dinner! Since this dish is very Italian, you might want to serve *Nanny's Simple Lettuce Salad* at the end of the cioppino dish, and then finish with a plate of cheeses and fruit. You can drink a red or white wine with this dinner. The white is traditional because of the presence of seafood, but the strong marinara can handle a robust red like a Chianti Classico or an old vine Zinfandel.

CHRISTMAS PORK LOIN

For years, I was the king of turkey. I would fix a turkey on Thanksgiving and again for Christmas, and no one complained, because my bird was the best in the land. Then in 1993, I decided to do something different. I had read that Julia Child had fixed a pork loin for one of her Christmas dinners, so I thought I would experiment. Here is the final result. This recipe will serve 12 people, and if you have leftovers, they are marvelous cold and in salads a couple of days later.

6 1 lb. pork tenderloins
½ cup soy sauce
1/4 cup olive oil
3 cloves garlic – crushed
1 Tbsp onion – diced
1 Tbsp vinegar
1/4 tsp crushed red pepper
½ tsp sugar

1 10 oz pkg. chopped spinach
1/3 cup Gorgonzola cheese
½ cup pignola nuts – toasted
salt

Butterfly and pound the tenderloins flat. Spread the spinach, cheese and pignola nuts evenly between the tenderloins. Salt the tenderloins to taste, roll them, and tie with string. Marinate the tenderloins in the soy sauce, olive oil, garlic, onion, vinegar, red pepper, and sugar in a covered dish for 3 to 4 hours. Place tenderloins and marinade in open pan and bake at 350-degrees for 1-½ hours.

Make gravy from pan drippings by adding water, milk, and flour.

Serve with *Red Bells and Blue Crabs Soup, Caesar Salad, Twice Baked Potatoes*, green beans, fresh bread, and white wine.

FESTIVE PIGGIE

This one works anytime of the year—Christmas or Cinco de Mayo and all the other holidays in between. You should have four people at the table to do this justice. The roast is a big one, but it is important to have a good-sized leftover for sandwiches the rest of the week. Holidays are busy times, so this recipe will be welcome, because it is a nice touch and very easy to prepare. This meal will give you time to spend with your guests and not be worked over by the time you have to put the meal on the table. Elegance comes from the way you serve the meal and how you enjoy your table guests, not how complex the recipe is.

6-7# boneless pork loin roast
15 oz apple juice
1 oz Galiano
365 Caribbean Jerk Rub
fresh cilantro
1 slice thick-cut bacon
1 green pepper

Place the roast is a large turkey roaster. Mix the apple juice and Galiano together and pour it over the roast. Shake a liberal amount of the Caribbean rub on the roast. Don't be afraid to put a lot on. Place a handful of fresh cilantro sprigs on top of the roast and add the slice of bacon over them. This will keep the cilantro in place and moisten the meat while it roasts. Cover the pan and let the roast stand at room temperature for 30 minutes. Place in a cold oven—cover off—and set the heat at 350-degrees. Roast approximately 2 hours, or until the internal temperature reaches about 150 degrees. Remove from oven, cover, and allow to rest for 15 –20 minutes prior to slicing. Remove the green peppers from the pan and serve the juice over the sliced meat.

I served *Texas Rodeo Cream Corn* (which I made ahead of time) and *Mixed Trading,* along with some store-bought biscuits, and I had everybody coming back for seconds!

TIDEWATER BLACK EYE PEAS

I am a sucker for traditions. Every region in the country and every ethnic group have holiday traditions, and the nice part of living today, is that you don't have to belong to that particular group to share and enjoy their traditions. For example, the Old South, particularly Virginia, has a New Year's Day tradition of black eye peas for good luck. They call it ***Hoppin' John***. This recipe will get you close to the Hoppin' John. Some add rice or serve it just as it is. You can decide—after all, it is now your tradition! Whatever you do with it, I hope it brings you good luck at any time of the year.

1 32 oz bag of black eye peas
3 slices of onion – diced fine
4 strips of thick-cut smoked bacon or ¼ lb. pancetta
2 ribs of celery – diced
clove of garlic
5 14 oz cans chicken broth
1 bay leaf

Soak the peas overnight in a bowl covered with water. Drain and rinse before final prep.

Sauté the bacon, onion, and garlic in large, heavy-gauge stockpot. Add the remaining ingredients and simmer on top of the stove for about 2 hours. Add salt and pepper to taste.

Here comes the good part—serve just as it is, or throw some fire into it with a little Tabasco sauce!

Now go whip up some *Phoenix Corn Bread,* and serve up some of *Nanny's Simple Lettuce Salad.* You'll have an easy Sunday night supper.

HOLIDAY HAM

Easter is the traditional time to serve and eat ham. Early Christians, who were converts from Judaism, celebrated this holiday with ham as a symbol of being set free from the Judaic Law that forbid the eating of pork. While ham is eaten all across this great country, there are many different varieties of ham and many, many different ways of preparing ham. For this recipe, Mom and I suggest you buy a fully-cooked shank portion. In reality, all you are doing is heating the ham for consumption, and it takes a lot less time and work to do this.

1 7 to 10 lb. ham
½ cup brown sugar
½ cup crushed pineapple w/ juice
½ cup orange marmalade
½ cup rum

Trim off the hide and excess fat from the ham and then criss cross score the ham with a sharp knife.

Mix all 4 ingredients together, cover the ham with the glaze, and bake in a covered roaster in a pre-heated 300-degree oven for 2 to 2 ½ hours. The sauce can be used to garnish the ham slices when they are served.

This ham will feed six to eight people, and the left over bone and meat will be perfect for *Granny's French Pea Soup* or *New England Boiled Dinner.* Check out the Veggie section for the *Texas Rodeo Cream Corn,* and the *Tidewater Black Eye Peas* for a couple of side dish options for this dinner.

Maximize your 401K contributions while you are working, but when you leave, roll them over into a self-directed IRA.

NANNY'S EASTER CHEESE PIE

The Italians have a tradition about an Easter cheese pie. I have seen a number of variations on this recipe, but this is my favorite. The "pie" is baked in a cake dish or large Pyrex or Corning casserole dish, but it is called a pie, nonetheless. This recipe takes a little bit of effort, but it is a great two-person job. Perhaps the most difficult part of this recipe is finding the citron. I remember Nanny and I driving all over Denver one time trying to find citron. Persevere; the zesty flavor of the citron will be worth it!

3 lbs. fresh ricotta cheese
1 ½ cups sugar
9 large eggs
juice of ½ lemon
2 tsp vanilla
½ tsp cinnamon
1 Tbsp corn starch
½ cup citron
½ cup semi-sweet chocolate chips
½ cup maraschino cherries – halved
¼ cup sliced almonds

Fold together, in a very large mixing bowl, all of the ingredients above until a smooth creamy consistency develops. Do this by hand. In fact, if you are feeling really sensual, use your hands to mix this together. Set aside until crust is ready.

Crust

2 ½ cups flour
3 large eggs
½ stick butter
2/3 cup sugar
2 tsp vanilla

Mix crust items in a large mixing bowl with electric mixer until the mixture begins to pebble. Finish mixing by hand. Sprinkle flour on clean surface, and flour hands to knead dough until consistent. Roll out to a rectangular pattern and transfer to a 10 x 12 x 3 baking dish that has been buttered. You may have to pull off excess pieces from one side to fill in the crust. You have to be sure the crust comes all the way to the top of the baking dish. Otherwise, your filling will run down between the crust and the dish, and that is a big mess! Pour filling into the baking dish once the crust is in place.

Bake in a pre-heated 350-degree oven for 1 1/4 hour on the middle rack. Turn off oven, open door, and let stand 30 to 60 minutes in the warm oven. Remove from oven and let stand at room temperature for an additional 30 minutes before serving.

If you have any left over, it means you did not invite enough people for Easter dinner. This recipe will feed a dozen. If you have leftovers, I would recommend refrigeration to maintain the moistness.

Prep time can take anywhere from 30 minutes to an hour. You have an additional 1 hour and 15 minutes of baking time, plus another hour of standing time, so it is a good idea to do this recipe early in the day. You can even do it the night before and serve it at room temperature.

BREAKFAST

Everybody knows this is the most important meal of the day, and yet few cookbooks give much attention to this subject. There are a couple of reasons for this, not the least of which is the argument that breakfast should be cereals and juices and not fat and cholesterol. I agree. We really do not need too much advice on how to pour our cereal or cut the banana that goes on the top of it. Most people that I know tell me that breakfast is the healthiest meal that they eat most of the days of the month, but they also like to indulge once in awhile on weekends and give their arteries a little surprise.

If you have made an effort to fix a first-class meal the night before, you may want to go the extra distance and really put on the dog for breakfast the next morning. If that is the case, get out of bed, take a shower, and go to a restaurant.

If you really do not want to go to a restaurant—or even a truck stop—then the following pages may be of some help to you.

Please note, however, that every breakfast that follows requires that you quietly get up before the rest of the house and put on a pot of coffee. I do not personally drink coffee—other than espresso and then only after dinner—but I love the aroma that it gives off when it is brewing. We are into setting the right mood, so if you do not drink the coffee, make it anyway and when it gets cold, you can water your plants with it. When your partner wakes to the smell of fresh coffee brewing, you can do no wrong if you serve a cup of it in bed (or fresh o.j., if neither of you drink coffee). It may even make breakfast unnecessary. It could also go a long way in forgiving any "rubber" eggs that may follow.

In any case, these are neither fancy nor, in most cases, complicated offerings for breakfast—just simple day starters that you should find tasty and satisfying. A good start to any day.

EGGS JOSHUA

When they are done right, there is nothing like some light fluffy scrambled eggs. When they are done wrong, they usually are served on an airplane. The secret to these eggs is to cook them over low to medium heat, and not to overcook them. Take your time and start your day off to a good beginning.

5 large eggs
3 Tbsp cream cheese
½ cup sharp cheddar cheese – shredded
1 Tbsp chives
1/3 cup milk
2 Tbsp butter
black pepper

Beat the eggs, milk, chives and pepper in a bowl until they are smooth and frothy. Fold in the cheeses, breaking the cream cheese into large chunks.

Heat a non-stick pan over low to medium heat. Add the butter and the eggs. Keep turning the eggs until the liquid appearance is gone and the eggs begin to clump together in a mound in the center of the pan. Cover the pan and turn off heat, but let stand on the stove for 4 or 5 minutes. Serve with *Wonder Fries*, sliced fresh tomatoes, toasted bagels, and a frosted mug of milk.

You have servings for four normal people or two teen-agers.

Prep Notes: This is a perfect two-person menu if one person does nothing but the eggs, and the other does all the other preparation.

It is critical that you use a large, non-stick sauté pan for the eggs, and that means you need a wooden or plastic spatula for turning them.

A common kitchen fork will beat the eggs just fine, but a whisk can be useful if you want to add a little flair to your preparation.

TRUCK STOP EGGS

Everyone knows the best industrial grade eggs come from a truck stop, but the problem is finding the truck stop. Here is your road map.

1 cast iron frying pan
4 large strips thick bacon
2 large eggs
black pepper

Fry the bacon in the frying pan over medium heat. Set bacon aside and crack the eggs into the pan. Grind lots of pepper on top of the eggs. Use your spatula to bathe the bacon fat over the top of the eggs until the yolk is slightly white in color.

Serve with *Big Frank's Pan Fried Potatoes*, toasted whole-wheat bread, and hot coffee.

EGGS SCAMPI

Remember that an egg is nothing more than an oval blob of glue waiting for some flavor to attach itself to. I don't think that an egg by itself has much flavor, and at the same time, an egg will take on any flavor that you give it. Here I cook my eggs much the same way I would shrimp scampi.

2 large eggs
1 Tbsp olive oil
1 tsp butter
1/8 tsp garlic powder
black pepper

For these eggs, you need a small cast iron frying pan that is covered with ceramic or some other non-stick frying pan.

Heat the olive oil and butter, add the garlic powder, and stir until it begins to brown. Immediately add the eggs, dust with some freshly ground black pepper, and cook with a cover until eggs are done according to your preference.

Serve with fried ham, English muffins, and a slice of fontina cheese. A tall, cold Mimosa is an ideal drink with this breakfast.

SAUSAGE GRAVY & BISCUITS

This is a real Southern favorite that can be found on many tables of the Old South. I have often imagined that Big Daddy played by Burl Ives in ***Cat on a Hot Tin Roof*** must have had this for breakfast on the set every morning. It is a big item on the menu at Bob Evans restaurants along the interstate system, so if you want the real thing, you can either travel the interstates or make your own at home. This is the easy way to do it.

GRAVY

1 lb. pork sausage
1 ½ cups milk
2 Tbsp flour
black pepper

BISCUITS

2 1/4 cups Bisquick
2/3 cup Milk
2 Tbsp Romano cheese – grated

Fry the pork sausage over medium heat until it is completely cooked. Be sure that you break it into small pieces while it cooks. You can fix this part a day ahead of time and refrigerate the meat (with the oil) and break it into even smaller pieces when it is cold. In a mixing bowl, combine the flour and milk and stir it until all the flour lumps are dissolved. Add to the hot meat and stir until it begins to bubble. Grate some fresh black pepper on the meat, cover the pan, and turn off the heat. Once again, this part can be made a day ahead of time and refrigerated until you need it. This makes the actual prep time at breakfast limited to the biscuits and squeezing the juice.

In a large mixing bowl, combined all 3 biscuit ingredients, mixing and kneading until you have a nice, round ball. Flour your hands and the counter top and roll the ball into a log about 9 or 10 inches long. Slice the log into 9 or 10 pieces. Bake in a 450-degree oven for 9 to 10 minutes. Split biscuits and spoon hot gravy over them. If you feel guilty about the fat and cholesterol, eat a bowl of fresh blueberries and drink a glass of hand squeezed orange juice.

If you want absolute authenticity, you must look over the top of your eye glasses and in your best Southern drawl say, ***"Mendacity, sister woman".***

EGGS CHESAPEAKE

In my infinite love affair with the Blue crab, I had to come up with a legitimate way to have them for breakfast. It is a close take-off on the famous eggs benedict, but I think that you will find them much more rewarding if you can obtain fresh crab meat.

2 English muffins
cooked chopped spinach
3-4 Tbsp lump crab meat
1-2 tsp mayo
lemon juice
cayenne pepper
2 poached eggs
Béarnaise sauce

Mix the crab meat, mayo, a squirt of lemon juice and a dash of cayenne pepper together to make a little crab mix.

Toast the muffins lightly and spread a little spinach on the bottoms of the muffins. Butter and set aside the smaller top portions to eat later or while you are putting the rest of the breakfast together.

Carefully build a nice thick crab layer over the spinach and top with a poached egg and a spoon of béarnaise sauce. (Use the store-bought stuff—this is breakfast, and there are more important requirements on your time than cooking all day.) Place muffins on a baking sheet and bake in a 450-degree oven for about 5 minutes. Serve hot. This sure beats a bowl of Wheaties with sliced bananas.

This is an elegant offering, so you could consider making a pitcher of Mimosas to go with the breakfast. If you make a Mimosa, you really should use freshly squeezed oranges and a decent bottle of champagne. Decorate the glass with a slice of orange and start the day in fine style.

PIZZOLA EGGS

I guess I may have been part of the original pizza generation that grew up just as national pizza franchises were beginning to come into being. In college, I can remember being so fond of pizza that we would leave the unfinished pizza sitting on the kitchen counter and polish it off for what was loosely called "breakfast" the next morning. Now you know why mothers worried when we went off to college. This is a much more elegant—and healthy—rendering of that "breakfast pizza".

2 small Boboli shells
4 strips bacon
2 slices tomato
grated cheddar cheese
sprinkle of basil
sprinkle of chives
2 eggs – basted sunny side up
freshly ground black pepper

Cut the strips of bacon in half and fry them the way you like them. Remove from pan and put on paper toweling. Fry the eggs (sunny side up) and remove from pan.

Place 4 pieces of bacon on each Boboli shell and top with 1 slice of tomato. Grate some cheese directly on top of the tomato and sprinkle basil and chives on top of cheese. Use fresh herbs if you have them. Put 1 egg on each Boboli and grind some fresh black pepper on top of the egg.

Place the Bobolis in a pre-heated 425-degree oven and bake for 5 to 6 minutes, until cheese is soft.

Serve on a plate and eat with a knife and fork. If you want to make believe you are still in college, you can indulge in a bottle of beer with your pizzolas.

NO NAME CAFÉ HEUVOS RANCHEROS

My son lived in a Latino neighborhood in Denver, and we would walk to a little café on Santa Fe Boulevard for breakfast on Saturday mornings. This café had no name but wonderful green chile and mouth-watering breakfast offerings. It took me nearly a dozen visits to figure out how they made this particular recipe. I was quite excited when I was able to make this recipe with ingredients that I was able to buy in Annapolis, Maryland. There are a number of ingredients in this recipe, but if you make the green chile a day or two ahead of time, it will not be that much of a chore, since the other items can be store-bought without compromising the recipe.

2 eggs per person
2 corn tortillas per person
1 pkg. hash brown potatoes
1 can refried beans
grated Monterey Jack & cheddar cheese

GREEN CHILE
4 pork chops
paprika
salt & pepper
3 Tbsp corn oil
1 small onion – diced
2 cloves garlic – sliced
6 poblano peppers – sliced
3 cups chicken stock
1 tsp cumin
1/4 cup fresh cilantro – chopped

CHICKEN STOCK
3 quarts water
1 chicken leg
1 chicken thigh

2 chicken bouillon cubes
1 Tbsp parsley

Chicken Stock

In a medium stockpot, bring the water, chicken, bouillon cubes, diced carrot, and celery to a hearty boil. Cover and cook for a couple of hours. The chicken meat should fall right off of the bones. Pick out the bones and skin and run the remainder through your food processor or blender. Set aside. You can do this part as much as three days ahead of time.

Green Chile

Trim the meat off the pork chops and cut into 1-inch cubes. Dust with salt and pepper and paprika and brown in corn oil over medium high heat in a large sauté pan, along with the bones. When the meat is well browned, remove the cubes and bones from the pan, reserving the oil. Add the onion, garlic, and poblano peppers, stirring frequently while they brown. Remove the onions, garlic, and peppers with a slotted spoon and blend in your food processor. Return the mixture to your pan, along with the chicken stock, pork meat, cumin and cilantro. Cover and cook over moderate heat for 1-½ hours. This step can also be done at least three days ahead of time.

The Finale

Fry the eggs, sunny side up, heat the refried beans, and fry the hash browns. Heat the corn tortillas in a little corn oil, about 10 seconds on each side, putting one tortilla under each egg. Add a spoon of refried beans and hash browns to each plate, and top with the green chile and a sprinkle of grated cheese over the entire plate.

Heat some flour tortillas and dig in. If you feel like you need a little cold beer to wash this down, go right ahead—they do it that way down in old Monterey.

FRANK'S BIG BREAKFAST

My maternal grandfather was a physical man—old country stout and strong in both his physique and spirit. Because he did heavy physical work on his job, it was important to eat a hearty breakfast. To my relatives who knew him, I must say clearly that this is a young boy's recollection of how it was, and moreover, it is my own license on how I now think that it should have been. I seem to remember these huge breakfasts of whatever was left in the refrigerator from the prior day. My grandmother would rise early and have the entire stovetop in action to create these legendary feasts. Here is what I think the Big Breakfast should look like.

Eggs Joshua
Truck Stop Eggs
sauerkraut
Polish sausage
fried ham steaks
Big Frank's Pan Fried Potatoes
Pigs in the Blanket **(take your pick on which kind)**
chicken legs
Mom's Apple Pie
sweet cinnamon rolls
Honey-Cointreau Banana Nut Bread
toasted rye bread

This is a breakfast worthy of the entire rugby team. Invite them over on a Saturday morning and serve an ice-cold European beer like Beck's or Heineken, and watch them come alive!

If you really want to do this Paul Bunyan style, toss in a couple of pasties!

WHAT TO DRINK

Let me be perfectly clear about this issue, I am not a wine expert. In fact, I know very little about wine. I do not pretend to know one vintage from another and am not sure what a good year for any given grape might be. This is far too extensive a field for my limited skills, but I do have some sense about what makes a good companion to certain types of foods, and I guess that has some merit and value. If this concerns you, then do your shopping and dining at good wine stores and restaurants and simply ask for assistance. Over time, if you get good advice, you will know more about the subject than I do.

I have learned, for example, that the finest of wines when stored, decanted or served improperly may end up being no better than something that you drank at college fraternity parties. What I would like to do is give you a few tips on the following pages on how to best enjoy whatever you may chose to drink.

There are no ironclad rules when it comes to drinking, anymore than there are ironclad rules when it comes to eating—other than moderation. So much of what and how we eat is governed by convention—we simply learned to do it that way. Italians learn to eat their salad after the main course, while most Americans eat it before the main course. Is one right and the other wrong?

As a general rule, a red wine is the better choice for red meats, and a white wine a better choice for seafood and poultry. But there are exceptions. Oftentimes the choice of the proper wine selection hinges on the simple matter of, *"I do not like white wine, or red wine gives me a headache"*, in which case, it makes little sense to force something upon someone when they have determined that they do not like it.

It is also a general rule that white wine should be chilled and red wine served at room temperature, but I also know people who chill their red wines. Not too chic, but people do it. Hopefully, a little education will correct some of these disgusting, ugly, and positively boring social blunders! Just kidding!

Here is everything that you will ever need to know about drinking before, during, after, or without your meal.

WATER

It is not only good for you—it is good. Americans need to drink more red wine and more water. Most of us ignore water for one simple reason—we do not honor it properly. Serve your water in a big glass, and serve it with lots of ice. Top it with a generous slice of lemon, lime or orange, and you have an elegant drink that complements any meal you can serve. If you have bad tasting or tasteless tap water, you can always buy spring water (This is not mineral water.) in most grocery stores and that will solve that problem. You may be surprised at how good water actually tastes when it is properly chilled and served.

DESIGNER WATER

I suppose this is the next best thing to ordinary water, but the cost makes it questionable. Once again, this is simply water, so follow the same guidelines offered above. Large glass, good crystal, lots of ice, and dress it up with a slice of lemon, lime, orange, kiwi, or strawberry. Place the bottle or bottles on the table so people can refill during the meal. It also dresses the table and encourages consumption. San Pellegrino is always my first choice in bottled dinner water.

MILK

Sometimes nothing will do other than a good, cold glass of milk. I always keep a couple of very large frosted mugs in my freezer, and I can tell you that there is nothing like a frosted mug of milk when the occasion calls for it. That is it—simple. Skim milk is best for your heart if you are over 21 years of age. Milk does provide a good source of calcium and that, too, is important. The key here is to make the service as cold as possible.

SODA

I enjoy the fact that we call it different things in different parts of the country. Some places it is called *POP*, and in others it is *SODA* and then some call it *SODA POP*. It is great on picnics and with sandwiches, but like water, you need to make it good and cold and do not be afraid to give it a garnish. Colas do well with lemons and limes, and uncolas appreciate oranges and strawberries.

SCOTCH

Not everybody likes scotch. For many, it is an acquired taste that comes over a period of time. I guess the truly good thing about scotch is the simplicity of it. You do not drink it with Coke or Seven Up, so about the only question is whether to drink it straight or on the rocks. If you follow the lead of the Scots, you will probably drink it straight up with a splash of water, but I like mine on the rocks with a twist of lemon, if it is a blended scotch. If it is a single malt, then I definitely take it "neat" or straight. As with most of the finer things in life, the older the scotch, the better it generally is. I have had some Highland single malt scotch that is 30 years old, and it is smooth as silk. For some reason, a blended scotch seems to be a good before-dinner drink. However, a well-aged single malt after dinner in a brandy snifter or a nice cut-crystal can be quite a memorable treat. In any case, most people tend to serve it more frequently in the cooler times of the year.

COGNACS

Most folks drink cognac after dinner while enjoying a good cigar in front of the fireplace—Well, you get the idea. If you truly like this stuff, you recognize that we are not talking about brandy and we do mean old. Many people argue that cognac needs at least 75 years to really mellow out. I can tell you that I have had Louis XIII on more than one occasion, and the texture and smooth quality is unmatched in anything of lesser age and quality. Any cognac is going to be expensive, so buy the best you can afford and use it only on very special occasions. Please buy what is known as a brandy snifter—large ones so you can get your nose into the opening and savor the bouquet while you drink it. Never serve it even remotely chilled, and try to heat the glass in your hands or stick it in the microwave for 15-25 seconds for a really fine release of the bouquet.

GIN

Gin is to the Brit's what beer is to the Germans. I think the cost of a good British gin like Tanquerey, Bombay Sapphire, or even Beefeaters is worth the price. In the summer, a gin and tonic after a day on the boat or a gin martini with a couple of olives in it by the fire on a cold winter day, is about as good as it gets.

BOURBON

Jack Daniels is not bourbon but Kentucky Whiskey. It is my inclination that anything that is brown in color and is consumed before meals should be drunk on the rocks, maybe with a twist of lemon and a splash of water, but nothing else. In any case, you should remember that carbonated sweet sodas would most likely tear up your head and stomach if you drink more than one of them. Most people think that terrible hangover came from the alcohol, but if they were drinking carbonated and sweetened soda in their drinks, that is probably the biggest reason for their ill feelings. I have known hardcore bourbon drinkers (such as my dad and John Wayne) who testify that Jim Beam is a good as it gets and it does, in fact, come out well in blind tests. I like a 100-proof Old Grandad as the base for a good Manhattan. There has been a resurgence of bonded, single barrel bourbons as an after dinner drink served straight up with a waterback. Blanton is one of the best you can find with an 8-year old Basil Hayden giving it strong competition. Jefferson Reserve is mild and finishes smoothly—try a single barrel instead of single malt next time.

RUM

Rum makes a great summer drink on your boat. It does well in tonic with a slice of lime, just as you would a gin and tonic. It is also finely complemented with Schweppes Bitter Lemon and a piece of lime on the glass. Most rum is made from sugar beets, but if you find the one that is made from sugar cane, you are in for a treat. Mount Gay bottles some at the cost of a bottle of good blended scotch.

VODKA

The Russians created vodka as the Brit's did Gin. I still like the Stoli

Crystal kept in the freezer and served on the rocks or in a vodka martini, **"shaken, not stirred"**. If you want to go for the top shelf, you won't be disappointed in real potato-distilled Chopin. That is about as good as you are going to get in the form of vodka. Don't scrimp with the olives or onions.

MARTINIS

People still drink them, and I guess they will always be around. You can make them with gin or vodka, and they can be on the rocks or straight up. Some people like an olive, while others prefer a twist of lemon. If you put a cocktail onion in it, it becomes a Gibson. I think the secret to a good martini comes from a couple of sources. First, make it very cold. If you keep your vodka in the freezer, that helps. Use a lot of ice when you mix it. Vodka martinis should be shaken to wake up the flavor, but not gin, because it bruises the gin. Use a fresh glass each time, and use lots of ice if it is on the rocks. Chill your glasses if they are being served straight up. Most people like their martinis very dry. In other words, put very little vermouth (dry) in the mix. Three ounces of gin with a splash of dry vermouth will usually make a good, standard martini. Many people just whisper the word "*vermouth*" over the top of the glass....

MANHATTANS

I can remember, when I tended bar many years ago, that from time to time someone would order a Manhattan, and I always thought it was such an elegant drink. It is an easy drink to make and is much like a martini in that it can be up or on the rocks. It can also be made from bourbon or rye, but if it is made with scotch it is called a Rob Roy. The measurements are simple in that you have two parts rye to one part sweet vermouth, with a dash of bitters. If you want a "perfect" Manhattan, that takes two parts rye and one part vermouth (half sweet and half dry). Once again, the drink should be very cold, so you need to shake it vigorously in the cocktail mixer with ice before your pour it. A Manhattan is finished with a maraschino cherry at the bottom of the glass and looks very regal when served straight up. If you are a woman, own some elbow-length white gloves, and can talk like Bacall, just whistle, and I will make your Manhattans all day!

SHOPPING SKILLS

Because our lives are so filled and demanding, most of us need "how to" instructions to accomplish most of our tasks successfully. Most of us do not have the time to delve into the inner mechanics of how things work; we simply want to be able to make them work. A good case in point is the computer. Today, every successful executive can, and does, use a computer in his or her daily business functions. Do they understand DOS and programming languages? Probably not, but that does not prevent them from being skillful in the use of the software. It is simply a matter of efficient application of time.

I remember hearing someone say that what he or she really needed was to know how to shop. Forget knowing how to cook, I do not even know how to shop! I first thought of their plea in terms of discerning a good tomato from a bad one. I was mistaken. The need is much more fundamental than that. Many people have never really learned how to actually go shopping. Incidentally, I speak not only of groceries, but also of everything from houses and cars to silk blouses and boating shoes.

I began to realize the tip of the iceberg when I thought of how many times I have heard people say; "I should never shop when I am hungry because I buy a lot of junk when I do." That, my friends, is Rule Number One, and if we violate that so often, then there must be more, so pay attention, weary traveler, and maybe the next few minutes will bring great relief.

Never shop when you are hungry because you buy the wrong things. You tend to buy things that you think you are going to eat when you get home. This often includes things that have a high spoilage rate and things that really don't fit into the rest of the week. It is sort of like going out to buy a new car the same day the old one just broke down and would cost you an arm and a leg to repair it. Dangerous!

Shop at a regular time every week. For example, shop at the same time of the week and the same time of the day. A good routine is to go work out, eat a light meal, and then do your grocery shopping.

Limit your trips to the store. You should try to do your basic shopping on a weekly or bi-weekly basis. This will usually be a big order, since it will include detergents, paper products, canned and packaged goods, etc.

Stock up on non-perishables. I visited a friend's house one time and opened a closet door and found it filled with toilet tissue from top to bottom. Literally, an entire closet filled with Charmin—I expected to see Mr.

Whipple in there. It makes sense,though, because giant sizes are cost effective and volume buying does save money, as well as trips to the store. Your shopping will be more pleasant if you are only buying fresh edibles.

Avoid rush-hour shopping. Fighting traffic on the Capital Beltway is punishment enough for one life. You do not need to replicate the experience in the supermarket. I try to shop late at night or early in the morning. Late at night (even after midnight), you pretty much have the store to yourself. But that means no deli or fish market and little bakery, as well. If you hit the place at 7:30 or 8:00 a.m., you find all departments staffed and working, but few shoppers. You may get better service at this time since the staff is still fresh.

Always make a list. A list will keep you honest and it will avoid Twinkies mysteriously appearing in your basket. Most markets are laid out with a similar floorplan, so my Shopping List in the back of this book should be helpful. I have my list on my computer and print out a copy every time I go shopping. You should do the same; it is worth the initial time required to load it on your hard drive.

Give shopping a priority. This is an important part of your life; do not relegate it to the bottom of the pile. Plan your list and plan your shopping and make an event of it instead of an ordeal.

I have heard it said that some of the better grocery stores have become the upscale meeting places for members of the opposite sex. The grocery store in my little hometown in Michigan is, indeed, one of the meeting places of the town. You see a lot of people stopped in the aisles talking about their weekend plans, etc. Let's make a pact to bring some fun back into the shopping place. Next time you need to go shopping, why not get dressed up like you were going to a special party and see if you can make an impression on somebody in the store. You might make some new friends.

Index

A

Antipasto Classico, 55
A.J.'s Hometown Pasties, 113
Annie's Crab Balls, 35
Appetizers
- **Annie's Crab Balls, 35**
- **Bandito Nacho Grande, 41**
- **Big Deale Hot Crab Dip, 33**
- **Colorado Red Salsa, 36**
- **Crostini Olivio, 45**
- **Denver Chicken Wings, 42**
- **Honest Guacamole Dip, 40**

Iron Gate Hummus, 50
- **John B's World Famous Onion Rings, 49**
- **Oysters Italiano, 48**
- **Piasano Olive Spread, 46**
- **Susie's Salsa, 39**
- **Trade Winds Chicken Wings, 44**
- **Trail Drive Salsa, 38**
- **Warehouse Mussels, 47**

Anytime Salmon Patties, 242
Arizona Hacienda Pasta Sauce, 197
Asparagus
- **Asparagus & Bacon Soup, 99**

B

Bananas
Bananas Pisciotta, 320

Bandito Nacho Grande, 41
Barbeque
    Bitch'n Bull, 119
    Boss Hog, 117
    Championship Brats, 123
Clarke's Choice, 122
Crazy Coyote Chicken, 120
Royal Champion Chicken, 121
Basic Burgers, 128
Beef
    Braised Short Ribs, 227
    Dad's Better Than A Diner Meat Loaf, 216
    Dana's Delight, 225
    Grandpa Fred's T-Bones, 224
    Maryland Pot Roast, 226
    Mission Hills Porcupine Balls, 218
    Mixed Grill Supreme, 236
    Poncho's Cheese Steak, 106
    Sloppy Who, 108
    Stuttgart Batavia & Curried Rice, 237
    Veal Toscano, 174

Big Daddy Burgers, 135
Big Daddy's Shrimp Etouffee, 266
Big Deale Hot Crab Dip, 33
Big Ron's Original Colorado Chili, 79
Big Sailor Chocolate Chip, 314
Bitch'n Bull, 119
Blue Burgers, 129
Border Town Rice, 304

Boss Hog, 117
Braised Short Ribs of Beef, 227
Braised Spinach, 306
Breakfast, 341-350
  Eggs Chesapeake, 346
  Eggs Joshua, 342
  Eggs Scampi, 343
  Frank's Big Breakfast, 350
  No Name Café Heuvos Rancheros, 348
  Pizzola Eggs, 347
  Sausage Gravy & Biscuits, 344
  Truck Stop Eggs, 343
Burgers, 125-135
  Basic Burgers, 128
  Big Daddy Burgers, 135
  Blue Burgers, 129
  Guido Burgers, 130
  King Leo Burgers, 131
  Pueblo Pauly's Pepper Burgers, 132
South of Border Burgers, 134

C

Caesar Steak Salad, 64
Calling Signals in the Kitchen, 75-78
Campbell's Wedding Soup, 100
Campfire Rainbow Trout, 245
Carlo's Housewarming Pasta Salad, 70
Carolina Pork Chops, 232
Cavill's Cioppino, 167 & 330
Championship Brats on the Grill, 123
Chesapeake Soft Shells Con Romano, 244

Chicken
- **Chicken Cutlets Italiano, 188**
- **Chicken Pottery Pie, 259**
- **Crazy Coyote Chicken, 120**
- **Cugino's Chicken Cacciatore, 162**
- **David's Grilled Chicken, 252**
- **Denver Chicken Wings, 42**
- **Fiesta Chicken Breasts, 210**
- **Gina's Peachy Pollo, 254**
- **Jack's Fried Chicken, 258**
- **L.A. Deli Chicken Salad, 110**
- **Mason-Dixon Line Jambalaya, 268**
- **Moving Day Chicken, 257**
- **New Mexico Chicken Roast, 212**
- **Pollo di Pesco, 166**
- **Rib Stickin Chicken & Dumplings, 261**
- **Royal Champion Chicken, 121**
- **Saigon Fire Dragon Chicken, 262**
- **Santa Fe Chicken Breasts, 210**
- **Sherry's California Chix, 255**
- **Stay at Home Chicken Fajitas, 206**
- **Sunday's Chicken Feast, 251**
- **Trade Winds Chicken Wings, 44**

Chicken Cutlets Italiano, 188
Chicken Pottery Pie, 259
Christmas Pork Loin, 332
Cindy's Marinated Shrimp, 249
Clarke's Choice, 122
Country Frittata, 194
Colorado Red Salsa, 36
Corky's Holiday Meat Pie, 329
Cooper Mountain Chili & Rice, 81

Crab & Corn Chowder, 94
Crab Town Muffins, 250
Crawdaddies & Crabs in the Hip Pocket, 112
Crazy Coyote Chicken, 120
Crostini Olivio, 45
Cugino's Chicken Cacciatore, 162

D

Dad's Better Than A Diner Meat Loaf, 216
Dana's Delight, 225
David's Grilled Chicken, 252
Deep Dish Santa Fe Pie, 201
Denver Chicken Wings, 42
Desserts, 313-321
- **Bananas Pisciotta, 320**
- **Big Sailor Chocolate Chip, 314**
- **Doug's Peachy Cobbler, 317**
- **Home Place Pecan Pie, 316**
- **Mom's Apple Pie, 315**

Doctor Nanny's Chicken Soup, 102
Doug's Peachy Cobbler, 317

E

Eastern Shore Crab Cakes, 240
Eggs Chesapeake, 346
Eggs Joshua, 342
Escanaba Bologna Salad, 111

F

Farfelles & Friends, 178
Festive Piggie, 333
Fiesta Chicken Breasts, 210
Four Star Lasagna, 157
Frank's Big Breakfast, 350
Fredo Ronaldo, 181

G

Gina's Peachy Pollo, 254
Goo-Goots, 308
Grandpa Fred;s T-Bones, 224
Granny's French Pea Soup, 87
Grilled Rainbow Trout, 246
Grilled Salmon Steak, 248
Guido Burgers, 130

H

Health Issues, 287-288
Heros, Hoagies, & Subs, 105
High Plains Pinto Beans & Ham Hocks, 214
History of the Burger, 125-126
Holidays, 325-337
- **Cavill's Cioppino, 330**
- **Christmas Pork Loin, 332**
- **Corky's Holiday Meat Pie, 329**
- **Festive Piggie, 333**

Holiday Ham, 335
Holiday Turkey Stuffing, 326
Nanny's Easter Cheese Pie, 336
Tidewater Black Eye Peas, 334

Turkey, 325
Wild Rice Stuffing & Side Dish, 328

Home Place Pecan Pie, 316
Honest Guacamole Dip, 40
Honey Banana Nut Cointreau Bread, 283

I

Insalata Ronaldo, 57
Investment Grade Italian Gravy, 152
Iron Gate Hummus, 50
Italian Zucchini Boats, 193

J

Jack's Fried Chicken, 258
John B's World Famous Onion Rings, 49

K

Kimmie's Kalzones, 115
King Leo Burgers, 131
Kitchen Needs, 15-18

L

L.A. Deli Chicken Salad, 110
Las Cruces Chicken Club Salad, 66
Linda's Loins, 233

M

Manhattan Deli Lentil Soup, 88
Mara's Magic, 176
Maryland Pot Roast, 226
Mason-Dixon Line Jambalaya, 268
Measurements, 28-29
Mex-Italiano Macs, 196
Michigan Cole Slaw, 63
Mid Vail Black Bean & Chicken Chili, 82
Mid Winter Vegetable Beef Soup, 90
Milwaukee Potato Salad, 62
Mission Hills Porcupine Balls, 218
Mixed Grill Supreme, 236
Mixed Trading, 291
Mom's Apple Pie, 315
Mom's Potato Salad, 61
Mongo's Green Chili, 198
Moving Day Chicken, 257

N

New England Boiled Dinner, 229
New Mexico Chicken Roast, 212
New Orleans Red Beans & Rice, 269
Nanny's Easter Cheese Pie, 336
Nanny's Giant Stuffed Shells, 154
Nanny's Simple Lettuce Salad, 58
Napolitano Italian Gravy, 149
No Name Café Heuvos Rancheros, 348
North Country Stuffed Peppers, 219

O

Oinkers in the Woods, 185
Oysters Italiano, 48

P

Pantry Items, 19-27
Pasta
- **Arizona Hacienda Pasta Sauce, 197**
- **Farfelles & Friends, 178**
- **Four Star Lasagne, 157**
- **Fredo Ronaldo, 181**
- **Investment Grade Italian Gravy, 152**
- **Mara's Magic, 176**
- **Mex-Italiano Macs, 196**
- **Nanny's Giant Stuffed Shells, 154**
- **Napolitano Italian Gravy, 149**
- **Oinkers in the Woods, 185**
- **Pasta alla Strasburg, 179**
- **Pasta Chairman of the Board, 143**
- **Pasta Patti, 141**
- **Penne alla Proud Mary, 182**
- **Penne with 3 Cheeses & Porcini Mushrooms, 183**
- **Pesto Rotini, Artichokes & Olives, 173**
- **Ron's Rigatonis & Meatballs, 153**
- **Ronnie's Ragu, 148**
- **Ryan's Grate Baked Ziti, 160**
- **Sean's Favorite Pasta, 145**
- **Shrimp & Pasta Medley, 68**
- **Summer Rigatoni & Ricotta, 147**
- **Toni's Timpano, 164**
- **Tuxedo Crabs, 171**
- **Vito's Linguini & Clams, 170**

Pasta alla Strasbourg, 179
Pasta Chairman of the Board, 143
Pasta Patti, 141
Patti's Perfect Pork Chops, 231
Penne alla Proud Mary, 182
Penne with Three Cheeses & Porcini Mushrooms, 183
Pepi's Goulash Soup, 84
Pesto Rotini, Artichokes & Olives, 173
Piasano Olive Spread, 46
Pigs in the Blanket, 221
Pizza, 275-279
- **A Crust for all Reasons, 276**
- **Crisp Crust, 277**
- **Gary's Choice, 278**
- **Pesto Sauce, 276**
- **Red Sauce, 275**
- **Thin Crust, 278**

Pizzola Eggs, 347
Phoenix Corn Bread, 281
Polish Navy Bean Soup, 85
Pollo di Pesco, 166
Poncho's Cheese Steak, 106
Popeye's Spinach, 305
Pork
- **Boss Hog, 117**
- **Carolina Pork Chops, 232**
- **Christmas Pork Loin, 332**
- **Corky's Holiday Meat Pie, 329**
- **High Plains Pinto Beans & Ham Hocks, 214**
- **Holiday Ham, 335**
- **Linda's Loins, 233**
- **Mongo's Green Chili, 198**
- **New England Boiled Dinner, 229**
- **Patti's Perfect Pork Chops, 231**
- **Roxie's Choice, 235**

Santa Rosa Posole, 215
Sausage & Peppers, 190
Sausage Potatoes & Onions, 191
Zydeco Pork Chops, 271

Potatoes, 293-303
Baked, 293
Bay Country Potato & Cheddar Pie, 298
Big Frank's Pan Fried, 299
Buttered Parsley New Potatoes, 294
Chicken Roasted Garlic Mashed, 297
Garlic Mashed Potatoes, 296
Grilled Roasted Redskins, 301
Old Fashioned Mashed, 295
Potato Pancakes, 300
Real French Fried, 294
Scalloped, 302
Twice Baked, 294
Wonder Fries, 303
Pueblo Pauly's Pepper Burgers, 132

Q

Quiche Laredo, 207

R

Red Bells & Blue Crabs, 98
Rib Stickin Chicken & Dumplings, 261
Ron's Rigatoni & Meatballs, 153
Ronnie's Ragu, 148
Roxie's Choice, 235
Royal Championship Chicken, 121

Ruth's English Muffin Bread, 282
Ryan's Grate Baked Zitis, 160

S

St. James Parish Roux, 264
Salads
- **Antipasto Classico, 55**
- **Caesar Steak Salad, 64**
- **Carlo's Housewarming Pasta Salad, 70**
- **Insalta Ronaldo, 57**
- **L.A. Deli Chicken Salad, 110**
- **Las Cruces Chicken Club Salad, 66**
- **Michigan Cole Slaw, 63**
- **Milwaukee Potato Salad, 62**
- **Mom's Potato Salad, 61**
- **Nanny's Simple Lettuce Salad, 58**
- **Shrimp & Pasta Medley, 68**
- **Sicilian White Bean, 71**
- **Tomato & Mozzarella, 60**
- **Uncle Jimmy's Italian Tomato Salad, 59**

Seafood
- **Annie's Crab Balls, 35**
- **Anytime Salmon Patties, 242**
- **Big Daddy's Shrimp Etouffee, 266**
- **Campfire Rainbow Trout, 245**
- **Cavill's Cioppino, 167 & 330**
- **Chesapeake Softshells con Romano, 244**
- **Cindy's Marinated Shrimp, 249**
- **Crab Town Muffins, 250**
- **Crawdaddies & Crabs in the Hip Pocket, 112**
- **Eastern Shore Crab Cakes, 240**

Grilled Rainbow Trout, 246
Grilled Salmon Steak, 248
Oysters Italiano, 48
Shrimp della Susan, 187
South County Crab Cakes, 241
T-N-T Jumbo Gumbo, 265
Tuxedo Crabs, 171
Warehouse Mussels, 47

Saigon Fire Dragon Chicken, 262
Santa Fe Chicken Breasts, 210
Santa Rosa Posole, 215
Sausage Gravy & Biscuits, 344
Sausage & Peppers, 190
Sausage, Potatoes & Onions, 191
Sean's Favorite Pasta, 145
Sherry's California Chix, 255
Shopping Skills, 361-362
Shrimp della Susan, 187
Shrimp & Pasta Medley, 68
Sicilian Sausage Bread, 279
Sicilian White Bean Salad, 71
Sloppy Who, 108
Social Aspects of Eating, 139-140

Soup
Asparagus & Bacon Soup, 99
Big Ron's Original Colorado Chili, 79
Campbell's Wedding Soup, 100
Cooper Mountain Chili & Rice, 81
Crab & Corn Chowder, 94
Doctor Nanny's Chicken Soup, 102
Granny's French Pea Soup, 87
Manhattan Deli Lentil Soup, 88
Mid-Vail Black Bean & Chicken Chili, 82

Mid-Winter Vegetable Beef Soup, 90
Mongo's Green Chili, 198
Pepi's Goulash Soup, 84
Polish Navy Bean Soup, 85
Red Bells & Blue Crabs, 98
Santa Rosa Posole, 215
S.S. Hesper Lobster Bisque, 96
Waterman's Crab Soup, 92
Yooper Corn Chowder, 95

South County Crab Cakes, 241
South of the Border Burgers, 134
S.S. Hesper Lobster Bisque, 96
Stay at Home Chicken Fajitas, 206
Stuttgart Batavia & Curried Rice, 237
Summer Rigatoni with Ricotta, 147
Sunday's Chicken Feast, 251
Susie's Salsa, 39

T

T-N-T Jumbo Gumbo, 265
Taos Enchilada Stack, 203
Texas Rodeo Cream Corn, 309
Tomato & Mozzarella Salad, 60
Tidewater Black Eye Peas, 334
Toni's Timpano, 164
Trade Winds Chicken Wings, 44
Trail Drive Salsa, 38
Truck Stop Eggs, 343
Turkey, 325
Turkey Ole, 213
Tuxedo Crabs, 171
Two Day Cabin Baked Beans, 289

U

Uncle Jimmy's Italian Tomato Salad, 59

V

Veal Toscano, 174

Vito's Linguini & Clams, 170

W

Warehouse Mussels, 47
Waterman's Crab Soup, 92
Weenie Rollers, 109
What To Drink, 353-357
- **Bourbon, 356**
- **Cognacs, 355**
- **Designer Water, 354**
- **Gin, 356**
- **Manhattans, 357**
- **Martinis, 357**
- **Milk, 354**
- **Rum, 356**
- **Scotch, 355**
- **Soda, 354**
- **Vodka, 356**
- **Water, 354**

Wild Rice Stuffing & Side Dish, 328

Y

Yooper Corn Chowder, 95

Z

Zucchini Dingies, 307
Zucchini Rustica, 307
Zydeco Pork Chops 271